Democratizing the Hegemonic State
Political Transformation in the Age of Identity

This book provides a new, comprehensive analytical framework for the examination of majority-minority relations in deeply divided societies. Hegemonic states in which one ethnic group completely dominates all others will continue to face enormous pressures to transform because they are out of step with the new, emerging, global governing code that emphasizes democracy and equal rights. Refusal to change would lead such states to lose international legitimacy and face increasing civil strife, instability, and violence. Through systematic theoretical analysis and careful empirical study of fourteen key cases, Ilan Peleg examines the options open to polities with diverse populations. Challenging the conventional wisdom of many liberal democrats, Peleg maintains that the preferred solution for a traditional hegemonic polity is not merely to grant equal rights to individuals, a necessary but insufficient condition, but also to incorporate significant group rights through gradual or megaconstitutional transformation. The future of societies divided over ethnic relations remains critically important to the possibility of global harmony.

Ilan Peleg is the Editor-in-Chief of *Israel Studies Forum* (since 2000) and the author of *Begin's Foreign Policy, 1977–1983: Israel's Turn to the Right* (1987) and *Human Rights in the West Bank and Gaza: Legacy and Politics* (1995, selected as Choice Outstanding Academic Title in 1996) and many other scholarly books and articles. His recent studies have appeared in journals such as the *Middle East Journal* and *Nationalism and Ethnic Politics*. Dr. Peleg's expertise is in ethnic relations in deeply divided societies, Middle East politics, Israeli society, and U.S. foreign policy, and he has spoken on these topics on CNN, Voice of America, and National Public Radio. Dr. Peleg is the Charles A. Dana Professor of Government and Law at Lafayette College in Easton, Pennsylvania.

To my son Gil

Democratizing the Hegemonic State

Political Transformation in the Age of Identity

ILAN PELEG

CAMBRIDGE
UNIVERSITY PRESS

CAMBRIDGE UNIVERSITY PRESS
Cambridge, New York, Melbourne, Madrid, Cape Town, Singapore, São Paulo, Delhi

Cambridge University Press
32 Avenue of the Americas, New York, NY 10013-2473, USA

www.cambridge.org
Information on this title: www.cambridge.org/9780521880886

First published 2007

Printed in the United States of America

A catalog record for this publication is available from the British Library.

Library of Congress Cataloging in Publication Data

Peleg, Ilan, 1944–
     Democratizing the hegemonic state : political transformation in the age of identity / Ilan Peleg.
        p. cm.
     Includes bibliographical references and index.
     ISBN   978-0-521-88088-6 (hardback) – ISBN   978-0-521-70732-9 (pbk.)
     1. Democratization – Case studies.   2. Nationalism – Case studies.
     3. Ethnic conflict – Political aspects – Case studies.   4. Hegemony – Case studies.
     5. Political stability – Case studies.   I. Title
        JC423.P342   2007
        321.8 – dc22   2007019993

ISBN   978-0-521-88088-6 hardback
ISBN   978-0-521-70732-9 paperback

Contents

Preface

This volume is the result of several years of focused intellectual reflection and deeply felt anxiety about the fate of our ever-shrinking but increasingly conflictual world. It started with writing about the seemingly endless conflict in the Middle East but gradually evolved into intense interest in other, similarly intractable blood feuds. The breadth of the volume reflects my current thinking about the origins of interethnic or intranational conflict in a number of the world's polities and possible ways of solving that conflict using a variety of governmental structures.

Numerous individuals and several organizations should be thanked for being of assistance to me, and I do thank them with genuine delight and deep gratitude. The University of Oxford invited me to spend the academic year 2002–2003 on its "campus," this hallowed ground of intellectual pursuit for almost 800 years. Special thanks are due to Sir Marrack Goulding, St. Antony's gracious Warden, and to Professor Avi Shlaim, who sponsored my membership at the college. While at St. Antony's, I maintained a "dual citizenship" at the Oxford Centre for Hebrew and Jewish Studies (OCHJS), located in the village of Yarnton, outside Oxford. I would be remiss if I did not thank OCHJS's president, Professor Peter Oppenheimer, and the other Fellows at the centre. Several Oxford professors were particularly helpful in commenting on my early thinking, especially Peter Pulzer of All-Souls College and Renee Hirschon of St. Peter's College, as well as the Oxford/New York publisher Dr. Marion Berghahn.

I spent part of the academic year 1999–2000 at Rutgers University as a guest of, again, two outfits: the Center for Russian and East European Studies and the Bildner Center for Jewish Life. While there, I took part in a weekly seminar on "Democratization in East Europe, Israel, and Beyond," writing a paper that eventually became part of the current book. My thanks are extended to Professors Jan Kubic and Myron Aronoff, the seminar's able leaders, for their insightful comments; to Professor Yael Zerubavel, Director of the Bildner Center for Jewish Life; and to Professor Israel Bartal, a member of the same seminar.

Throughout the last few years, I have discussed the ideas included in this book with numerous individuals who, thus, contributed to the volume, often without ever knowing it. Among them I would like to give special thanks to three individuals who have read the entire manuscript and have given me priceless advice on improving it: Alan Dowty, Adrian Guelke, and particularly William Safran. I am also grateful to a long list of colleagues with whom I have discussed through the years the ideas included in this volume: Gad Barzilai, Kevin Cameron, Eliezer Don-Yehiya, Uri-Ben Eliezer, Katalin Fabian, Bob Freedman, David Forsythe, Naomi Gal, Asad Ghanem, Hanna Herzog, Edward Kolodejei, Sandy Kedar, Ian Lustick, Howard Marblestone, John McCartney, Jonathan Mendilow, Joshua Miller, Joel Migdal, Luis Moreno, Benny Neuberger, Emanuele Ottolenghi, Yoav Peled, Gil Peleg, Nadim Rouhana, Gershon Shafir, Sammy Smooha, Jeff Spinner-Halev, Ilan Troen, Dov Waxman, Robert Weiner, Oren Yiftachal, Yael Zerubavel, and Eric Ziolkowski. Special thanks are also due to the organizers of the International Political Science Association (IPSA) seminar on "Ethnic Conflict in Divided Societies" in Belfast, Northern Ireland, in the summer of 2001 (and particularly to Professor Adrian Guelke), to the organizers of the IPSA's seminar on judicial issues in Jerusalem the very same summer (and especially Professor Menachem Hofnung of the Hebrew University), and to Drs. Guy Ben-Potat and Eiki Berg, organizers of the March 2006 workshop on "Partition or Power Sharing? The Management of Borders and Territories in the Globalized World" of the Mediterranean Programme of the Robert Schuman Centre for Advanced Studies at the European University Institute in Florence, Italy.

Thanks are also due to the members of the "home front." My Lafayette College assistants Chantal Pasquarello, Metin Aslantas, Noah Goldstein, and Dustin Antonello for researching the cases included in this volume and David Greenberg for designing the graphical artwork. My secretary for decades, Ruth Panovec, has been helpful in numerous ways.

Last but not least, special gratitude is due to my wife Sima and the rest of my immediate family: my daughter Talia, my daughter-in-law Harpreet, and my grandson Seth, a source of happiness and hope for a better world. To one member of my wonderful family, my son Gil, this book is dedicated with love.

Introduction

True peace is not merely the absence of tension: it is the presence of justice.

Martin Luther King, Jr.

National Conflict in Multinational States

The vast majority of states in the contemporary world are ethnically mixed. Their populations are divided into two or more groups that view themselves, and are often perceived by others, as different in some fundamental way from other groups within the same polity. The differentiation between groups might be based on history and origins, language or religions, narratives and myths, or even hopes and aspirations. Regardless of the source of the difference, what is important politically is that individuals and groups often have a deep sense of being unlike others who live with them in the same political space and that as social animals they adopt "us-them" identities (Sartori 1997, 58).

This subjective reality is often a source of long-term, severe internal conflict within the political system. Deep social divisions – whether their origins are in religious prejudice, economic gaps, or ancient historical hatreds – frequently result in massive bloodshed. The establishment of a democratic regime in divided societies might be perceived as a solution for internal strife, however, it rarely is in reality. Key social divisions often prevail despite democracy. Multinational democracies, more than multinational nondemocracies, are often torn between the requirement of unity and homogeneity and the reality of diversity (Taylor 2001, xiii).

This book is about intergroup conflict within multinational polities and especially about political confrontations within democratic or semidemocratic multinational systems. The volume focuses on polities in which one ethnopolitical group dominates society's political process by controlling state institutions and policies so as to promote its interests more or less exclusively. Today there is growing interest in recognizing the differences between national groups that live in the same polity, even within long-standing democracies such as Belgium, Canada, or the United Kingdom (e.g., Requejo 2001b). Such "internal" but distinct national groups often challenge the existing institutions in multinational democracies and demand that those institutions be transformed, recognize diversity more readily, and become more inclusive.

This study will analyze possible solutions to such interethnic conflict within the multiethnic polity. It is intended to be a broadly conceptual analysis of the democratization process (real and potential) of hegemonic ethnic states, the process through which such polities might become more open, inclusive, and egalitarian. This analysis is based on the examination of several empirical cases, multinational or multiethnic polities facing internal conflicts.

The persistent conflict between various national or ethnic groups is, simply put, a permanent characteristic of our age. However, there are at least three sets of questions that are far from being simple: (1) The way such internal ethnonational conflict might be resolved (primarily a theoretical question); (2) the way such conflict is usually resolved (an empirical question); and (3) the way intranational conflict should be resolved (a normative dilemma that depends, at least in part, on the values of the analyst).

Thus in an internal conflict of the type this study is interested in, the dominant ethnic or national group may try to "solve" the internal political dilemma by assimilating the minority, although that particular option often might be resisted not only by the minority but also by some members of the majority. A second and diametrically different solution to the conflict might be for the warring ethnicities to separate, although this theoretical solution is often unavailable in reality due to demographic, geographic, and other considerations. There is also a long list of options that could be termed "inclusive," "liberal," or (in the language of this study) "accommodationist." Such options include the granting of autonomy to ethnic minorities, offering them participation in the central institutions of the regime ("consociationalism" in the language of Arend Lijphart), the establishment of federal power-sharing schemes, and so forth. Several scholars have offered comprehensive lists of "positive/pluralistic" approaches to the easing of ethnic tensions (e.g., Safran 1991, 1994).

Although this study deals with these methods of managing conflict, its point of departure is in the analysis of multinational or multiethnic regimes that have established, primarily, elaborate systems of uni-ethnic or uni-national control, in spite (or because) of their multinational setting. This study does not accept this common reality of control as inevitable. It notes, empirically, the fact that not all multinational polities could be characterized as "control systems," an empirical realization that could give us, normatively speaking, hope for a better future for some of today's hegemonic systems. One of the most important theoretical distinctions offered by this study is the one between accommodationist regimes and inclusivist regimes. The study notes that accommodationist policies often reduce the demands for secession. Examples of an accommodationist regime and an inclusivist (or hegemonic) regime could bring the options open to multinational polities into sharper relief.

An example of a fairly clear-cut inclusive policy toward a minority is provided by looking at the political history of Finland, and particularly in the approach of the Finnish state toward the relatively small Swedish minority. Although Finland is close to being a homogenous nation-state, and could have easily adopted an assimilationist posture toward its Swedish minority or, at least, avoid granting that minority any special rights, it did neither. Finland made Swedish one of the state's two national languages and has allowed the Swedes to retain their cultural and educational institutions (Linz and Stepan 1996a, 24). The Finnish example demonstrates the centrality of the state not merely as a potentially controlling institution but also as a facilitator of inclusion.

An opposite example is Sri Lanka, where the state has often been a leading force for exclusion, control, and domination. It is a case demonstrating the difficulties of maintaining an inclusive and open democracy in a society facing deep ethnic divisions, where the political elite of the majority group adopts a nationalistic stance toward the minority. In the case of Sri Lanka, a series of state-sponsored policies created majority-minority estrangement. At least some analysts have seen the state as acting hegemonially (in the terminology of this study) by declaring the language of the majority as the only official language of the nation, conferring special status on the religion of the majority (Buddhism), discriminating against members of the minority in public employment, encouraging members of the majority to migrate into traditional minority zones (Kearney 1985, 1904–5), and so forth.

The example of Sri Lanka, and that of numerous other polities discussed in this study, suggests that the primary instrument for the promotion of the interests of the dominant group in a multinational setting is often the state, its institutions, and its structures, although the state ought to be always understood in its interaction with society (Migdal 1988, 2001). I call a state that energetically promotes the interests of a single ethnopolitical group in a multinational setting a *hegemonic state*. Similarly, but in a significantly broader manner, I refer to the regime built around such a hegemonic state and designed to sustain it an *Ethnic Constitutional Order* (ECO). Such order persists through an established and "dominant symbolic framework" within the society (Laitin 1986, 19), an acceptable, unchallenged social reality (Gramsci 1971).

Although some contemporary states define their role as promoting the interests of all their citizens as individuals and as members of the "nation," a political principle associated with the legacy of the French Revolution, the hegemonic state and the regime on which it is based perceive their role as limited to the promotion of the interests of members of the ethnic majority and, above all, the promotion of what is considered to be the collective agenda of the dominant ethnic or national group. In view of this common position of hegemonic-ethnic regimes, it is useful to adopt the distinction between "civic" and "ethnic" nationalism (Greenfeld 1992; Smith 1991) and develop it by focusing in some detail on the consequences of both types. The hegemonic regime, on which this study focuses, is often a regime promoting ethnic nationalism and ignoring the requirements of civic nationalism, although often it might create the illusion that it is committed to the principles of civic nationalism.

Although civic nationalism and civic citizenship are inherently liberal, egalitarian, and contractual, ethnic nationalism and the citizenship model that seems to emerge from it in hegemonic settings are fundamentally illiberal, discriminatory, and organic. The two forms are hard to reconcile, although in many a polity they live side-by-side, in tension and with unease. The resolution of the confrontation between these two models could be and sometimes is achieved only by far-reaching political transformation. Some analysts have argued that there is a strong association between liberal democracy and civic nationalism (Keating 2001b, 30). Similarly, it could be maintained, there is a direct link between ethnic nationalism and illiberal forms of government, including hegemony.

Approaches to Solutions: Political Engineering and Megaconstitutional Transformation

The widespread conflict between ethnic groups within multinational states requires careful analysis so that possible solutions for this long-term, pervasive phenomenon can be identified and adopted. This volume begins the process of identifying solutions for ethnic conflict in multiethnic settings by offering an analytical framework integrating a fundamental distinction between solutions based on the recognition of the equal rights for individuals and solutions based on the recognition of group rights. The debate between those who support individual-based liberal democracy in its purest form (Barry 2001; Horowitz 1985; Offe 1998, 2002; Snyder 2000) and those who endorse group-based solutions for ethnic conflict (Gagnon and Tully 2001a; Keating and McGarry 2001b; Kymlicka 1995, 2002; Tamir 1993) is extensively assessed. The analysis sheds light on the theoretical and practical possibilities for finding solutions for ethnic conflict in multinational, democratic societies.

More specifically, this volume offers a systematic analysis of several concrete methods that might be used for dealing with conflict within multinational settings. Although the liberal-democratic solution tends to recommend, straightforwardly, an equal treatment of all citizens as individuals and the principled abandonment of any and all group rights, group-based approaches, arguing that the path to ethnic peace requires the recognition of group rights, tend to be more complex, varied, and differentiated. Such group-based approaches require, therefore, more detailed and nuanced analysis.

In this volume, I will analyze specifically several group-based solutions to ethnic conflict in multinational democracies. Among these solutions there is the full-fledged or partial consociationalism, federalism in both its symmetrical and asymmetrical forms (the latter particularly "admired" by contemporary group-rights enthusiasts), cantonization, autonomy in its territorial and nonterritorial forms, and other such mechanisms for power sharing or power division. The consociational model of Arend Lijphart (1968, 1997) has been analyzed extensively by both supporters and opponents. I will attempt to identify those elements of consociationalism that might be saved in the interest of civic peace, political stability, and enhanced justice in multinational states, especially those experiencing ethnic hegemony. A similarly detailed analysis will be applied to various forms of federalism, yet another mechanism for managing intergroup conflict in multinational settings. The same will be done with regard to different forms of autonomy and cantonization.

In brief, this volume will attempt to go beyond a mere identification or even description of various mechanisms used to settle conflicts within multinational or multiethnic settings. It will analyze such mechanisms in a broad comparative and theoretical fashion and, most importantly, will attempt to develop new conceptual tools for assessing the usefulness of various mechanisms for managing intergroup conflict. These mechanisms will be conceptualized as potentially effective countervailing forces to ethnic hegemony.

The main theoretical contribution of this volume will be in the extensive assessment of a governmental model that will be called an Ethnic Constitutional Order, a regime type identified in several of this author's previous writings (Peleg 2001, 2002, 2003a, 2004a, 2004b). An Ethnic Constitutional Order is a regime based on the "management" of interethnic relations by granting a single ethnic group full dominance within the polity, often by the use of the state as a primary instrument of control. Although in an authoritarian setting, such as the USSR, the hegemony of the dominant ethnic group might be easily identifiable, in democratic multinational polities an ECO is likely to be based on a creative and complicated mixture of individual and group rights that could easily obfuscate the reality and confuse the observer as to the true nature of the regime. More specifically, in such a regime several seemingly contradictory conditions might prevail simultaneously (Peled 1992; Smooha 1990, 1992, 1997). First, extensive (although not necessarily full) individual rights might be granted to all citizens, including members of the minority group(s). Second, limited group rights, such as language rights and religious rights, might also be granted to all groups, or at least to the most important groups in society.

Despite those "concessions" regarding both types of rights (individual and group rights), the primary goal of an Ethnic Constitutional Order, its "essence," is invariably to maintain and even enhance the dominance of a single ethnic or national group within the polity. This goal is achieved through a multifaceted system of control (Lustick 1979, 1980a, 1980b) by maintaining the majority's monopoly over the determination of the "public good" (Peled 1992), differentiating the citizenship rights of members of the majority and all other citizens (Shafir and Peled 2002), maintaining the unwavering support of the democratic majority (Peleg 2001), and by other means. Thus although the regime might appear to be fully democratic, the "depth" of its democracy or its quality has to be carefully examined. This is among the reasons that this study prefers to call such a regime an ECO rather than an "ethnic democracy" (Smooha 1990, 1992).

An ECO might not be what Yiftachel calls an "ethnocracy." His argument that an "open ethnocratic regime" cannot be classified as democratic (Yiftachel 2006, 32) is wrong; an ethnocratic regime, although democratically flawed (Peleg 2000), still might have many, even most, characteristics of democracy. Moreover, the emergence of democracy might lead to the establishment of an ethnic regime (Spinner-Halev 2002), either in response to popular demand or due to elite manipulation (Snyder 2000). My conceptualization of the role of ethnicity and its relations to democracy is different than the ones offered by either Smooha or Yiftachel.

In terms of a solution to protracted interethnic conflict within democratic polities, an Ethnic Constitutional Order is a unique hybrid, combining individual rights that characterize liberal regimes with group rights that often rely on consociational arrangements. Yet in the case of ethnic order, both types of rights are granted to minorities, as individuals or groups, in a purposely limited manner designed to maintain ultimate political control in the hands of the ethnic majority, exclusively and in perpetuity. The hybridity of the ethnic order and the limited nature of rights granted to minorities put this order in constant tension with some of the principles of democracy. It often invites long-term instability.

The most important analytical focus of this study is the discussion of the possibilities for fundamental transformation of Ethnic Constitutional Orders. The conditions under which such transformation is likely to occur are analyzed through a series of case studies, focusing on polities where transformation in different directions and intensity has actually occurred. This empirical approach, complementing the theoretical framework offered in the earlier chapters of the book, is promising in terms of identifying the conditions that might facilitate the transformation of Ethnic Constitutional Orders into more open, inclusive and stable polities.

The focus of this study is on the notion of political transformation (either as a gradual and sometimes even unintended by-product of societal developments or as a result of dramatic, substantial, and purposeful change in a country's regime). It raises questions in relation to the possibilities of political engineering in the complicated world of ethnic conflict. It is self-evident that the transformation of any regime, whether gradual or dramatic, intended or not, is a highly complex process. Such transformation might occur as a result of revolution (the French, Russian, Chinese, or Cuban revolutions are classic regime-transforming events) or as a consequence of a sound defeat in a major war (such as the political transformations of Germany and Japan at the end of World War). Dramatic and fundamental transformations are significantly more difficult to introduce, implement, or stabilize in the absence of the physical collapse of the regime's institutions.

Nevertheless, major regime transformations are evidently possible, even in peaceful times and even in the absence of significant violence. Such transformations usually occur, as will be demonstrated especially in Chapters 4 and 5, when an existing hegemonic regime has proven to be fundamentally and inalterably unable to deal with the challenges confronting it. Interethnic confrontations of great intensity, duration, and violence of the type dealt with in this study could produce such transformative experiences.

In the absence of either a major defeat in a war or an internal violent revolution that produce transformative experiences as a matter of necessity, political analysts might have a larger role to play in bringing about transformations than they might have otherwise. The role of such analysts might complement the role played by other political agents such as leaders or opinion makers within the polity. Thus political analysts – acting consciously as political engineers – might be able to develop ideas on reconstructing Ethnic Constitutional Orders as more stable and just polities. Political analysts could be particularly helpful in systematically weighing the possibilities of what some of them have called "mega-constitutional change" (De Villiers 1994; Russell 1994).

Over the last generation or so, there have been several attempts to comprehensively transform the constitutional order in diverse countries such as Russia and South Africa, Czechoslovakia and Spain, and Northern Ireland and Switzerland. Several of these efforts have led successfully to fundamental political transformations – South Africa, Czechoslovakia, and Spain are but three examples for such a change. They testify for the possibilities of constitutional growth and development of multiethnic societies. Such transformations were brought about by both political actors and political analysts, frequently working together.

This book is based on the assumption, the hope, and, in several cases, the concrete evidence that megaconstitutional change is not only necessary in situations of protracted ethnic conflict but also possible and desirable. Although by no means an easy process, the implementation of new political designs might be looked upon as a highly attractive alternative to endless ethnic conflict, particularly in hegemonic situations. In the process of democratization, in which the abandonment of hegemonism is only one specific situation, there is a place for the "crafting" of new regimes (Huntington 1996, 4; Linz and Stepan 1996a, 17, 23), although preconditions for that process, to be discussed in Chapter 7, ought not to be ignored.

The Structure of the Book

This volume is organized in a manner that facilitates a systematic and orderly inquiry into the issues raised in the opening section. This introduction emphasizes the ethnic diversity of most contemporary countries and the frequent conflict resulting from this reality, especially in polities dominated by a single ethnic or national group. It introduces the notion of a "hegemonic state" and the broader notion of Ethnic Constitutional Order as the institutional focal point for such a state, as well as the idea that solutions for intranational conflict could be based on equal rights for individuals and/or the recognition of group rights through consociational, federal, or other governmental structures. The introduction finally presents some of the elements of an Ethnic Constitutional

Order – a unique combination of individual and group rights – and discusses the possibilities of its transformation, dwelling in particular on the promise of political engineering at the service of a mega-constitutional change.

The rest of this introduction reviews the book's seven substantive chapters, presents the methodological strategy of the study, and formulates some of the major questions with which the study deals. Chapter 1 discusses the emergence of ethnic conflict in the post–Cold War era, emphasizing the enormity of the problem at hand. It deals then with the moral and ethical imperatives for finding a solution for ethnic conflict, particularly in hegemonic circumstances, by identifying five major reasons for doing so: preventing human suffering, guaranteeing political stability, advancing human rights, establishing a just society, and promoting democracy. The chapter emphasizes the necessity of distinguishing analytically between individual and group rights as a way of systematically analyzing solutions for intranational conflict. It identifies liberal, consociational, and federal mechanisms for dealing with such conflict. The *hegemonic option* is discussed at some length and the thesis of the volume is presented in great detail.

Chapter 2 deals with several essential concepts employed by this study for the analysis of intergroup conflict in a multinational setting: democracy, statehood, and hegemony. It refers to the complex interaction between these three concepts as the "Crucial Triangle" because, in the final analysis, the fate of any multinational political system is likely to be determined by questions relating to the precise and often delicate balance among these three forces. One central question, for example, is whether in a multiethnic setting a state is likely to become an instrument for the domination of the majority or, alternatively, used as a tool for the enhancement of democracy by actively limiting the hegemony of the majority and extending protection to the minority.

Because this is a book about the process of democratizing hegemonic states, Chapter 2 begins by offering an analysis of the often used but variably defined notion of "democracy." A definition of democracy that differs from several other common definitions is presented so as to facilitate the subsequent analysis of intranational relations within ethnically diverse countries. The definition offered by this study is purposely broader than many alternative definitions; it tries to bring into sharper relief the inherent difficulty of maintaining genuine democracy in a multiethnic society.

The second part of Chapter 2 deals with the multinational state as a common, global phenomenon and the third part (essential for the analytical focus of the study as a whole) deals with the state as an instrument of uninational hegemony, exercised in and often despite a multinational setting. The consequences of uninational hegemony are then being assessed and, finally, the possibilities for transforming the hegemonic state are evaluated. It is the purpose of this chapter to begin the development of an *explanatory model identifying the general conditions under which political transformation might occur*. This explanatory model pays attention to factors external to the multiethnic polity (e.g., international pressure on the hegemonic state to change), as well as internal factors (e.g., the "dissonance" created between hegemony and democracy, the resistance to domination on the part of the ethnic minority, opposition within the ethnic majority).

At the conclusion of Chapter 2, the heavily psychological concept of the "other" is introduced into the discussion. It is a concept that might be thought of as the glue that holds together some hegemonic polities (or is unable to hold together other such polities). In a hegemonic situation the majority and the minority view each other as the complete negation of themselves (Habermas 1998; Peleg 1994). It is by definition a hierarchical situation (Kristeva 1991; Memmi 1967). This psychological disposition makes genuine democracy, which requires equal treatment under the same law, practically impossible.

Chapter 3 offers a comprehensive classification of deeply divided, multinational states, countries that must deal politically with the diversity of their population. Such classification is absolutely essential if we are to truly understand ethnic hegemony contextually and, more specifically, if we are to analyze alternatives to such a regime. The first fundamental distinction offered in Chapter 3 is between what is called accommodationist multinational states and exclusivist multinational states. The former exhibits a fundamental commitment for cooperation between individuals and groups regardless of their ethnic or national background and on the basis of both formal and real equality, while the latter is characterized by the superiority of one national group over all others and its determination to keep this condition unaltered. Following the introduction of two types of exclusivism, one based on minority domination (sometimes referred to as *apartheid*) and the other on majority dominance, the chapter proceeds by identifying several variants of accommodationism, based closely on the distinction between individual- and group-based political systems. Two somewhat different individual-based systems are identified: *liberal democracy*, a governmental framework that rests primarily on equality of all citizens as individuals and *jacobin democracy*, a system that while granting extensive individual rights emphasizes the collective "will" of the people and the unified nature of the polity. Among group-based schemes, the classificatory system introduced in this volume distinguishes between power-sharing and power-division mechanisms for settling ethnic conflicts. Consociationalism and multinationality are among the power-sharing systems identified. Federalism, cantonization, and autonomy are identified as power-division governmental designs.

The analysis of different forms of exclusivism, a system built on the superiority of a single national group within a multinational political space, is of particular importance for this study. The distinction between the two variants of exclusivism, a system based on the hegemony of the minority and an exclusivist system based on the hegemony of the majority, is especially essential. The latter system is significantly "softer" than the blatantly discriminatory minority hegemony. It typically grants substantial rights to individual members of the subservient group and might even give such groups what might be regarded as "cultural rights" in areas such as education, language, and religion. The political process in a majority hegemonic polity is, however, controlled exclusively by the superior group. This exclusivity might become a problem for stability and justice alike. Various modes of hegemony will be analyzed in this chapter (e.g., marginalization, assimilation, discrimination).

The last part of this central chapter deals with the dynamics of hegemony, asking questions about the motives for establishing such a potentially unstable system and the mechanisms through which it is implemented. The fundamental motive for establishing hegemony, it is argued, is the deep-seated fear of the hegemonic group toward the subservient group. This fear might be based on a long-held sense of victimhood (evident are such cases as Serbia and Israel), bitter historical memory of past conflicts (e.g., Mečiar's Slovakia), anxiety about the future (the Baltics), and so forth. A multifaceted set of mechanisms used by the hegemonic state is then identified and numerous examples given to its use. Finally, Chapter 3 addresses the consequences of hegemony for majority and minority alike. It distinguishes between short-term and long-term results, noticing that while the former might be fairly beneficial for the hegemonic group, the latter rarely are.

Chapters 4 and 5 evaluate empirically, albeit not in great detail, the transformation of several uninational hegemonic polities in divided societies, either through "grand political engineering" (a conscious and purposeful mega-constitutional change) or through a more gradual and modest process. Both forms of change are theoretically possible and, as demonstrated in these chapters using concrete examples, both occur in the real world. Opening with the identification of five possible modes of transformation, the chapter introduces a distinction between the direction and the intensity of the systemic change. In terms of the intensity, it is suggested, there is a difference between a limited, moderate, and gradual revision of the system (discussed in Chapter 4) and its radical, abrupt, qualitative transformation (dealt with in Chapter 5). In terms of direction, a hegemonic polity in a deeply divided society could change either in the direction of further ethnicization by strengthening the power of the dominant group within the political system, or it can change in the direction of further democratization, so that increasing equality, openness, and inclusion characterize the overall trend within the political system. If those distinctions are combined, it seems that there are five routes open to the polity: maintaining the status quo, radical ethnicization, moderate ethnicization, radical democratization, and moderate democratization. Chapters 4 and 5 include not only examples of these different types but also a set of empirical questions that ought to be asked in assessing the transformation of hegemonic systems.

Chapter 4 proceeds by identifying four specific cases of limited historical transformations; it dwells on political systems that have gone through significant but confined change. The cases chosen to demonstrate the different types of change, in terms of the substantive results, are the following: (1) the transformation of post-Franco Spain from an authoritarian, hegemonic system to an ethnoterritorial, semifederal country (Arel 2001; Keating 2001a, 2001b; Moreno 1997, 2001a, 2001b; Requejo 2001a, 2001b), a process that, in all likelihood, has not been completed yet; (2) the transformation of Canada over the last two generations into a system recognizing the "distinctiveness" of its minority (although not to the extent demanded by all members of that minority) through an elaborate, robust federalism and multiculturalism (Arel 2001; Cannon 1982; de Villiers 1994; Gagnon and Tully 2001a, 2001b; Keating 2001a, 2001b; Kymlicka 1995, 2002; Resnick 1999; Russell 1994; Seidle 1999; Taylor 1992); (3) the adoption of devolution by the U.K. government as a technique for recognizing the uniqueness of its constituent groups (Bogdanor 2001; Bradbury and Mitchell 2002; Keating 2001a; Pilkington 2002); and (4) the unique case of Swiss cantonization and, particularly, the division of the Canton Berne and the establishment of the Canton Jura within Switzerland (Erk 2003; Fleiner 2002; Freitag and Vatter 2004; Linder 1994; Steinberg 1996).

Chapter 5 deals with several historical cases of more fundamental change, radical transformation of the political system designed to completely alter its character: (1) the transformation of an hegemonic system through peaceful separation as reflected in the case of Czechoslovakia where the leaderships of two nations, the Czechs and the Slovaks, decided to separate and have done so peacefully (Butora and Butorova 1999; Kraus and Stanger 2000; Leff 1988; Malova 1994, 2001; Rhodes 1995; Tatar 1994); (2) the case of the Republic of Cyprus where partition was achieved through the use of force (Herlich 1974; Hitchens 1989; Yiftachel 1992); (3) the effort to transform Northern Ireland from a Protestant-led province of the United Kingdom through the establishment of a consociational system (McGarry 2002; McGarry and O'Leary 1993; O'Leary 1999, 2001b); and (4) the transformation of South Africa through liberalization and the establishment of majoritarian rule, a case in which a society with long-term racist legacy has changed into a full-fledged liberal democracy (Friedman 2004; Gloppen 1997; Guelke 1999, 2005; Horowitz 1991; Maphai 1999; Taylor 1990, 1991).

Obviously, the theoretically interesting "story" in each of these cases of limited or radical change is that each of them can be used as a model for other cases with similar characteristics. Be that as it may, Chapters 4 and 5 put a great deal of "meat" on the theoretical "bones" of Chapters 1, 2, and 3, although also in those mostly theoretical chapters large number of examples are given to any and all general arguments.

Chapter 6 presents data in regard to what could be called the "reverse trend," cases where hegemony has been sustained or even strengthened by already hegemonic systems or where it has been introduced by previously accommodationist systems (Datta 1999; Greenway 2001; Kearney 1985; Lustick 1979, 1980a, 1980b; Melman 2002; Misra 1999; Peled 1992; Peleg 2004a; Shafir and Peled 2002; Stuligross 1999; Tamir 1993). Several systems called "ethnodemocracies" (Snyder 2000, 312), "Ethnocracies" (Ghanem 2001; Rouhana 1997; Yiftachel 1998, 2000a, 2000b) or "ethnic democracies" (Kretzmer 1990; Smooha 1990, 1997) are examined in this chapter. Cases where hegemony has been sustained using "cosmetic" changes (maintaining the status quo) or even mild or radical ethnicization are analyzed, albeit relatively briefly.

Chapter 7 attempts to bring into unity and coherence the diverse data (covering a large number of cases) and the analytical conceptualization offered by the previous chapters by presenting a preliminary theory of the transformation of hegemonic systems. The theory identifies the internal and external factors (or variables) that might produce the transformation of hegemonic systems and dwells on the often-complicated interaction between these factors. Chapter 7 tries to answer two interrelated questions: (1) what explains transformation of hegemonic ethnic polities (as against inertia or nontransformation) and (2) what explains mild, limited, and gradual transformation (as against radical, metaconstitutional transformation).

This chapter reflects the author's conviction that domestic intranational, interethnic conflict will dominate the political milieu of our world through most of the twenty-first century and the hope that this volume will be regarded as at least a modest contribution to the possibility of alleviating that conflict.

Some Methodological Considerations

The study of hegemonic transformation – the process through which ethnic constitutional orders might be transformed into more open, inclusive, and multinational polities – is clearly at its infancy. Although numerous case studies can be found in the scholarly literature, especially within what is generally known as "area studies," these studies are often a-theoretical or use a great variety of conceptual tools, making them useful but insufficient for studying the phenomenon of transformation in general. There is clearly no coherent framework for analyzing the transformation from ethnic hegemony to liberal democracy in a methodical and comparative manner. The current volume should, therefore, be regarded as a first step toward the alleviation of this problem. It is a "preliminary cut," an extensive proposal for researching systematically the possibility and likelihood of constitutional transformation in polities dominated by ethnic conflict.

The methodology adopted in this volume for studying hegemonic transformation fully reflects this reality. This methodology includes four primary elements:

1. *The introduction of key concepts.* This study introduces a series of new concepts such as hegemonic states and Ethnic Constitutional Orders as a way of focusing on political structures dominated by a single national group. The study also distinguishes between individual-based and group-based approaches for dealing with intranational conflicts, identifies various governmental mechanisms for achieving stability and enhancing democracy in deeply divided societies (e.g., liberal democracy, consociationalism, federalism, autonomy, and cantonization), and calls attention to the complex relations within the triangle of democracy-statehood-hegemony (which Linz and Stepan, 1996a, define as the "Stateness" Nationalism-Democratization link). Those concepts and additional ones (such as the notion of the "other") are the building blocks in the conceptual framework of this study. They are essential for the systematic development and testing of concrete hypotheses regarding hegemonic transformation

and, eventually, the establishment of a theory of hegemonic transformation, goals that this study can achieve only partially.

2. *The development of an analytical framework*. The study offers several analytical tools, over and above the definition of useful concepts, for dealing with the democratic transformation of Ethnic Constitutional Orders. First, the volume introduces (Chapter 3) a detailed classification of regime types, placing the two types of hegemonic polities (minority and majority) in their proper relations to other political systems. Second, the book identifies the crucial elements that must be focused on, in an effort to understand hegemonic behavior: its dynamics, motives, mechanisms, and forms, as well as its typical consequences. Third, the analysis includes a model of the relationships between the requirements of contemporary democracy, the modern state as the ultimate arbiter of power and justice in a democratic regime, and the practice of hegemonic behavior within a multinational setting. It is these complex relationships that determine the possibilities for hegemonic transformation, a subject covered in Chapter 7.

3. *The testing of basic questions and concrete hypotheses*. The ultimate goal of a study of the type presented here is to put to empirical test and focused examination the basic questions that the work addresses (see the following text). Although allusions to numerous cases of hegemony and transformation will be made throughout the exposition of the analytical framework (mostly in Chapters 1, 2, and 3), Chapters 4 and 5 will test in considerable detail the concrete hypotheses regarding the possibilities for hegemonic transformation. It does so by examining several paradigmatic cases of hegemonic transformation. Four of these cases (Chapter 4) deal with limited or modest transformation from hegemony to semifederalism and autonomy, recognition of minority distinctiveness, initiating devolution, and strengthening cantonization (Spain, Canada, the United Kingdom, and Switzerland, respectively). Four other cases (Chapter 5) represent radical transformation through peaceful separation (Czechoslovakia), forced partition (the Republic of Cyprus), an attempt to install a consociational regime (Northern Ireland), and a transformation from minority hegemony to majoritarian rule (South Africa). The cases introduced in Chapter 6, the third empirical chapter of the book, could be looked upon as the "control cases" insofar as that they deal with situations where hegemony is sustained by an established Ethnic Constitutional Order through relatively modest changes, either in the direction of further democratization (Israel and Turkey) or in the direction of further ethnicization (Estonia and Latvia). Chapter 6 also deals with cases in which ethnic hegemony is strengthened vigorously through violent action (Sri Lanka, Milosevic's Serbia, and Rwanda in the 1990s). Although it is possible that in the future the theory and hypotheses presented in this study could be tested by using more sophisticated quantitative data and analysis, in addition to the use of case studies, in this exploratory stage it is too early to do so. The most effective way to study hegemonic transformation today is through the careful analysis of case studies.

4. *The development of a preliminary theory of the democratic transformation of hegemonic systems is offered* (Chapter 7). The theory identifies the factors that are typically associated with such transformation, as well as the interaction between them. Although at this stage of studying hegemonic transformations it is not possible to offer a highly developed theory, and do so with a high degree of confidence, it is the goal of this study to offer a preliminary theory, a structure that could be further developed in the future.

The Basic Questions

By now we can formulate a series of fundamental research questions running through this study in its entirety, questions that will be dealt with in the chapters that follow. These questions are both empirical (dealing with "what is" questions) and normative (dealing with "what ought to be" issues). It is obvious by the enormity of each one of these questions that none of them can be dealt with exhaustively within the confines of a single book. The function of the volume is as much to raise these important questions as it is to answer them. More importantly, the study aims at presenting these questions in relation to each other and within one theoretical-conceptual space as a way of creating a new academic research focus – the transformation of hegemonic ethnic orders to more democratic, inclusive regimes.

Here are some of the basic dilemmas tackled by this volume, with reference to main places in the book where they are addressed:

1. What is the nature of interethnic conflict within a multinational state today (Chapter 1) and what are some of the normative reasons, the "values," that require a solution to such conflict (Chapter 1)?
2. Could large-scale political engineering assist in solving interethnic conflict? In what ways (introduction and Chapters 4 and 5) and under what conditions is such metaconstitutional transformation possible (Chapter 5)?
3. What are some of the principal strategies for solving ethnic conflict (Chapter 1), and what are some of the political structures that might be adopted in implementing those strategies (Chapter 1)?
4. Can "hegemony" by one ethnic group within the polity provide a short-term solution or even be sustained in the long run, and under what conditions (Chapter 1, Chapter 2, Chapter 5)?
5. What are, normatively and empirically, the requirements of democracy in our time (Chapter 2), and is the multinational state (including the hegemonic one) capable of meeting those requirements, and in what manner (Chapter 2)?
6. What are the costs involved in the establishment of a uninational hegemony (Chapter 2)? What are the forms of ethnic hegemony (Chapter 3) and its dynamics (Chapter 3)?

7. If and when the cost of hegemony is judged to be too high, can the hegemonic state be transformed and under what conditions (Chapter 2)? What direction is the transformation likely to take (ethnicization vs. democratization) and what intensity is it likely to exhibit (limited vs. metaconstitutional change, Chapter 4)?

8. How can one classify political regimes in a manner that might facilitate the orderly and systematic analysis of hegemonic polities by comparing them to nonhegemonic polities (Chapter 3)?

9. What are the implications of the battle royal between "hegemony" and "democracy," and between the centralized state and its ethnic "components," for the possibilities of establishing genuine democracy in the twenty-first century?

Undoubtedly, these are serious, difficult questions. Although none will be fully covered and satisfactorily answered, they must be addressed so as to shed light on the phenomenon of statist hegemonism and the possibilities for its transformation. This is the fundamental goal of the current volume.

The Thesis

The thesis of this volume is that due to the emergence of a new global governing code – emphasizing democracy, equality, human rights, and self-determination (understood as self-governance by sizeable ethnic and national groups) – Ethnic Constitutional Orders and ethnonational hegemony in general experience today and will experience in the future enormous pressure to transform. In an era of cultural liberalism, multiculturalism, and the spread of postmaterialist values (Inglehart 1990), the dominance of one ethnonational group over other groups is likely to be resisted by dominated minorities within hegemonic polities, objected to by liberal elements within the dominant majority, and severely criticized by important players within the international community.

To avoid the intensification of civic strife, increasing instability, massive violence, and loss of international legitimacy and support, ethnicized political systems (and particularly their governing elites) will need to seriously consider gradual or mega-constitutional changes in their Ethnic Constitutional Orders, regimes that typically include discriminatory laws and practices. This consideration might lead some ethnic orders to further ethnicize their regime and to establish a full-fledged "ethnocracy" (Yiftachel 2006; Yiftachel and Ghanem 2004a, 2004b), especially when there is intense "ethnic outbidding" among elites within the political system (DeVotta 2005, 141). It is hypothesized here, however, that more often transformation in the direction of further inclusion and enhanced equality (i.e., more profound form of democracy) would govern the response of dominant groups and their leaders.

Any transformation of an established hegemonic system could be expected to be extremely difficult, particularly because (1) the discriminated minority, supported by the international community and liberal elements within the majority, is likely to demand full equality by law and in practice, and (2) many individuals and even organized groups within the hegemonic majority are expected to resist the dismantling of the majority's preferential power position that often relies on well-developed ideology and well-established, entrenched interests. The transformation process whereby an ethnicized order becomes significantly more inclusive is likely to be protracted, difficult, and violent.

Although the transformation from a hegemonic or "exclusivist" system to an "accommodationist" system, where all individuals and at least the major social groups are treated equally, is the normatively preferred solution in terms of the contemporary *zeitgeist* (particularly in the West), it is the thesis of this book that even in cases where such transformation is implemented one should resist the temptation of endorsing an identical solution for all political systems characterized by deeply divided social structures. From the dual perspective of order, the enhancement of political stability (a utilitarian rationale), and that of congruence with the principles of justice, democracy, and human rights (a Kantian rationale), the preferred solution for a traditionally hegemonic polity in a deeply divided society might be in establishing a political system based on *a combination of extensive individual rights and the recognition of at least some group rights*. Yet in seeking to leave its hegemonic tradition behind, each hegemonic polity will need to define its own unique mix of individual and group rights. Although in theory one may wish to endorse, in terms of individual rights, the principles of Western liberal democracy and combine them with some recognition of groups (as long as such recognition does not violate the equal treatment of individuals), in reality different systems would have to seek a balance that is compatible with their unique traditions and the demands of the evolving "world culture."

More specifically, the argument of this book is that in terms of the requirements of democracy, and particularly that of full equality for all citizens as individuals, there is very limited if any room for flexibility in moving from an exclusivist to an inclusive system. Substantial flexibility in choosing an appropriate group-rights regime is not only possible but required and desirable. In terms of collective rights, various deeply divided societies might want to adopt different modes of consociationalism, federalism, autonomy, cantonization, or other forms of group rights, responding to their particular conditions. Although the group-rights regime should be chosen through extensive and open public dialogue, its specific variant cannot be determined without close attention to the historical, demographic, and political conditions under which this regime had been erected.

In general terms, this book maintains that political solutions based on a balance between the universalistic principles of liberal democracy, and especially individually based equality, and the particularistic demands of major groups within society have the greatest likelihood of achieving long-term stability in deeply divided societies. Unity and diversity may live in relative harmony in a deeply divided society if and only if the constitutional framework of the society – its political essence – is perceived as the product of genuine dialogue between society's major groups rather than as a reflection of the hegemonic imposition by society's dominant group.

This book argues theoretically as well as empirically (by examining many specific examples) that in deeply divided societies – where divisions are not merely a matter of preference but long-developed historical realities resonating in individuals' and groups' identities – the recognition of group rights as a fundamental constitutional principle is a necessity. By definition one cannot find an overarching identity in deeply divided societies. Moreover, in hegemonic Ethnic Constitutional Orders, divisions are not merely a product of history and identity. They are also institutionalized realities, often existing for generations. The most effective way of moving toward a solution of an interethnic conflict based on history, identity, and institutions is by erecting a regime that combines the egalitarian principles of liberal democracy with the innovative structures of group representation.

My thesis will, undoubtedly, raise objections by purists on the liberal-democratic side, arguing that any recognition of group rights, by definition, must result in individual inequality. My response will be that (1) group rights must be "allocated" with special care so as not to harm (or at least to minimize harm to) individual equality and (2) that in establishing group rights we ought to look at the overall good of society – in the cases of this study a society that had witnessed long periods of ethnic hegemonism – and, in doing so, we might conclude that on balance group rights are justified and beneficial for both the traditionally discriminated minority and society as a whole.

In developing the thesis that a combined mix of extensive and equal individual rights, on the one hand, and some form of substantive and substantial group rights, on the other hand, is a preferred regime in deeply divided societies, we need to assess the alternatives to that proposed regime. It ought to be emphasized that what is known in the political literature on deeply divided societies as "ethnic democracy" (Smooha 1997) – the institutionalized hegemony of the majority group with "liberal rights" for all individuals (Peled 1992) – is a recipe for (at best) an inherently flawed democracy (Peleg 2000, 2004a) and, at worst, a nondemocracy (Yiftachel 1998, 2001, 2006). Furthermore, it would be argued in this study that liberal democracy with its principled but unidimensional focus on individual rights often ignores the sociopolitical reality of numerous societies where the peoples' identities have been shaped for generations by the divided nature of their societies. But even "multicultural democracy" (McGarry 2002), with its commitment to the preservation of different cultural communities through support for endangered languages, religions, and cultures (e.g., recognizing dress codes) often does not respond to the real needs of distinct communities, needs that could be fulfilled only by granting these communities substantial political power in the determination of their own fate.

My analytical framework leads me to the belief that there are four types of regimes in deeply divided societies. The first is an exclusivist regime based on the rule of the minority (e.g., South Africa under apartheid or Sunni-ruled

Iraq under Saddam Hussein). This regime, called *Herrenvolk democracy* in the case of South Africa (a misnomer of the first order), lacks internal or external legitimacy insofar as it is obviously nondemocratic and therefore suffers from severe problems of instability. The second type of regime, sometimes called *ethnic democracy* (also a problematical term) is based on the hegemony of the majority and its control over the state, although it grants all members of the polity fundamental rights on an individual basis and maintains an overall democratic façade in the form of regular election, free press, and independent judiciary. The problem with both minority and majority hegemonism is that neither recognizes the equality of groups within society despite the deep sociopolitical divisions within them, and both take affirmative steps to establish the hegemony of one group over all other groups. These regimes, therefore, either produce blatant nondemocracy (in the case of minority hegemony) or an inherently flawed democracy (in the case of majority hegemony).

Based on these theoretical distinctions and empirical observations, we are left with two relatively accommodationist options designed to create (although often unsuccessfully) stable democratic orders: (1) liberal democracy: a regime based on the principle of individual equality while intentionally ignoring group-based sociopolitical divisions as unimportant or immaterial, and a political order that maintains sociopolitical cohesion through French-style (Jacobin) centralism and commonality of culture or through American-style overarching patriotic identity; (2) Group-Rights Regimes: a regime where the social divisions are recognized as politically pertinent and a governmental structure erected to reflect those divisions through the institutionalization of power sharing or even the adoption of formal multinationalism or where power is divided (through federalism, autonomy, or cantonization) to accommodate all or most groups.

The two exclusivist regimes, minority controlled or majority controlled, imply the existence of ethnic hierarchy within the polity. Moreover, in the case of minority-controlled polity, the system is characterized by *ethnic exclusion* – the majority does not participate in some or all of the most important aspects of political life. In the case of majority-controlled systems, the ethnic relations might be more complex. The majority may adopt a policy of *ethnic assimilation* (trying to absorb the minority) or, if it believes that such policy is doomed to failure, *ethnic marginalization*. Moreover, in extreme cases and under unique circumstances, ethnic majorities might resort to a policy of *ethnic destruction* (Yegen 1999, 557). The nature of majority-minority relationships within an accommodationist regime is likely to be very different. While liberal democracy does not ordinarily promote or recognize group rights, unless it is specifically committed to multiculturalism, it is a regime that by its emphasis on broad-based fundamental rights might facilitate *ethnic preservation*, if such preservation is desired by the ethnic group. In the case of group-rights regimes, *ethnic enhancement* is assumed as a positive value to be promoted by the regime.

On the basis of these distinctions, this study argues that accommodationist regimes are clearly more democratic than exclusivist ones. At the same time, although there might be a likelihood of more stability in accommodationist regimes, stability is never guaranteed in any deeply divided society. Moreover, it is the thesis of this book that there is no *prima facie* reason to believe that individually based accommodationist regimes are inherently more democratic or more stable than group-based accommodationist regimes. In societies with relatively shallow divisions and the ability to establish overarching identity among all or most citizens (often the characteristics of immigrant societies such as the American or the Australian), individually based liberal democracy seems to be the preferred variant. Although it maximizes individual liberties, it does not harm the ability of ethnic and other groups to express themselves or work for the promotion of their particular interests. In other societies, particularly those in which deep sociopolitical divisions based on history and identity are an inherent part of the essential reality, some type of group right regime is simply inevitable or highly desirable. It is the thesis of this book that *the deeper the division, the more likely it is that a group-based approach ought to be adopted for the benefit of all if the goal is enhancement of democracy and stability*.

In the final analysis, this study argues, the solution to the "hegemonic problem" – the unilateral domination of the state by one ethnic group within a deeply divided society – could be found only in *balancing the interests of the ethnicized state and its dominant majority with those of the minorities within it*. Finding an optimal balance is a difficult task, but in principle the goal is to identify a solution that guarantees the existence and integrity of the state while, at the same time, enhancing the rights of its minorities and their sense of belonging. An example of such solution could be found in the establishment of non-territorial autonomy in countries with distinct minorities (Coakley 1994). Although territorial autonomy might lead to secessionist and separatist pressures, nonterritorial autonomy is considerably less dangerous from the perspective of the existing state and its majority. Chapters 4 and 5 will explore empirically a variety of modes of balancing interests adopted by several very different systems.

I

Ethnonational Conflict in Multinational Polities

> Governments exist to protect the rights of minorities. The loved and the rich need
> no protection: they have many friends and few enemies.
> Wendell Phillips, 1811–1884, an American abolitionist

The Emergence of Ethnic Conflict

Serious clashes among different ethnic and national groups within societies
are among the most prevalent forms of contemporary conflict. This conflict
could be found within nondemocratic polities (e.g., Saddam Hussein's Iraq or
the People's Republic of China), within new democracies (e.g., post-Franco
Spain, Slovakia after the "Velvet Divorce," or the Baltic Republics in the early
1990s), or even within traditional, long-standing democracies (e.g., Canada or
Belgium). Democratic tradition or an active process of democratization does not
guarantee the absence of internal ethnic conflict. In fact, they often facilitate it.

Ethnic conflict of the type we see today in every corner of the earth is intimately linked to the emergence of nationalism in the modern world, a process analyzed comprehensively by scholars such as Benedict Anderson (1993),
Ernest Gellner (1983, 1997), Eric Hobsbawm (1990), Hans Kohn (1944), Ernest
Renan (1996), Anthony Smith (1986, 1991), and many others. Within the
framework of modern nationalist ideology, regardless of the precise course or
causes of its development, the supreme human value in the political arena has
always been the total commitment of all individuals and groups to the interests
of the nation. Moreover, there has been an intimate link between the somewhat
amorphous concept of a "nation" and the more easily defined notion of the
"state," reaching the ultimate level of their complete identification in the concept of the "nation-state." Therefore, Hobsbawm has argued that a nation "is
a social entity only insofar as it relates to [a] certain kind of modern territorial
state, the 'nation state'" (1990, 9–10), and Smith has stated rather decisively
that "nations can only be fulfilled in their own states" (1971, 21).

Classical theorists in the nineteenth century have gone even further in identifying the nation with the state. Thus John Stuart Mill (1861), an altogether liberal thinker, argued that a homogenous state (i.e., a uninational polity) is a precondition for political liberty (or what is termed "democracy" in this study). The Italian Giuseppe Mazzini and German theorists of nationalism such as Fichte and Hegel also identified the nation and the state. Herder emphasized the importance of language and culture in what today would be called "nation building."

Yet if these classical and contemporary analysts are right (normatively and empirically alike) about the centrality of the national spirit and its claim for an exclusive place in the modern state, an internal conflict within almost all so-called nation-states is virtually inevitable. The reason is that the vast majority of the so-called nation-states are multinational or at least multiethnic polities with several ethnicities or nations within them. If individuals have (or should have) supreme loyalty to their nation, as theorists of nationalism assume, and if most states have more than one nation within them, severe internal conflict is unavoidable.

But there are good reasons for deep pessimism in regard to the possibility of civic peace in multiethnic environments not merely due to general ideological considerations but also due to the particular character of our own era. The end of the Cold War seems to have ushered in an even more intense period of intranational, ethnic conflict than we have witnessed before. Above all, the post–Cold War era has signified the decline of politics defined in ideological terms, politics focused on the struggle between democratic capitalism and statist communism. The dismemberment of the Soviet Union and the Warsaw Pact brought to an end, at least temporarily, the confrontation between the Right and the Left, giving rise to the middle-of-the-road, however ill-defined, "Third Way" (Giddens 2000).

Yet the *annus mirabilis* of 1989 did not "end history" as we know it (Fukuyama 1992). On the contrary, from the perspective of ethnonational conflict within existing states, it gave "history" a shot in the arm; it energized it. The end of the ideological Cold War shifted the focal point of world history from the struggle for world domination between ideologically committed capitalists and socialists to a new arena, the ethnonational one. The decline of intense ideological debate led to the rise of an ethnic, religious, or nationalist conflict and the "emergence of antagonisms" (Mouffe 2002, 56) that are less likely to be resolved peacefully.

The 1990s and the early years of the twenty-first century in particular have seen the emergence and the intensification of intergroup conflicts defined in ethnic terms. These conflicts have been described often in almost apocalyptic terms. Notions such as "the coming of anarchy" (Kaplan 1994), where state-based order is completely undermined and shattered, or the "clash of civilizations" (Huntington 1993), where monumental confrontations result from ethnocultural differences, came to greatly influence, if not totally control, the thought processes of many analysts. Some observers saw the use of religious nationalism and its challenge to the West as "a new Cold War" (Juergensmeyer 1993). Several analysts thought that the reappearance of "hyper-nationalism" would surely make many observers miss the good old, orderly, and predictable Cold War (Mearsheimer 1990).

It is with this emerging intrastate ethnonational conflict that this book is most concerned. Although this type of conflict is by no means new, the geopolitics of the old Cold War covered up its most powerful and persistent features, elements that were present for generations in numerous countries just under the surface. When this geopolitical condition withered away, numerous dormant conflicts abruptly erupted. Several federations (or, better yet, sham federations) imploded, splitting into their old ethnic or national components: the Soviet Union, Yugoslavia, and Czechoslovakia fall into this category. This process quickly led to ethnic conflicts in numerous places including Chechnya, the Baltic States, and the former Yugoslav territory. But, severe ethnic conflicts also flared up in countries with relatively marginal links to the evaporating Cold War: the conflicts in Rwanda and Burundi, Kashmir and Iraq are but merely some examples.

Despite the strides of "globalization" (especially in its economic form), precisely at the time that the Cold War came to an end, ethnic identity was not broken down but, on the contrary, was strengthened and energized, often at the expense of the national state that lost its centrality in the economic sphere and as a security provider. While neoliberal scholars have argued that globalization will reduce what was called "pre-modern forms of identity" (Keating and McGarry 2001a, 4), such forms of identity – ethnic and national in nature – were sustained and even invigorated. Moreover, although certain analysts thought that universal human rights will quickly spread all over the world, possibly as a by-product of globalization and the emergence of civil society in previously nondemocratic countries, the world has seen numerous ethnic conflicts accompanied by massive violations of human rights since the early 1990s. Ethnic bonds have been revitalized, and globalizing trends did not weaken them in the least.

In view of the reality of increasing ethnic and national conflict, it is not surprising that some analysts found it necessary to defend, on normative grounds, the need for endorsing the old model, where state and nation coincided (Miller 1995, 82; Tamir 1993). This position could be described as somewhat naive: it simply does not fit the multiethnic social reality in the vast majority of contemporary states. But even if one is reluctant to normatively legitimize the forces of nationalism and ethnicity, and especially their claims for superiority and exclusivity within the contemporary state, there is no doubt that these forces are alive and well and likely to play an important political role in the foreseeable future, on all continents, in all regions, and within most countries.

A strong argument could be made that ethnonational feelings are on the ascendance, in the contemporary world often (but not exclusively) as an antidote to the forces of globalization and integration (Ben-Porat 2006). Moreover, multiple national and ethnic identities often emerge in the contemporary world in response to the countervailing pressures. The model of globalization versus national identity is probably an incorrect oversimplification. More often the two forces act side-by-side today or even in interaction, and they tend to reinforce one another.

Even some of the most stable European states (e.g., France or the United Kingdom) are challenged today by the revival of ethnic feelings and, sometimes, the political aspirations of their minorities. In this new political environment, any state, including the traditional hegemonic state, finds itself under increasing pressure to introduce reforms and even to fundamentally transform itself. Such action might be needed to calm down rising ethnic, subnational demands, although it is not always effective.

When internal pressures lead to significant violence, as they often do, there is an even more urgent need for the contemporary state to act decisively. It ought to be noted, however, that in the case of the hegemonic state, the state is not merely a reactive force to ethnic demands and violence. The polity's own hegemonic behavior – its aspiration to dominate other group(s) within its borders – could be a primary cause for conflict. Thus Byman and Van Evera found that of thirty-seven conflicts between the fall of the Berlin Wall and 1996, no less than twenty-five resulted from a clash between hegemonic ethnic groups and other groups (1998, 5). They have identified a long list of conflicts resulting from what they have termed "communal hegemonism," including the Azerbaijani-Armenian wars, the clash between Hutus and Tutsis in Burundi, the conflict between Georgians and Abkhazi, the Hindu-Muslim confrontation in India, the Arab-Kurdish struggle in Iraq, the Tamil-Sinhalese civil war in Sri Lanka, the Sudanese conflict, the Turkish-Kurdish strife in Turkey, the numerous conflicts within the territories of the former USSR and Yugoslavia, and many more (Byman and Van Evera 1998, esp. Table 4, 23).

In general, most contemporary conflicts are internal and most of them involve hegemonism. By some counts, only about 10 percent of all conflicts are international. None of the thirty-one active conflicts around the world in 1994 was found by Baker to be classical interstate wars (1996, 563). Many analysts believe that "ethnic conflict has become today's most pervasive and dangerous expression of organized strife" (Aklaev 1999). Moreover, among internal conflicts, most are based on old interethnic rivalry or historic feuds, and many stem from the drive of the majority to dominate the minority, the "hegemonic drive" to which this volume is dedicated.

The Need for Solution

The reality described in the first part of this chapter makes it clear that serious thought ought to be given to solving interethnic, intranational conflicts wherever they might occur. Over the last decade or so, authors and analysts have called the attention of policy makers to the fact that in numerous countries minorities are at risk when caught up in an ethnically based conflict, that such minorities are the principal victims of serious human rights violations even though they most often tend to demand greater rights within existing states rather than insist on separation, and despite the fact that they are inclined to use nonviolent political action rather than rebel (Gurr 1993).

Some analysts have focused on dealing with ethnonational conflict from the perspective of a global view. Thus Walter Morris-Hale authored the book *Conflict and Harmony in Multi-Ethnic Societies* (1996). Others have focused on the process of democratization as the key for "ethnic peace" (Aklaev 1999). Although some analysts offered broad conceptual frameworks for studying ethnic conflicts, others have dealt with case studies and area studies approaches or conducted statistical analyses. Some political commentators have focused more specifically on ways of regulating, managing, or solving ethnic conflicts (e.g., Baker 1994; Ghai 2000; Guelke 2004; McGarry and O'Leary 1993).

Recognizing the centrality of ethnic conflict in and the nature of protracted conflict all over the world, a few analysts offered complex classifications of methods for eliminating differences between ethnic groups in multinational societies (e.g., through integration, assimilation, or even partition or secession) or "managing" differences through consociational methods (power sharing), cantonization, federalism, and even hegemonic control (McGarry and O'Leary 1993, 4). Those alternatives for dealing with pervasive ethnic conflict will be covered later in the volume.

But before we turn to alternative strategies, methods, and mechanisms for dealing with ethnic conflict, including the hegemonic option, it is important to ask a preliminary, fundamental, and primarily normative question: Why should we dedicate our limited resources – economically, militarily, politically, and even intellectually – to the resolution of ethnic conflict given the fact that such conflicts are often as protracted and complex as they are, that a failure to resolve them could lead to further deterioration, and that the chances of success are invariably low?

Solution for internal ethnic conflict is important, indeed crucial, for at least five reasons: (1) as a means of saving human life; (2) as a way of assisting in the full and genuine democratization of a country; (3) as a tool for promoting political stability; (4) as an instrument for advancing human rights; and (5) as a way of enhancing justice. These five reasons will be taken in turn. They establish, in combination, the normative basis for this study.

First, and most directly, ethnic conflict in the contemporary world has proven to be extremely costly in terms of human lives. Large numbers of people, mostly noncombatant civilians, were killed in ethnic conflicts in most parts of the world: in the 1994 Rwandan genocide, the Balkan wars during the 1990s, the conflict between the Kurds and the Turkish state as well as between Kurds and the Iraqi regime, the Russian-Chechnyan wars, the Indian-Pakistani conflict over Kashmir, the Sinhalese-Tamil clash in Sri Lanka, the Sudanese civil war, the Northern Ireland bloodletting (especially after 1969), and the Israel/Palestine conflict, to mention but several of the better known ethnic conflicts. With terrorism on the rise and weapons of mass destruction more available than ever, those numbers are likely to dramatically increase in years to come.

The number of casualties of ethnonational conflict is likely to be high particularly in hegemonic situations when a dominant nation is trying to solve its ethnic problem "once and for all" (as in Serbia's operations in Bosnia and Kosovo, Russia's operation in Chechnya, or the Rwanda genocide), when a dominated group feels that it is fighting for its very existence (as in Chechnya, Kurdistan, or Sri Lanka), or when a conflict between majority and minority has become simply "a way of life," a protracted existential reality (as in Northern Ireland or Israel/Palestine). Only a fundamental political solution of the type tried in Ireland's Good Friday agreement or a mega-constitutional transformation of the type implemented in post-Franco Spain and in post-apartheid South Africa can possibly put an end to massive killing or pervasive oppression associated with such ethnic conflict.

A second reason for trying to find solutions for long-term ethnic conflicts is that such solutions are likely to be essential for full democratization of practically any polity. It is interesting to note that over the last fifteen years or so there has been a dual, simultaneous process – the rise of ethnic conflict and widespread democratization. But the relationships between the two processes have been clearly adverse, with the increase in ethnic conflict preventing full democratization (e.g., Russia's Chechnya campaigns, Serbia's wars). In general, the democratization process might be hampered, and even stopped, by an ethnic conflict, and, moreover, an ethnic conflict might cause the quality of an existing democratic regime to deteriorate. Several analysts (e.g., Snyder 2000) have noticed that democratization might "exacerbate existing ethnic problems" (Aklaev 1999, 255). By the same token, however, ethnic politics, and particularly an active ethnic conflict, might make full democratization impossible or impact the quality of an existing democracy rather negatively.

Hegemonic states, in particular, are likely to be influenced negatively by the complex relation between ethnic conflict and democracy. What Fareed Zakaria called "illiberal democracy" (1997, 2003) is the best regime a hegemonic state can hope for; that is, a hegemonic state might be able to maintain a procedural democracy based on majority rule and periodic elections, but not a full-fledged, substantive democracy based on the entire gamut of rights and genuine equality (Chapter 2). Hegemonic policy may deteriorate to civil war and massive bloodshed, accompanied by wholesale violations of human rights.

There are several examples for the negative consequences of hegemonic behavior on the quality of a country's democracy. Vladimir Mečiar's ethnicized policies in 1990s Slovakia are a case in point. The deterioration of Sri Lanka's democracy since its 1948 independence is another case. In this island nation, the Sinhalese majority initiated government-sponsored migration into traditional Tamil areas, instituted its language as the exclusive official language of the country, and conferred a special status on its religion, Buddhism (Kearney 1985). A bloody civil war has been fought for decades as a result of such hegemonic behavior. A more recent and by now better-known example of the relationships between hegemonic behavior and bloody conflict is the history of Serbian policy during the 1990s.

Third, solutions to ethnic conflicts are essential for creating any semblance of political stability. The relationship between ethnic homogeneity and political liberty was recognized already by John Stuart Mill, who believed that the former is necessary for the latter (1861). Gabriel Almond returned to that theme, maintaining that political stability requires cultural homogeneity (Almond 1956). Rabushka and Shepsle, in their important book on plural societies, have noted that these societies are often polarized because political elites rationally appeal to the interests of their constituency (1972), a conclusion that seems to have been confirmed by numerous ethnic conflicts such as the one in the former Yugoslavia.

Although it is not hard to find anecdotal and even systematic support for what we may want to term the *pessimist school* (analysts who believe in the inevitability of serious violence in multinational societies), it is possible to adopt a more positive outlook on the interaction between ethnic heterogeneity and political stability. Such different observers as Lord Acton, Otto Bauer, and Arend Lijphart have argued, in rather diverse settings and in different analytical styles, that multiethnicity is not an insurmountable barrier to political stability. Arel maintains that at the end of the twentieth century, "a solid majority of analysts find themselves in the optimist camp" (2001, 67).

Although the debate between pessimists and optimists is intellectually quite important, from a public policy perspective it is clear that because most societies are already multiethnic, and because ethnic identity within them is often a source of conflict, maximal effort should be exerted to solve this conflict as a way of enhancing the stability of the political system. In a hegemonic context this is even clearer than in other contexts: the very essence of political stability in hegemonic polities depends on the ability of the dominant group to adopt a policy of inclusion toward the minority.

Fourth, a solution for internal ethnic conflict should be achieved as a means for advancing the cause of human rights within the polity (Peleg 2003). Hegemonic ethnic regimes, in particular, are prone by their very nature to violate the human rights of their minorities. This is especially the case when the "core nation" (Brubaker 1996) controlling the state enjoys multidimensional superiority in all important areas (e.g., education, the economy, armed forces, technology), if there is a bitter and violent conflict between the constituent ethnic groups, if the country lacks a tradition of respect to human rights (and political tolerance in general), and if there is no significant international pressure on the majority to treat the minority in accordance with acceptable norms of human rights.

When it comes to human rights violations, the role of the political elite of the majority is critical. It might be the single most important group in terms of solving the internal ethnic conflict and, thus, alleviate the conditions of human rights. Thus, for example, while under Vladimir Mečiar, Slovakia was led toward the marginalization of its Hungarian minority, and post-Mečiar Slovakia was led toward a Slovak-Hungarian accommodation (Butora and Butorova 1999). The importance of leadership, particularly as it relates to human rights, can also be discerned in cases such as those of India, Israel, and Spain (Chapters 4–6).

Accommodationist policies in deeply divided societies could make a great and immediate difference in the area of human rights. Consociational and federal solutions, in particular, could restrain the majority and grant the minority significant human rights. Thus the consociational deal negotiated for Northern Ireland (O'Leary 2001a) and the still incomplete federalization of Spain (Moreno 1997, 201) have led to positive results in this regard. Without an overall accommodationist policy, human rights cannot be maintained in deeply divided societies. The new position of human rights in the contemporary world, where they have become "global core values," has provided the outside world an effective lever, enabling it to greatly influence the behavior of ethnic elites and restrain their behavior, thus enhancing the status of human rights in deeply divided societies.

Finally, solutions to or improvement in ethnic relations are an important consideration in the advancement of justice in deeply divided societies. Ethnic conflict results invariably in great injustice to numerous individuals, particularly to those who are members of the minority, as well as to minority groups. Spokespersons on behalf of minorities have argued for promoting the politics of identity, difference, or recognition as a way of establishing a just political system and correcting existing discriminatory practices against minorities (Connolly 1991; Kymlicka 1995; Taylor 1992; Young 1990). Thus Young argued that "a just polity must embrace the ideal of the heterogeneous public and accept and publicly acknowledge group differences, especially insofar as nationality and ethnicity is concerned" (1990, 179–80). Gagnon maintains straightforwardly that justice requires that minorities be recognized (Gagnon and Tully 2001), and many minority spokespersons endorse, specifically, the idea of asymmetrical federalism and correcting existing discriminatory practices against minorities as a recipe for the establishment of an equitable if not equal situation in countries characterized by tense majority-minority relations.

Opponents of special recognition for minority rights have made arguments in terms of the general principles of liberal democracy, objecting particularly to the violation of the foundational idea of individual equality. They have argued that the recognition of minority rights would divide society rather than integrate it (Snyder 2000) or "affirm group difference at the expense of commonality" (Miller 1995, 140).

In the final analysis, however, although both positions could be defended in theory, each situation has to be considered empirically within its fullest context and in light of both principles: liberal equality among individuals and the necessity of group recognition. In countries that have been historically hegemonic, political action must be taken to make the polity at least minimally hospitable to long-discriminated ethnic minorities. Unless the minority is publicly "recognized" in a symbolic manner, and unless aggressive action is carried out to substantively correct past discriminatory policies and present inequities, a just solution cannot be achieved in hegemonic situations.

This volume promotes more fully the argument that although equal rights to individuals, in the tradition of liberal democracy, are normatively the best foundation for equality and stability, democracy, and human rights, elements of recognizing the special identity of certain groups could and should be integrated into a liberal regime, as long as they do not violate substantively the principle of equality before the law. This general, principled position applies particularly to ethnic groups that have suffered from long-term discrimination, institutionalized at the hand of a dominant majority.

Strategies for Solutions: Individual- and Group-Based

In the previous section, an argument for the imperative of solving ethnic conflict was presented from a fundamentally normative perspective. The normative approach is important if one remembers that the tackling of ethnic problems is invariably costly and requires serious societal commitment. Moreover, some of the issues of dealing with ethnic problems are rather controversial and require a fully informed, reasoned intellectual choice. Thus the normative debate on whether group differences ought to be recognized by the political system or ignored as irrelevant (as would be the clear preference of liberal democrats) remains unresolved. Other issues are argued on more empirical grounds (e.g., the debate between what were termed "optimists" and "pessimists" about the possibility of establishing a stable and free society in a multinational setting; a debate that is not yet settled).

In this section, a discussion of the appropriate fundamental strategy to the solution of interethnic conflict is launched. It is a crucial discussion about the proper approach to sociopolitical ethnic division, and it will lead us organically to a more specific analysis of the mechanisms and the methods that could convert these general strategies to concrete governmental structures.

Theoretically, the number of strategies for solving ethnic conflict is endless. In devising a strategy for dealing with social and political division, some analysts have distinguished between approaches based on actions taken by the state versus actions taken by the international community (Keating and McGarry 2001b, 25). Thus states may attempt to calm internal restlessness by granting ethnic groups rights in the area of religion (e.g., the recognition of the Church of Scotland by the United Kingdom or religious rights given to Palestinians in Israel), and/or in the area of languages (e.g., the dual language policy of Canada, the less generous policy of Spain toward the Basques and Catalans, or the language policies of India and Israel [Harel-Shalev 2006]). States may also adopt a general policy under the banner of "multiculturalism," improve the resource allocation schemes (from their minorities' perspective), or adopt strategies such as consociationalism, devolution, federalism, or autonomy.

The international community might take actions to deal with ethnic conflicts within sovereign states. The long-held principle that such conflicts are internal matters has "evaporated" over the last thirty years or so, with massive international involvement in conflicts in countries entangled in ethnic wars, including Rhodesia and South Africa, the former Yugoslavia, and now numerous countries in Eastern Europe (e.g., the Baltic States, Slovakia, Romania).

In this section, however, it is argued that, first, the most fundamental issue in regard to a solution of long-term ethnic conflict in a multiethnic polity is whether it adopts an individual-based approach or a group-based approach as a fundamental strategy for dealing with majority-minority conflicts. Second, it is argued that although in a traditionally hegemonic ethnic polity it is significantly easier for the dominant majority to adopt an individual-based strategy for dealing with its minorities than a group-based approach, some combination of the two is likely to prove necessary for a stable long-term solution.

The individual-based approach to the resolution of ethnic conflict is the simpler of the two approaches. Associated with a regime type known as liberal democracy, an individual-based approach argues that in all societies, homogenous and heterogeneous, ethnically divided or unified, all individuals must be treated as equal. While liberal democrats recognize that most societies are divided into ethnic groups (whatever the exact definition of *ethnicity* might be), they view ethnic status, and loyalties and commitments of any kind, as a private matter that ought not to be "politicized." Those who believe in the individual approach are convinced that it is the best way of maintaining at least four essential values: equality, liberty, unity, and stability. Their "show cases" for the success of their approach are "Anglo-Saxon" countries, such as the United Kingdom, the United States, Canada, Australia, and New Zealand, but also other liberal democracies, such as postwar Germany and the Scandinavian countries.

The alternative, group-based approach starts with the assumption that because most states are heterogeneous, and some are deeply divided along ethnic lines, a collectivist, group-based strategy for managing internal conflict is necessary. Moreover, many group-based theorists believe that the only way for achieving justice, equality, and stability in deeply divided societies is through the public recognition of different identities within the polity.

The group-based approach is extremely complex, especially if compared to the straightforward individualistic approach. First, the idea that groups within existing polities are entitled to any type of recognition, let alone self-determination, immediately raises a series of questions as to what groups are entitled to such a right (e.g., only ethnic groups?), and how and by whom is the decision on self-determination and its implications to be made (e.g., the group alone or the polity at large?). Second, it ought to be recognized that even if the principle of the self-determination of a group is conceded, it leads to a series of complex issues. For example, could this self-determination be achieved either "externally" – by secession (as in the case of Bangladesh) or partition (Cyprus, Israel/Palestine, the Indian Subcontinent, Czechoslovakia, Yugoslavia, and the USSR) – or only "internally," by the "reconfiguration of the existing constitutional association so its multinational character is reorganized and accommodated" (Gagnon and Tully 2001, 3).

It must be realized that although hegemonic states are likely to resist strenuously either a comprehensive individual-based approach for solving their ethnic problems or a group-based approach, the opposition to the latter is likely to be more severe than to the former. If the majority group enjoys overwhelming superiority over the minority (demographically, economically, politically, and unilaterally), as is often the case in "hegemonies," it can sustain its dominant position even if a full-fledged liberal democracy with all of its individual free-doms, rights, and liberties is established. Agreeing to substantive group rights for the subservient minority might be viewed as endangering the very essence of the polity.

The adoption of a group-based approach for the resolution of ethnic conflict in a hegemonic ethnic state is likely to be looked upon by the dominant ethnic group as being completely unacceptable. Granting group rights to any ethnic group – other than the hegemonic one – is, by its very nature, an act of violence against the very essence of the regime. Hegemonic states that have accepted group rights as a strategy for conflict resolution despite those inherent difficul-ties have, therefore, gone through a rather painful process of transformation.

The general approach adopted in this volume is that, for analytical purposes, it is useful to distinguish between the individual-based and the group-based strategies for dealing with ethnic conflict. Yet from a policy-making perspective it could be beneficial in at least some cases to combine the two approaches to solve specific ethnic dilemmas. Thus it is important to recognize that, theoret-ically, the individual approach is the more universalistic among the two; it is based on the supposition that all citizens are equal regardless of their identities or group membership. The group approach is particularistic by definition: it assumes that a society ought to take into account the uniqueness of at least some groups. It is interesting to note that although some countries have adopted fun-damentally the universalistic approach of equal individual rights (e.g., Canada's policy under Trudeau), others have decided that a particularistic approach has a better chance of establishing a just and stable order (e.g., Belgium's move toward federalism or Switzerland's traditional cantonal system). Yet some coun-tries (e.g., post-Franco Spain) have established a "mixed" regime, combining equality of individuals in the tradition of liberal democracy with significant group recognition, even on an asymmetrical basis.

The battle royal between those who support an individual-based approach and those who endorse a group-based approach is likely to continue in the fore-seeable future, despite the fact that from time to time partisans have declared that "their" formula is the clear winner. Liberal democrats continue to argue that any deviation from strict equality for individual citizens is dangerous. Jack Snyder, for example, believes that the granting of group rights in emerging democracies "might serve to lock in divisive national identities, unnecessarily heightening distrust between groups" (2000, 33). He clearly prefers an institu-tional setting that deemphasizes ethnicity (36) and promotes "civic identities" and "rights on the individual level" (40). Snyder's recommendations are a direct and logical extension of Horowitz's proposals for the depoliticization of eth-nic identities through a variety of institutional arrangements (Horowitz 1991b, 451–76).

Other Western analysts (e.g., Brian Barry 2001) have joined in supporting the individual approach and rejecting group rights as a primary mechanism for the resolution of interethnic conflict. Thus David Miller rejects what he calls "radical multiculturalism" that, to him, emphasizes "the politics of difference" and embraces the ideal of heterogeneous public especially in regard to ethnicity (Young 1990, 179–80). This group-based ideology, suggests Miller, "celebrates sexual, ethnic, and other such identities on the expense of national identities" (1995, 135). The implication is that it induces instability.

Similarly, Claus Offe argues that the granting of group rights might generate "a dynamic of potential conflict" that could be limited by "overarching identity of commonality of shared nationhood" (2002, 14). It is Offe's opinion that "liberal universalism and individualism is a more promising and more realistic project of maintaining unity" than recognizing group rights (ibid., 15). Although Offe concedes that in some cases group rights might be necessary, a position accepted by the current volume, he believes that in general the integration of groups into society is best served through individual rights (1998, 137–40).

Although the position of those who support individual rights as the best and only approach for conflict resolution is extremely attractive on purely normative grounds, it is rather problematical on an empirical basis:

1. In numerous societies today inequalities are already well established, historically built in, and even perpetuated for the foreseeable future. The "divisive national identities" that Snyder fears are already there, often established for generations. In the interest of equality, justice, and stability such inequalities need to be corrected, and group-based differentiation or even preferential treatment for discriminated groups might be the most effective way (or at least one effective way) of dealing with the problem.

2. Supporters of liberal democracy view it as invariably committed to overarching societal identity and common citizenship (which it often calls "civic" citizenship), in contrast to group-rights regimes that seem to assume that such overarching identity is simply beyond reach. Supporters of group rights for minorities point out that liberal democracy may camouflage what is, in reality, the domination of the majority. It seems that the extent to which a particular liberal democracy is based on "commonality," rather than exclusively on the majority's culture and interests, is primarily an empirical question. For that reason, this volume looks at concrete cases. The level of "neutrality" of liberal democracies cannot be assumed; it must be examined.

3. Although liberal democrats argue that group rights threaten equality and liberty, in all Western democracies group rights "work within the constraints of liberal democratic constitutions" (Kymlicka 2002, 25). This means that individuals are protected from overzealous minorities even if these minorities enjoy group rights.

The last point is extremely important for the overall thesis of this volume. In resolving ethnic conflict it may be advisable to engineer solutions based on the primacy of liberal democracy (i.e., individual equality) but, at the same time, adopt provisions that allow for group rights. In principle, that is the way to structure a just and stable solution for polities facing internal division along ethnic lines.

Although the type of solution offered in this volume is by no means radical, and although in principle the combination of individual and group rights might make sense, the disagreement among the camps is intense. Those who insist on group rights see those as absolutely necessary for solving ethnic conflict in deeply divided societies. Those who endorse an individualistic approach to rights tend to view any deviation from an exclusive individual approach as fatal.

The best-known comparativist supporting group rights in divided societies as possible and inherently essential has been Arent Lijphart. In a series of books and scores of articles, Lijphart has argued on behalf of what he called "consociational" or "consensus" democracy, a complex agreement on power sharing among the leaders of the most important groups within society. While Lijphart's model has not been designed specifically for dealing with ethnic divides, his fundamental idea ought to be seriously considered for that particular context.

Lijphart's approach on behalf of group rights has received substantial support from political philosophers such as Will Kymlicka (especially 1995), Charles Taylor (1992, in particular), and others (e.g., Baker 1994; Patten 2001; Young 1990, 2000). Moreover, over the last decade or so, a long series of publications supporting the group rights of minorities have appeared, endorsing the claims for recognition of the Basques and the Catalans (Keating 2001b; Requejo 2001b), Hungarians in Slovakia (Butora and Butorova 1999), the Quebecois (Keating 2001a; Keating and McGarry 2001b; Kymlicka 1995, 2002), Israeli Arabs (Ghanem 2001; Peled 1992; Peleg 2001, 2002, 2003b, 2004; Rouhana 1997; Shafir and Peled 2002, 1998; Yiftachel 2000a, 2000b), the Tamils of Sri Lanka (Kearney 1985), Irish Catholics in Northern Ireland (Morris-Hale 1996; McGarry and O'Leary 1993; O'Leary 2001b), and other minorities.

Moreover, and very interestingly, some analysts have even made passionate arguments on behalf of the majority's rights to its group privileges (Miller 1995; Tamir, 1993). Thus, for example, although Miller offered a general defense of nationalism, Tamir suggested that nationalism could be liberal, and Smooha developed a model of ethnic democracy (1990, 1997, 2002) that, in effect, accepts ethnic dominance. Needless to say, from the perspective of hegemonic control of a majority over a minority, a perspective taken by this study, these conceptualizations are highly problematical.

Kymlicka, who wrote some of the most sophisticated essays in defense of group rights, summed up his position well: "Liberals can and should accept a wide range of group-differentiated rights for national minorities and ethnic groups, without sacrificing their core commitments to individual freedom and social equality" (1995, 126). He believes that minorities need protection from the decisions of the majority (e.g., rights in the area of culture and language), and that they are entitled to that protection especially if historical agreements are on their side. Moreover, the value of cultural diversity is also important (ibid., 127). Kymlicka is particularly concerned with situations in which the minority faces "unfair disadvantage which can be rectified by a group-differentiated right" (ibid., 8). He maintains that group rights are not inherently in conflict with individual rights as long as these group rights refer to the right of the minority group to limit the economic or political power exercised by the larger society over the group and are not used to limit the liberty of the individual members of the minority (ibid., 7).

The type of analysis offered by Kymlicka – differentiating carefully between legitimate and illegitimate minority rights – may hold the key for progress toward the resolution of majority-minority relations in many countries, including several hegemonic polities.

Mechanisms and Methods for Reducing Ethnic Conflict

The previous section attempted to clarify some of the fundamental strategies that might be adopted for dealing with internal ethnic strife, dwelling on the key distinction between strategies focused on the rights of the individual versus those focused on group rights. In this section, I will analyze several regime types compatible with those strategies: liberalism (and, more specifically, liberal democracy), consociationalism, federalism, cantonization, and autonomy. A more elaborate classification of regimes that might be available for multinational polities will be offered in Chapter 3.

Liberal democracy is surely a regime that has a reasonable claim for actively promoting individual rights and, to a lesser extent, accepting group rights. In such a regime – practiced in the Anglo-Saxon world, France, and in Scandinavia, for example – individual equality and the full gamut of individual rights, liberties, and freedoms are guaranteed by constitutional and legal provisions, protected by laws and by courts, and are widely accepted by the public as "foundational."

Group rights are somewhat more problematical in liberal democracy. Although ethnic and other identities are known in liberal societies, the great number of which are immigrant or even settler societies, in most of them ethnicity (and other group-based identities) is privatized, voluntary, and noncoercive. Most important, ethnicity is not recognized by the state in any formal institutionalized manner, and it is not a source of advantage or disadvantage for individuals.

In some liberal democracies the state is not entirely free from the ethnocultural particularistic effects that are, quite naturally, linked to the majority or to the sociopolitical prominent group. Thus in the otherwise liberal-democratic United Kingdom, the monarch is the head of the national church (the Anglican Church), and the separation between church and state is not recognized. The link between the two is formally emphasized. In various liberal democracies the national church is involved, in one way or another, in public affairs, albeit in a mostly formal, ceremonial manner. The important fact, however, is that in liberal democracy the "national church," the majority religion, or other ethnocultural, particularistic institutions should not have substantial and substantive advantage over other identities or considerable control over the state. Moreover, in no liberal democracy is the discrimination of a minority, as a group or individuals, accepted, and in most liberal democracies minorities are specifically and aggressively protected from such discrimination. Ideally, the relationship between the state and the national church in a liberal democracy is mostly symbolic and ceremonial, not material and substantive.

Analysts who support group rights as a way of protecting minorities argue that even in liberal democracy, "the state has not been, nor can it be, culturally neutral" (Requejo 2001b, 110–32). In principle, this point is valid. Even by choosing a national language, let alone a state religion, a liberal democracy is "particularized." Similarly, by declaring a particular day as an official day of rest, the state has taken a particularistic stand. Yet it is important to recognize the huge difference between minimalist, unavoidable particularistic choice in liberal democracies and the maximal, pervasive particularism of "hegemonic polities."

Critics of liberal democracy might also be right in maintaining that such a regime treats cultural differences "as particularist trends or deviations" (ibid., 110). Such an attitude might be the essence of liberal democracy, although genuine liberal democracy should deal equally with all such "deviations" and facilitate their survival. Moreover, by guaranteeing all the possible liberties for individuals and groups, liberal democracies make it possible for groups to organize and promote their unique identities. As a matter of principle, liberal democracy treats all groups as equal and does not give any group substantial advantage over other groups, with the occasional exception of having a "national church" as previously described.

In some liberal democracies, however, the need for recognizing the special status of historically discriminated or disadvantaged groups has risen. Such special recognition, which often goes under the term *affirmative action*, is justified in terms of equality, justice, and stability, but it is often regarded as a deviation from the foundational norm of total equality among individuals. This practice might be applicable also in multiethnic, multinational settings as a way of responding to the demands of people with historical rights within multiethnic polities (e.g., the Quebecois in Canada, the Basques and Catalans in Spain), as long as the principle of individual equality is accepted as the supreme value within the polity.

The occasional deviation from the norms of liberal democracy found in affirmative action programs emphasizes rather than detracts from the main ideological goal of most liberal democracies: the creation of a transcendental and overarching identity that stands over and above all other identities and is equally shared by all citizens. The commitment to that ideal is particularly pronounced in the "classical" democracies such as France, the United Kingdom, and the United States. At the same time, it is self-evident that the establishment of such an overarching identity is a tall order, and in deeply divided societies (of the types that often produce hegemonic polities) might be doomed to failure.

In analyzing strategies for the creation of transcendental identity, some analysts distinguished between several varieties that are compatible with the general framework of liberal democracy. A distinction that is of direct relevance for the transformation of hegemonic polities has been offered, for example, by McGarry and O'Leary (1993, 17) and is based on the previous work of several other scholars: (1) the state might promote civic integration by creating a common civic, national, or patriotic identity. Horowitz calls such a common identity "inter-ethnic nationalism" (1985, 567); and (2) the state could promote ethnic assimilation by creating a common ethnic identity, a strategy sometimes referred to colloquially as "the melting pot."

These presumably distinct strategies are sometimes mixed in reality and from the perspective of this author some of them could be judged to be compatible with liberal democracy while others are rather hegemonic. Thus, for example, the notion of "Great Britain" (or the "United Kingdom") might reflect a serious effort on the part of the British state to integrate "civically" several nations or ethnicities (the English, Scots, Welsh, and Irish) by creating a common identity based on shared history (e.g., the spirit of Dunkirk and other such myths), shared ideals (e.g., democracy and the rule of law), common language and culture, and so forth. Similarly, the American nation is based on the promise of and the commitment to the Constitution, several real or constructed American ideals, and shared historical myths. For the French, civic integration has been predicated for a long time on the absorption of French culture and particularly the French language.

These cases and others are examples of civic integration that is compatible with the assumptions of liberal democracy, particularly because they allow ethnic groups to maintain their unique identities while "melting" into the larger society. Thus in the case of the United States (as well as Canada, Australia, and New Zealand), ethnicity is a private matter, an identity toward which the state is neutral and the public tolerant. Ethnic groups, like other groups, can and do organize and become active in all areas, including politics. Although in all of these cases, the dominant group, the "founding nation" if you will, is given certain advantages over other ethnic or national groups, these advantages are relatively minor and often unavoidable. Thus in all the Anglo-Saxon countries, English is the dominant language and its knowledge is a precondition for citizenship, as French is in France and other national languages are in their respective countries. Moreover, in these countries, the day of rest and several holidays are determined by the Christian tradition. These types of what might be called "majority prerogatives" are normatively acceptable in liberal democracies.

Coercive actions designed to assimilate ethnic minorities, particularly indigenous nonimmigrant minorities, are hegemonic and nondemocratic in nature. Although the boundary between the democratically acceptable and the hegemonically unacceptable is not always clear, the distinction is nevertheless important. Thus in terms of historical examples, although many observers might judge the efforts of the French state to turn peasants into Frenchmen (Weber 1976) as legitimate, maybe because they were carried out by a democratic republic and the "target" populations already spoke a variety of French dialects, the efforts of the Hungarians to "Magyarize" their territory after 1867 were generally judged as nondemocratic, heavyhanded, and, in the language of this volume, "hegemonic." The Russification policy carried out by czars and Commissars alike, and the Turkification policy since Ataturk fall under the same category.

In general, it has proven to be much easier for immigrant societies to carry out benign "civic integration" around the culture of the dominant founding nation (e.g., the United States) than it has been for societies constituted from several "indigenous" people living in their own historical homelands (e.g., Spain). Such societies have often resorted to coercive assimilation using hegemonic mechanisms.

The assumption of all integrative models – civic or assimilatory – have been that members of the target group, those who are asked to integrate into the larger society in which they are a minority, could be persuaded to give up their claim for autonomy or preferably any other political, collective right. In return, the dominant group and "its" state would grant members of the minority civic equality in all areas, equal opportunity, and guarantees against discrimination. It is important to note, however, that such a bargain is not offered in cases of hegemony, especially when the minority is considered unassimilable due to the severity of conflict between it and the majority or insurmountable gaps between the two groups in terms of religion, race, culture, and so forth.

What might be called "an assimilation bargain" is substantially more difficult to reach with ethnic groups living in their own place of origin, their real or imagined ancestral home, than it is with immigrant groups moving into new territory. Yet the bargain is also much more achievable when the state offering it is a genuine liberal democracy rather than an authoritarian state. In the case of liberal democracy, after all, the minority targeted for integration may continue to pursue its collective interests through private channels, under the full protection of the liberal state, albeit without its formal support.

Forced assimilatory policy of a minority is a different story altogether, especially when it is carried out by the stronger ethnic group and in contested territories. When such an assimilatory policy is carried out, it is a proven recipe for bloody conflict in today's world. There are numerous examples for such policy generating conflict: Ireland in the nineteenth century (Friel 1981), Turkey's policy toward the Kurds, Sri Lanka, and so forth. The transformation of polities carrying out such policies and their emergence as genuine democracies depends on the majority's recognition that assimilation is impractical, unachievable, and altogether counterproductive, especially once the distinct identity of the "target group" has been established. Such identity has traditionally been associated with the development of literacy consciousness, distinct language, political organization(s) that transcends the kinship level, and so forth (Anderson 1983; Cederman 1997, esp. 157–61; Hobsbawm 1990).

In some liberal-democratic polities, such as Canada, multiculturalism has been promoted as an alternative to heavy-handed assimilatory policy or even benign integrative policy. Nevertheless, such policy, even when strongly endorsed by the majority, has often been perceived by minorities as unsatisfactory or even threatening (Gagnon and Tully 2001; Keating 2001b; Requejo 2001b).

Although liberal democracy, especially in its pure form, is totally and somewhat exclusively committed to individual rights, several types of political systems (or regimes) are fundamentally group based. Such polities assume that in an era of intense nationalism the only way to restrain domestic ethnic conflict is by recognizing the group rights of ethnic collectivities. Although none of the group-based systems oppose individual rights – they all see these as essential – they view individual rights as insufficient for dealing with the most important political issues on the agenda of an ethnically divided society.

In this study, several regimes that might restrain hegemonic states through group-based systems are recognized. An important distinction is offered between regimes based on *centralized power sharing* (consociationalism or binationalism) and regimes based on *decentralized power-division* through federalization, cantonization, or autonomy.

One way in which the power of the dominant ethnic group in society might be restrained is through an agreement between it and other groups to share power in all of society's important institutions. Consociationalism, which was developed systematically in the writings of Arend Lijphart, has at least four characteristics:

1. Grand coalition representing the various segments of society (including joint control over the state's executive power).
2. Proportional representation throughout the public sector (including the elected parliament, civil service positions, and budgetary allocations).
3. Substantial autonomy and self-government for ethnic communities.
4. Constitutional vetoes for minorities.

Lijphart envisions a consociational "deal" as an agreement among the leaders of the main groups. He, thus, assumes that (1) the elites are genuinely interested in reaching a power-sharing deal (which in numerous situations has not been the case), and (2) the elites are capable of leading the "masses" in a moderating, compromising direction and, if they do so, are capable of withstanding the challenges of alternative and more radical elites. In the contemporary world, we have seen "elites jockeying for power within the ethnic group and having incentive to be immoderate" (Snyder 2000, 30) more often than elites leading their people toward compromise. Leaders who look for strengthening their position among their ethnic brothers are unlikely to be moderate, not even in the most liberal of places.

Although, theoretically, consociationalism is possibly the most attractive regime from the perspective of the minority, it is rather problematical even beyond the issue of the motivation and the capabilities of the ruling elite to create such a regime:

1. Lijphart's "model" was developed on the basis of cases where the main social cleavages were not ethnic but ideological (e.g., class, religion). In contemporary societies the ethnopolitical cleavage is more dominant (Arel 2001, 66) and on the whole substantially deeper than the divides

dealt with by Lijphart. It is possible that those ethnic cleavages are too deep to facilitate a consociational solution or to sustain it. Consociationalism requires the measure of trust and unity that are, simply put, not available in numerous divided societies today. More generally, it could be argued that identity politics are not conducive for consociational solutions.

2. Consociationalism is highly problematical from the perspective of democracy. In its essence, it is a "deal" between elites designed to give minorities preferential position relative to their size in the population. Thus it might violate the "will of the majority" by giving an extra weight to the prerogatives of the minority (e.g., veto power). Although consociationalism still might be the preferred solution in many situations (e.g., as a way of avoiding pervasive instability) the principled weaknesses that it has in terms of the requirements of democracy must be recognized.

3. In numerous situations, where consociationalism might be needed badly as a solution to ethnic conflict, one ethnic group enjoys overwhelming dominance within society. Such a group is most unlikely to agree to a full-fledged consociational deal of the type envisioned by Lijphart. While consociationalism might work in a relatively balanced situation (such as Northern Ireland), it is unlikely to be implemented in countries such as Canada, Israel, Estonia, Spain, Romania, or any other country where numerical balance is lacking. The applicability of the consociational model is thus rather limited.

4. For consociationalism to emerge, flourish, and be sustained, an appropriate political culture that promotes compromise and dialogue is needed. Yet most hegemonic situations with which this volume is concerned have developed when one national group defeated another by force of arms (Canada, Israel, Ireland, Spain are but some examples). In many of these situations, the defeated group believes it has scores to settle and the victorious group is unlikely to give up the fruits of its victory. Chances for a real consociational deal are not good in these conditions.

For those reasons and others, consociational deals are possible only when one has a relatively mild conflict, shallow divides, rough equality among the parties, and truly extraordinary leaders on both sides, a combination that is almost impossible to achieve. When you have such a rare combination, the possibility of establishing full-fledged consociational, binational, or multinational regimes is quite good. In existing "hegemonies," which are built on vast differentials of power between majority and minority, as well as hostility between the groups and the domination of ethnic politics, the likelihood of consociational deals is even smaller.

In view of these problems, we face today a pronounced decline of consociationalism, despite its considerable theoretical attractiveness. Several consociational systems collapsed completely in the last quarter of the twentieth century (Cyprus, Lebanon). Others have been described as less consociational than previously assumed (Netherlands, Austria). Most interestingly, though, a country such as Belgium has moved from a consociational model of centralized power sharing toward a robust federalism. Malaysia, a country described in the past by some analysts as consociational, is as hegemonic as ever and in Israel consociationalism is limited to the relationships among Jewish groups (Cohen and Susser 1996; Don-Yehiya 1999). India, also described as consociational by some observers (Lijphart 1996), has shown signs of Hindu nationalism and even mild hegemonism in the language of this study.

It is possible that among the highly conflictual societies today, only Northern Ireland would be moving in the foreseeable future in a consociational direction. Yet there are two interesting facts to remember in regard to Northern Ireland: (1) the proposed consociational deal that was adopted there in 1998 has not been implemented to date, to a large extent due to the inherent difficulties with the model; (2) because Northern Ireland is not an independent state, but part of the United Kingdom, it is a genuinely unique case with limited implications for other cases. Most important of all, in terms of this study, no independent, sovereign state that could be called "hegemonic" has moved in a consociational direction over the last several decades.

One radical form of consociationalism is *binationalism* or *multinationalism*, a regime in which a state is equally shared by two or more nations. Examples include Czechoslovakia, where even the name indicated the power-sharing arrangement, and Belgium before it moved decisively toward federal structure, as well as the Austro-Hungarian Empire. Binational or multinational structures are extreme cases of consociational power sharing. They rarely work in the contemporary world.

Although binationalism, multinationalism, or consociationalism as group-rights regimes are based on centralized power sharing, several other group-rights regimes take an alternative and in some ways more realistic approach by decentralizing and dividing power as a method of solving ethnic conflicts. Three such decentralizing regime types are of particular importance for this study: federalism, cantonization, and autonomy. The similarities between these three types are more pronounced than the differences, but because the emphasis in this volume is on transforming hegemonies into more inclusive systems, it is useful to look somewhat microscopically into the different variants of group-rights regimes that are available for such hegemonies.

Federalism is a highly complex system, with numerous variants of its own. Although the fundamental idea – dividing power between the central government and the territorial units of the state – is fairly simple, there are numerous important questions regarding the kind of polities that are likely to be successful in achieving stability through federalism, the specific division of power between the center and the "units," the right of secession, and so forth.

The most important issue from the perspective of this volume is whether a federal solution can resolve an internal ethnic conflict in a way that will achieve stability, justice, and democracy. One important characteristic of federalism is that "it allows for certain diversity which is not to be found in unitary states"

(Fossas, 2001, 63), thus responding to the concerns of the ethnic minority. The federal idea inherently combines unity and diversity, trying to maintain the integrity of the state along with the recognition of its components.

In terms of the present study, Juan Linz's distinction between different types of federal states is useful (Gagnon and Tully, 2001a, 323). Linz distinguishes between federal states that exist in mononational situations (post-1918 Austria, Australia, Germany after 1821, the United States) and federal states in societies characterized by political units with different languages, religions, and so forth. (Belgium, Canada, India, Spain, Switzerland). A similar distinction is the one between territorial federalism, where a large territory is divided to produce a more efficient form of government, and multinational federalism, designed to accommodate diverse national communities (Resnick 1999).

For obvious reasons this study has deep interest only in federal states where multiethnicity dominates the political scene. If hegemonic polities are already established in such polities, federalism could become a key for the resolution or the easing of their internal ethnic conflicts, however severe.

A federal "deal" for the resolution of ethnic conflict could be highly attractive, especially if several fundamental conditions prevail. Among these conditions are the absence of a total breakdown in relations between the ethnic groups (as a high level of trust is required for the federal solution to work) and a reasonable demographic and possibly historical distribution of the national territory (e.g., Belgium or Canada). The boundaries of the ethnic, federal units (e.g., states, provinces) must match the relevant criteria that define the ethnic group – language, religion, historical precedents, etc. – or a federal arrangement would not be possible. If and when such conditions exist, robust federalism is a possibility. The federal units, ethnoterritorial in nature, can be given real power in all areas, possibly with the exception of security, foreign affairs, and overall economic policy.

In a hegemonic situation, however, the dominant ethnic group is likely to be extremely hesitant in allowing a robust federalism of ethnoterritorial nature to develop. It may perceive such an arrangement as a prelude for secession and possibly even as actively encouraging it. The transfer of power from the centralized state to the federal components could therefore be quite problematical in a hegemonic state.

Nevertheless, at least several previously unitary states have moved in a federal direction over the last few decades. Spain and Belgium are good examples, and the United Kingdom may follow suit. The notion of "devolutionary federalism" (Lenaerts 1996) was introduced into the analysis as a result of these developments, and it is a notion that might have a great future. In such a regime, powers are systematically transferred from the center to the constituent units.

A federal arrangement within an ethnic context is, in general, highly attractive from a normative perspective. Such an arrangement may meet the demanding expectations of liberal democracy. In principle, a federal scheme is a reasonable way of dividing power between the sovereign state and its ethnic components. Most important, it gives the weaker parties – the ethnic minorities – a measure of protection against majoritarian arbitrariness, and it does so using constitutional means: written constitutions that cannot be easily revised, bicameral legislatures with overrepresentation for weaker groups and/or regions, supreme courts that keep a zealous eye on the integrity of the federal deal, and so forth.

Despite all the advantages of federalism in multiethnic polities, like other group-rights regimes, federalism is not free of problems, in both hegemonic and liberal-democratic states:

1. The creation of a federation in any unitary state, but especially in a hegemonic one, could generate a powerful drive toward full independence of the federal units. If federalization is perceived as a prelude to secession and an invitation for separatism, unitary states might resist it under any conditions. It is important to remember, in this context, that all three ethnofederal Communist systems – the Soviet Union, Yugoslavia, and Czechoslovakia – broke up immediately with the decline of the authoritarian state. The federal structure hastened the disintegration of the state. For that reason, many unitary states may see federalism merely as a last resort, and they are likely to have a fairly weak form of it when they adopt it (e.g., Spain).

2. Ethnic "hegemonists" and liberal democrats may look at ethnically based federalism with a measure of suspicion. To begin with, liberal democrats tend to oppose, as a matter of ideology, all group rights; they perceive these as establishing inequality (although many of them are willing to make an exception in the case of affirmative action). Moreover, some liberal analysts believe that "ethnofederalism tends to heighten and politicize ethnic consciousness" (Brubaker 1996, ch. 2; Snyder 2000, 327), thus generating conflict rather than solving it.

All in all, while this argument is valid, most countries that might be candidates for federalism are already thoroughly ethnicized long before ethnofederalism is seriously discussed. Be that as it may, most countries with a dominant ethnic group – Israel, Romania, Slovakia, or even Spain and the United Kingdom – are unlikely to look kindly on robust federalism as a solution for their ethnic problems. Federations are especially fragile in biethnic societies. McGarry and O'Leary argue that with the possible exception of Belgium, "there is not a single case of successful federalism based upon a dyadic or two-unit structures" (1993, 34). If Belgium disintegrates, it could be the final nail in the coffin for the ethnically based federal design in its binational application.

Federalism, however, might be more successful in multiethnic than in biethnic polities. Two cases, India and Spain, come to mind as moderately successful, although the jury is still out on both cases. In the case of India, a highly centralized form of federalism was established, leading some scholars to regard the system not as genuine federalism (Rajashekara 1997, 266). The Indian government has overriding powers over the power of the States, the constitution may be amended by the national parliament alone (unlike the United States), and state governments can be quite easily dismissed by the national government. Moreover, the ascendance of a nationalist government in India of the 1990s might be seen as a threat for the powers of the states, units that often represent diverse ethnocultural groups in this vast country (Datta 1999; Greenway 2001; Melman 2002; Mirsa 1999; Stuligross 1999).

India's Founding Fathers, especially Nehru, conceived of the country as centralized but secular and ethnically blind. India of the Congress Party was surely not ethnically "hegemonic." Although ethnically based complaints led the government to readjust some boundaries, so as to reflect more accurately ethnic divides, the basic principle of resistance to separatist and religious groups was maintained (Brass 1999). Although Lijphart described India as "consociational" (Lijphart 1996), others objected to that characterization. All in all, with the BJP rise to power, then its decline, and also with major violent outbursts on ethnic background, it remains to be seen how the Indian formal federalist system will evolve.

The Spanish case is equally interesting, especially from the perspective of the transformation of a hegemonic state into a democracy with at least some federal features. It is possible that in terms of preventing hegemony, the multiplicity of the ethnic or national groups, as well as their relative power, gives the Spanish case certain advantages over other cases. As will be explained later in some detail, Spain has gone through a dual transformation from authoritarianism to democracy and from being a Castilian state to a multiethnic republic, processes that seem to have reinforced each other.

Despite these changes in the Spanish political system, many Basques and Catalans find the Spanish model still lacking. While most federations are symmetrical in structure, in the sense that all subunits have identical powers, in the case of Spain, as in that of Canada, the historical nationalities have argued for asymmetry. This demand has not been fully accommodated by the state or been endorsed by other groups or regions within the country.

The idea of asymmetrical federalism remains interesting yet controversial. More specifically, asymmetrical federalism is often perceived by its opponents as contradicting the fundamental principles of democracy and equality. Moreover, in a federal system, the demands of one or more units for asymmetrical treatment are likely to be regarded by other units as fundamentally unfair. To the extent to which federalism in a multiethnic setting is an exercise in balancing unity and diversity, the insistence on special status for some ethnoterritorial provinces (e.g., Quebec or Catalonia) may generate disunity.

Another group-based method of managing ethnic differences is *cantonization*. McGarry and O'Leary view cantonization as a micropartition of a multiethnic state in which political power is devolved to small political units, each granted "mini-sovereignty" (1993, 31). One interesting feature of cantonization is that it could easily facilitate asymmetrical relations between the different cantons and the federal government. Even the semifederal, post-Franco, Spanish state has adopted the asymmetrical principle of cantonization and has done so quite successfully. Thus Catalonia and the Basque country have different relations with the central government in Madrid than all other internal units within Spain, and there are also significant differences between these two historic regions.

Although cantonization is a fairly rare form of government – the single classical example being Switzerland – it might be "usable" in other settings, especially when other group-based methods for settling conflicts are beyond reach due, principally, to the opposition of the dominant ethnic group within the polity. The cantonizational idea of allowing ethnically homogeneous units to make their own decisions on the lowest possible level of political organization is a simple but possibly effective solution for countries where interethnic cooperation on a higher level is not possible.

The principle of cantonization is straightforward: create uni-ethnic subunits in a multiethnic polity and endow them with the power to manage their own affairs. Although the overwhelming "Swiss nature" of this type of government may make it look unpromising for other countries, this governmental method could possibly be applied in other countries that are ethnically mixed and highly conflictual. The former territory of Yugoslavia (especially Bosnia, Macedonia, etc.) could benefit from the Swiss experience, but other polities (Canada, Northern Ireland, Israel) may try this model as well.

Although the cantonization of conflictual societies is fraught with challenges (e.g., the mere division of the territory is likely to be problematical), it has some clear advantages over other mechanisms for settling conflicts. Even though there is a sense of finality to partition or succession, and even to federal or consociational arrangements, cantonization is a more moderate, less final deal. It could be even experimental in nature, and thus more acceptable to the state and its ethnic majority.

Although cantonization has evolved in Switzerland over a period of several hundred years, it might be "usable" in areas where such historical depth is simply not possible. For example, it is a method that could be tried for dealing with local communities of Arabs in Israel, Hungarians in Romania and Slovakia, and other communities living in hegemonic polities.

The last group-based arrangement in a multiethnic state to be discussed is *autonomy*, with its territorial and nonterritorial forms. While McGarry and O'Leary (1993) do not even include autonomy in their scheme of methods for either "eliminating" or "managing" differences, there is a place in such a classification for *autonomy*, a frequently used term in the literature (Safran and Maiz 2000). Autonomy is a group-based regime type, which gives a particular ethnic group or region control over some public aspects of their lives, on a territorial or nonterritorial (i.e, personal) basis, but under the full and unhindered sovereign power of the state. Consociationalism is centralized power sharing, autonomy is not; federalism and cantonization are always territorial, autonomy is not; federalism might limit constitutionally the power of the central state, autonomy will not. So although autonomy shares with other regimes some characteristics, it also differs from them in important ways. Spain today, India since 1967, and possibly Belgium until 1993 are systems with elements of autonomy more than full-fledged federal systems, regardless of what they call themselves formally.

Jash Ghai views autonomy as "a device to allow ethnic or other groups a distinct identity to exercise direct control over affairs of special concern to them, while allowing the larger entity these powers which cover common interest" (2000, 8). It should be noted that Ghai's definition of autonomy does not include a territorial component or demand the transfer of sovereignty from the central government to the local one. As such, his concept of autonomy is clearly nonfederal. His notion of autonomy is clearly more compatible with consociationalism, although it differs from it in that consociational arrangements often imply power sharing on the level of the centralized state.

The vast literature on governmental arrangements suggests that there are not one but many views of autonomy. All in all, we should flexibly allow different power-sharing deals, with greater or lesser control by the center, to be included in this form of regime, as it is done by Lapidoth (1996, 33).

Despite the considerable level of semantic confusion over the precise meaning of autonomy – some analysts, for example, believe it to be further reaching in terms of self-rule than federalism – the notion of "autonomy" is quite popular today as a governmental tool for settling conflicts. The widespread acceptance among analysts of the legitimacy of group rights gives autonomy a measure of respectability (Baker 1996).

Several cases of autonomy in recent years have given this scheme a considerable "boost" as a model for conflict resolution. The devolution plan in the United Kingdom (a unitary state *par excellence* that gave its name to the centralized "Westminster" model), the Corsican autonomy plan by France (the state that gave the world the "Jacobin" centralized model), and less-known cases (e.g., the Danish Home Rule Act of 1979 by which Greenland was granted self-rule) offer autonomy as a possible solution to at least relatively moderate conflicts, potential conflict, or nonconflicts where special recognition of a particular ethnic group is necessary.

Despite the support for autonomy by many group-rights proponents, this model suffers from some of the problems of the ones that plague federalism and consociationalism:

1. Autonomy could be seen by the state and by the ethnic majority as a first step toward independence, especially if it is territorially based.
2. From the perspective of pure liberal democracy, autonomy could be perceived as unequal because those who enjoy autonomy might have more rights than others.
3. In an ethnically conflictual situation, leaders are likely to find it difficult if not impossible to offer autonomy, and the existence of a democracy may make concessions more difficult.

Most of those problems could be addressed effectively, provided that the proposed autonomy for a group is (1) limited in scope and (2) nonterritorial in nature. Even a hegemonic state – democratic or even authoritarian – could learn to live with nonterritorial autonomy (NTA), granting ethnic minorities rights in areas such as religion, culture, and language. Because nationalism plus territory equal statehood, states are understandably reluctant to give any territory to national or ethnic groups within them, even if such an arrangement is called merely "autonomy."

Nonterritorial autonomy could, of course, be highly attractive when ethnic groups are demographically spread (Coakley 1994). In such cases, individuals belonging to certain ethnic group(s) might be granted "personal autonomy," and the central state's fear of separatism could be substantially reduced. In some situations, territorial autonomy and nonterritorial autonomy could even be combined, as has been the case in Belgium (Hooghe 1993) and in Canada (De Villiers 1994).

Several interesting cases of nonterritorial autonomy stand out. Cyprus had a rather short-lived experience with that form of regime (1960–3), but Lebanon has lived with it for over thirty years (1943–75). Even in Israel, Arabs as individuals have certain rights in the field of education, religion, and culture (language), and so do Swedes in Finland.

In the case of Cyprus, the largely consociational constitution gave a great deal of autonomy to the two ethnic groups, establishing two separately elected communal chambers with legislative powers over religious, educational, cultural, and personal status matters. The system was advantageous in the sense that it set up a federal structure without actual territorial federalism, thus, it could be argued, blunting the edge of hegemonism. Yet the demise of the system is the best evidence for the inherent weaknesses in even such a relatively benign paradigm for interethnic peace.

Lebanon is another case in point. There, each sect had its schools, social and welfare organizations, courts for dealing with personal status matters, and so forth (Suleiman 1967). Yet the Lebanese NTA could not survive the ethnic strife after the mid-1970s (although that strife was greatly influenced by the intervention of outside powers).

In Malaysia (1955–69), a form of consociational democracy with autonomy features was tried as well. Each segment of the multiethnic population – Malay, Chinese, Indian, and Pakistani – enjoyed a high degree of internal autonomy (Lijphart 1997, 151). In this case the experiment proved unsuccessful.

Although NTA might not be a perfectly desirable solution for a weak ethnic group in a hegemonic state, it is clearly preferable to a condition of no autonomy at all, especially if the ethnic majority carries out a policy of coercive integration that is implemented by the state. A liberal-democratic regime with full-fledged personal equality, as well as NTA, allows an ethnic minority to conduct its affairs on its own. At the same time, NTA could serve as a coverup for hegemonic control, especially when it is implemented without the establishment of a genuine liberal democracy (Israel and South Africa are relevant examples).

In general, however, "there is something of value in non-territorial approaches to the resolution of ethnic conflict" (Coakley 1994, 312). The alternative to autonomy, in addition to the hegemony of the majority, could often be secession, but efforts to achieve it result in the vast majority of cases in long and destructive war. Although negotiating autonomy of any kind is not free of costs and risks for the political elites – especially in terms of possibly losing the support of the ethnic majority – some elites are strong enough, and sufficiently far-sighted, to push for an autonomy prior to the outbreak of major interethnic hostilities.

Eastern Europe today has become a large laboratory for autonomy. Thus although Moldova has accepted the idea, the Ukraine has adamantly refused. Several countries (Romania, Slovakia) have been under Western pressure to treat their minorities fairly, international pressure that has borne some fruits. The Russians offered the Chechens autonomy, they refused. A bloody war resulted. It is emblematic of the possible alternatives to the autonomous idea.

The Hegemonic Option: Long- vs. Short-Term Results

The previous section described and analyzed in some detail a number of regime types based on either individual rights or group rights. Emphasis was placed on the way in which ethnic conflict could be regulated, and possibly reduced, by various regimes. In this section, another option for managing ethnic conflict will be explored, the imposition of ethnic hegemony. Although Chapter 2 will explore in more detail the relationships between hegemony and democracy, the use of the state as an instrument of hegemonic control, the consequences of hegemony and the possibilities for transforming it, themes to which I will return in Chapter 3 (which offers a classification of multinational states), in this section I will discuss some of the basic characteristics of hegemony.

In terms of the distinction between individual- and group-based rights, the hegemonic regime provides often an interesting and complex mixture that could easily confuse the observer:

1. Many hegemonic regimes grant fundamental individual rights to all of their citizens, as do liberal democracies, although in most of them one finds subtle and often not-so-subtle distinctions, in law and in practice, between individuals belonging to the majority and those belonging to the minority (Kretzmer 1990).
2. In many hegemonic regimes, limited group rights are granted to ethnic minorities, especially rights in the areas of religion, regulation of personal status (e.g., marriage, divorce), language, culture, and even the running of an independent educational system.

Despite those "concessions" to individual and group rights of minorities, what is called in this volume an ECO is a political system that pursues relentlessly one primary goal: the maintenance and enhancement of the dominance of one ethnic or national group. This is the essence of such regimes.

Under the best of circumstances, ECOs may achieve a status of an inherently flawed democracy. In such regimes, which Smooha has called "ethnic democracy" (1990, 1997), the hegemonic state grants basic individual rights to all individuals but carefully guarantees the dominance of the majority over the public sphere in its entirety. Israel is among the best examples of that relatively benign variant of an ethnic order; post-Soviet Estonia and Latvia are others, as is Sri Lanka.

Under the worst of circumstances, an ethnic order could deteriorate and adopt full-fledged, discriminatory policies against the minority, a situation that might easily lead to a civil war, unless the minority is too weak to resist the majority's discrimination and must accept its fate quietly. While Smooha and Hanf (1992, 28–9) offer a distinction between stable and unstable domination, the argument of this book is that in today's world instability is inherent in hegemonic polities.

The notion of "control" by one ethnic group over another was first developed as an analytical concept by Ian Lustick (1979, 1980). McGarry and O'Leary, quoting Lustick, deal with "hegemony" and define it as a situation that makes an "overtly violent ethnic contest for state power either 'unthinkable' or 'unworkable' on the part of subordinated communities" (1993, 23). Although the McGarry-O'Leary definition is useful for analyzing the essence of political hegemony, as well as its political dynamics, it is important to note that in terms of rights, Ethnic Constitutional Orders amount to systematic discrimination between citizens on the basis of ethnic descent.

In relation to other regimes identified in this chapter, the following generalizations could be offered about ECOs:

1. ECOs are unavoidably in great tension with liberal democracy, a regime that is based on the ethnic neutrality of the state and on equal rights to all citizens (Chapter 2). The most that an ECO could achieve is a status of an "illiberal democracy" (Zakaria 1997, 2003), that is, a procedural democracy with periodic elections but not a status of a genuine democracy with emphasis on broadly defined human rights and tightly protected civil rights.

2. As for consociationalism, a regime based on genuine group accommodation and cooperation that is reflected in power sharing over the centralized state, ethnic orders cannot possibly achieve that (despite Lijphart's opinion of the Israeli case). Ironically, in an effort to maintain hegemony, groups within the majority may establish a consociational structure among themselves (Cohen and Susser 1996; Don-Yehiya, 1999) thus creating a hybrid of what could be called "consociational hegemonism."

3. A federal regime might be compatible with an ethnic order but only if it is a relatively nonrobust, feeble federalism of the type established in India. If the central organs of the state – its executive and legislative branches in particular – are firmly in the hands of the dominant ethnic majority, it could allow a subordinate, subservient minority to control some of the federal or semifederal units. After all, in such a structure the federal units can be "disciplined" by the center if and when they challenge the overall, hegemonic structure of the state. It remains to be seen whether several

federal or semifederal states (e.g., Spain) will move in a hegemonic or liberal democratic direction.

4. Cantonization and autonomy are two additional forms of regime that could, theoretically, live peacefully with a moderate hegemonic regime. These governmental forms could even strengthen "benign" hegemony by giving minorities at least minimal outlets for their desires. More robust hegemonies, however, are likely to fear these options and view them as a prelude to secessionary, separatist drives.

Of all the regimes analyzed in this chapter, liberal democracy might be the most dangerous from the perspective of the ethnically hegemonic state, although, on the face of it, the group-rights regime may look more immediately challenging. In a genuine liberal democracy one may find the seeds of hegemony's demise because the inherent logic of liberal democracy is so fundamentally incompatible with that of hegemonism. Once a liberal democracy is established in a society, even if in an imperfect form, its inherent tension with the hegemonic structure is likely to spill over and affect negatively the entire regime. In the battle royal between liberal democracy and hegemonism, the former might emerge victorious.

Several cases, to be more fully analyzed in Chapters 4 and 5, indicate that the power of democracy against the hegemonic state is awesome. Over the last two decades the growing federalization of Belgium, the ethnoterritorial semifederalization of Spain, the liberalization of several East European countries (e.g., Estonia, Latvia, Slovakia), the move toward consociationalism in Northern Ireland, and toward devolution in the rest of the United Kingdom, are all processes related to the spreading or deepening of democracy in its liberal form within and against a hegemonic political order.

The hope for the genuine democratization of a society is adversely linked to the strength of the existing ethnic hegemony within that society. Moreover, the more dominant the majority the less likely it is that the minority will be able to achieve its democratic rights within the existing system. If the domination of the majority is overwhelming, the minority's ability and, possibly, will to resist, may be paralyzed. Members of the minority group may conclude that "being second-class citizens is better than being first-class rebels" (Snyder 2000, 323), as may be the situation of the Arabs in Israel, the Chinese in Malaysia, and the Russians in Estonia and Latvia.

The Crucial Triangle

Democracy, Statehood, and Hegemony in Multinational Settings

> As long as differences and diversities of mankind exist, democracy must allow for compromise, for accommodation, and for the recognition of differences.
>
> Eugene McCarthy, 1916–2005, U.S. Senator

The thesis presented in this volume focuses on several fundamental concepts that require closer scrutiny, analysis, and reflection than the one given in Chapter 1. The function of this chapter is to provide such analysis. It begins by asserting that we face today the emergence of what might be called "a global governing code," a set of commonly held values emphasizing, primarily, democracy as the only universally acceptable regime form. Multinational polities, like other polities, are normatively assessed against the requirements of democracy. But this reality raises an immediate question that is at the basis of this and many other studies: "What is democracy?" This chapter will begin by addressing this cardinal question. If Ethnic Constitutional Orders (ECOs) are nondemocratic or if they promote, at best, "flawed" democracy, as argued in this study, we need to know as precisely as possible what are the standards of genuine democracy that such regimes fail to meet.

On several occasions in the introduction and in Chapter 1, references were made to the multinational or multiethnic state. Most states today deviate from Mazzini's ideal of "one nation, one state," and most are surely not "nation-states" at all; they are multiethnic and multinational. If multiethnicity is prevalent and if it is a source of conflict, then an exploration of the multinational state and its nature is important. Even more important, from the perspective of this book, is the role that the state, as a conglomerate of formal institutions, may play as an instrument of domination, used by one national group to control all other groups within the multiethnic state.

If the state is an instrument of domination, however, it is also a key for *solving* ethnic conflict through the development of integrative institutions and, possibly, through its own transformation. There is a need to study the state in some detail from the perspective of its ability to change. If the transformation of the "hegemonic state" into a more accommodating, inclusive structure is required – be it through federal, consociational, or other structures – closer attention to that transformative process is crucial.

These lines of analysis will be pursued in this chapter, in the hope of adding considerable depth to the concepts already introduced. This analysis will prepare the ground for the proposed classification of multinational states offered in Chapter 3 and the empirical examination of several cases where transformation from hegemony to inclusivity seemed to have occurred (Chapters 4 and 5).

The chapter begins with an examination of the notion of "democracy" and the requirements that are ordinarily connected to it or, better yet, the principles that ought to be associated with it. Special attention is given to what is often referred to as "liberal democracy," in view of the special place of that particular regime variant within this volume. Because my thesis is that Ethnic Constitutional Orders ought to adopt democratic principles as a mechanism for stability and even survival, a fairly detailed analysis of those democratic principles is necessary.

Equally important is a thorough understanding of the precise role of the state, because it is the state that seems to have been the dominant actor in contemporary ethnically hegemonic regimes. Although many analysts believe that the modern state has declined or already died (Camilleri and Falk 1992; Ohmae 1995; Van Creveld 1999), others believe that the rumors of the death of the state, or even its decline, are highly exaggerated (Weiss 1998). Regardless of the general trend of state power – as it is affected by globalization, integration, other processes – it is my purpose to examine in this volume the role of the state as an instrument of sociopolitical control in multinational settings and especially in hegemonic multinational settings.

In addition to the notions of "democracy" and "statehood," there is a need to look more closely at the concept of "hegemony," a notion developed by Antonio Gramsci and others and applied in this volume to one specific type of sociopolitical relations: ethnic relations in a multinational setting. Special attention will be given to the exploration of the relationships between hegemony and systemic transformation. But beyond these theoretical considerations, it is important to examine the empirical consequences of hegemonism and to assess the findings of such scholars as Ted Robert Gurr (1993, esp. Ch. 2–5; 2000), Daniel Byman and Stephan Van Evera (1998), and others.

Finally, the argument will be made that an understanding of the invariably complex and often hostile relations within a multinational setting requires the use of yet another analytical concept, "otherness," a social condition in which certain individuals or groups are perceived, described, and treated as fundamentally and irreconcilably different from the reference group (often the majority). Any and all negative qualities are projected onto the Other, often the qualities that the perceiver fears or even recognizes in himself (Peleg 1994, 261). Otherness is not only part and parcel of any hegemonic regime, but is the "glue" that holds it together, linking the different elements of such a polity.

Although none of these complicated notions would be given an extensive examination as such, the chapter will explore them as analytical tools for the understanding of ethnic hegemony in multinational settings. Moreover, this chapter will focus on the interactions between these concepts. More specifically, attention will be given to the relationships between genuine democracy and the vision of the state held by a hegemonic ethnic group and its leading elite within a multiethnic setting. This complex relationship will be called "the Crucial Triangle" because it could determine the very fate of the state that finds itself caught in this web of relations.

Prerequisites of Contemporary Democracy

There is a major paradox in regard to the concept of democracy in the contemporary world. On the one hand, it has become a controlling concept in everything related to the design of an appropriate, just, and stable regime for the modern polity. From a normative perspective, everyone argues that their system is genuinely democratic, while their rival's polity falls short, and there is a remarkable global, ideological consensus that this particular form of government – democracy – is the most desirable of all.

On the other hand, democracy is today, more than ever, the classic "contested concept" (Gallie 1962): it is given to numerous definitions, interpretations, claims, and counterclaims. Democracy as a useful concept for political analysis is too often in the eye of the beholder. One way around this problem is to define "democracy" as precisely as possible and do so more explicitly than has been done traditionally.

Although comprehensive discussion of democracy is beyond the scope of the current volume, because this concept is heavily used for assessing the status and the performance of hegemonic regimes and the possibilities for their transformation, it ought to be given clear, explicit, and concrete definition.

To begin with, democracy is not a dichotomous variable but a continuum. Most countries today are neither perfect democracies nor obvious nondemocracies. They fall somewhere in between, meeting some requirements of genuine democracy (see the following text) while failing to meet others.

Secondly, to make the concept of democracy useful for the type of political analysis offered in this volume, the concept has to be broken into its components. Breaking down the concept of democracy into its components could facilitate an empirical analysis. In the modern literature, democracy, or "polyarchy" in the language of Robert Dahl (1971), is often identified with three components: (1) contested elections; (2) an executive branch that is either popularly elected or responsible to an elected legislature; (3) basic civil liberties such as free speech (Russell 1993, 14). Huntington (1991, 7, 9) uses similar criteria to the ones used by Dahl, and so do other writers who approach democracy from a typically American perspective. Non-American writers join them quite often (e.g., Claus Offe, Ralf Dahrendorf).

Historically speaking, the definition of *contemporary democracy* began with the conduct of elections (elections that became increasingly "general"). In the second half of the twentieth century, however, civil rights were increasingly added to the standard definition of *democracy* (Dahl 1989). What some of the standard definitions are missing – a critical point from the perspective of this volume – is an emphasis on equality, possibly reflective of a traditional American perception that equality often contradicts liberty and many writers' preference for the latter.

As against Dahl and others, W. B. Gallie offers a broad definition for democracy, a definition that includes equality as a component. For Gallie, democracy is a regime where (1) the majority of citizens choose the government; (2) there is equality of all citizens regardless of race, creed, sex, and so forth; and (3) citizens can actively participate in their self-government (Black 1962).

It is interesting to note that equality is somewhat subdued and largely unspecified even in the definition given by three of the most accomplished analysts of comparative government, Diamond, Linz, and Lipset (1990, 6–7). For them, democracy is a system that meets three conditions: (1) meaningful and extensive competition among individuals and groups for all elective positions; (2) highly inclusive level of participation in the selection of leaders and policies, so that no major group is excluded; and (3) a level of civil and political liberties sufficient to ensure political competition and participation, including freedom of expression and freedom to form or join organization.

The concept of democracy developed for use in the current study is somewhat different from the definitions quoted so far. This definition is specifically tailored for the study of hegemonic ethnicity. It includes three components, and it rank orders them from a minimalist requirement, through a middle-range requirement, to a maximalist requirement, so as to offer a coherent approach to democracy and create an analytical tool that would facilitate *a distinction between fully democratic polities and flawed democracies.*

The definition of democracy developed in this study includes the following three components: (1) minimal requirement: the conduct of regular, free, and fair elections (an element included in most modern definitions and reflective of the idea of majority rule); (2) middle-range requirement: the protection of fundamental freedoms, an element included in most Western concepts of democracy but missing in so-called illiberal democracies (Zakaria 1997, 2003); (3) maximal requirement: equality before the law and in practice of all citizens, as individuals, and equality of the most important groups in society. This component is missing in many Western definitions, yet it is especially crucial in deeply divided societies, with which this study deals.

The most important element in the conception of democracy offered here is in its emphasis on equality as the most demanding component of such a democratic regime. This conception shares Charles Taylor's view (Gagnon and Tully 2001) that equality of all citizens is "a crucial legitimating condition of modern democracy" and that "discrimination in a modern society is seen as a challenge to the right to exist" (xiii), generalizations that are particularly true in divided societies where the ethnic majority views the state as its alone.

Moreover, it is important to remember that the principle of equality of all citizens is the key for the Western (mainly Anglo-Saxon and French) definition of a legitimate and democratic government, in contrast to the principle of ethnic distinctiveness and membership in the "organic" nation as developed by the Germans (Arel 2001, 69–70).

Equality is uniquely important in the context of this study because it is the single criterion, among the three, that distinguishes the hegemonic, ethnic regime from what will be regarded as a genuine, liberal democracy or group-based democratic polities. Put differently, although hegemonic regimes may meet the requirement of conducting regular elections, and may even grant all citizens – as individuals – basic rights, they deny, as a matter of course and by the imperatives of their very essence, equality to many of society's groups by singling out the hegemonic majority for preferential treatment.

Emphasizing equality, we should be fully aware of the tension inherent in including the third component of democracy, the demand for individual equality and the demand for group equality (in cases where group rights are recognized by the polity). Granting equal rights to all individuals, and them alone, is relatively simple – it is the most fundamental demand of democracy in general and of liberal democracy in particular. Once a polity grants group rights, and specific groups (majorities or minorities) within the polity are singled out for any special rights, other groups and individuals may perceive themselves as and, possibly, be victims of discrimination. Be that as it may, if a particular group in a democracy is given special rights, similar groups should be given the same rights, so as to maintain the principle of equality. Moreover, group rights should be carefully balanced against the damage or perceived damage they may do to individual equality.

In Ethnic Constitutional Orders group discrimination is a powerful force inherent in the very logic of the system even more than individual discrimination (although the latter is also quite common). Nationalizing polities by their nature discriminate against those who do not belong to the nation. Hegemony is embedded in the state as race might be in the "racial state" (Goldberg 2002), regardless of the country's ethnic or national heterogeneity.

Despite the problems inherent in group rights in any democratic regime, and specifically liberal democracy, strong arguments on their behalf could be made:

1. Group rights could be granted on the basis of historical rights. Thus in post-Franco Spain, the Basques were granted by the democratizing Spanish state some special rights in collecting taxes based on past agreements with the Spanish monarchy. The Quebecois have continuously argued that as one of Canada's 'founding nations' they are entitled to special group rights, over and above those given to other provinces, a claim that has been recognized only partially.

2. Group rights might be granted as a compensation for past discrimination. Thus affirmative action programs in the United States and other countries have been established as a means for equalizing the conditions of members of different ethnic groups if and when it was recognized that they have suffered from long-term, pervasive, and injurious discrimination that affects their ability to achieve equality at the present time.

3. Group rights might be dispensed to avoid negative, injurious results. Some analysts have argued that in deeply divided societies minority groups must be given special group rights if their interests, and possibly their very existence, will suffer irreparable damage in the absence of such rights. For example, many members of minority groups in democracies such as Spain and Canada believe that they should have maximal control not only over cultural, linguistic, and educational matters in their ancestral lands, but also over the immigration flow into what they consider their territory, a demographic and economic process that tends to favor the majority's culture.

The modern democratic (and especially liberal-democratic) nation-state has been ideologically unsympathetic to special group rights of any kind. From the perspective of group-rights advocates, it has exhibited interventionist impulses and has bought into the Jacobin notion of national unity (Fossas 2001, 67). Yet the awakening of ethnic groups even in the most Jacobinistic of polities has been duly noted even by typically centralized states; they have responded by granting group rights to minorities, although often to a lesser degree than demanded by these groups. In Ethnic Constitutional Orders the tension between the centralized state and minorities is much more severe than in other contexts because of the incompatibility between the essence of the regimes and genuine minority rights.

The three-pronged definition of democracy developed here is particularly fitting for the analysis of such hegemonic states. It is purposely hierarchical, recognizing that the first requirement of democracy (conducting regular elections) is easily achievable even in a nondemocracy. Although election is a necessary condition for democracy, it is an insufficient condition. Even the second requirement, instituting fundamental freedoms, could not but guarantee a democracy that is still incomplete or flawed. Only the adoption of the third requirement – equality – could assure the emergence of a genuine democracy. Although almost all countries today have instituted some kind of election, the adoption of constitutional freedoms requires a substantially higher level of long-term commitment to democracy. Achieving comprehensive equality for all individuals and possibly the most important sociopolitical groups is, within a comparative context, a truly demanding requirement. The strength of a hierarchical definition is that it can distinguish between different levels of democracy. Unlike other definitions, it captures the "depth" of democracy.

In focusing on the element of equality within a hierarchical definition of democracy, particularly as it relates to the evaluation of ethnic hegemonies, it is important to include several elements: (1) the equality of all citizens as individuals, a condition without which democracy cannot be achieved; (2) the equality of the most important groups in society: although in deeply divided societies, some groups might not be equal to other groups in certain respects (e.g., the public recognition of their languages), the demographically sizeable groups with distinct ethnic profiles ought to receive considerable recognition if the polity recognizes any group rights; (3) equality should be both formal and real, legal and practical: ethnic polities should not be able to "get away" with merely legislating equality, they should work on it proactively, energetically, and multidimensionally.

The definition of democracy offered here is not only useful but necessary for a comprehensive assessment of ethnically hegemonic polities. In the empirical chapters of the book, this definition will be used as rigorously as possible. Thus when analyzing the historical transformation of various hegemonic countries, one could usefully ask whether, and to what extent, they have met the different requirements of democratization. More specifically, the following questions ought to be asked in regard to polities that have presumably gone through democratic transformation and, especially, transformation from ethnic hegemonism to full-fledged, inclusive democracy:

1. Has a state established regular elections in taking the first step from authoritarianism to democracy? Spain in the post-Franco era, for example, has gone through the electoral process, even before the adoption of other elements of democracy.

2. Has a country adopted constitutional guarantees for fundamental freedoms and liberties of all of its citizens, in what form, and how strongly have those been guaranteed? Canada, for example, has been perceived by some analysts in the past as Anglo-Protestant in character. Whether this perception is correct or not, it is important to note that under the leadership of Pierre Trudeau, the Canadian state adopted a comprehensive bill of rights.

3. Has a polity committed itself to equality between all individuals and groups and has this commitment been multidimensional? Possibly the most important element of the 1998 Good Friday (Belfast) Agreement in Northern Ireland has been a commitment to such equality, especially equality between groups.

If a previously hegemonic polity has taken all these steps and has implemented them successfully, an undoubtedly monumental task under the best of circumstances, it could be judged to have crossed the line from hegemonic ethnicity to liberal democracy. If it has implemented only some of these requirements, it would be described in this volume as a "flawed democracy."

The identification of the three requirements of democracy as stages on the way toward full liberalization and democratization, not merely as three independent elements, is crucial. It sensitizes the analyst to the pitfalls, dangers, and difficulties inherent in this process. For example, the institutionalization of elections, although crucial, is by no means a guarantee for the adoption of subsequent constitutional guarantees for constitutional freedoms (Zakaria 1997, 2003). Moreover, regular elections and even the institutionalization of basic freedoms may or may not lead a dominant ethnic group to deethnicize its polity. Some analysts believe that democratization may deepen sociopolitical conflict rather than solve it (Snyder 2000), and an ethnic conflict could be the type of strife that would escalate in the process of democratization (as happened in Slovakia under Mečiar, in Serbia under Milosevic, and even in Estonia and Latvia in the early 1990s). A democratized ethnic majority is often as zealous in clinging to its ethnically based prerogatives as any authoritarian elite, and the leadership of such a majority may have less flexibility in designing compromise solutions than the leadership of a nondemocratic polity.

The Multinational State Facing Diversity

The establishment and development of genuine democracy in multinational polities, especially in traditionally hegemonic states, depends to a large extent on one social institution, the state, although the state is greatly influenced by the society within which it operates. Thus fundamental societal attitudes of estrangement, or "otherness" (see the following text), may limit the options open for state institutions in terms of solving internal ethnic conflict.

While the state has often been declared to be, especially in the recent past, "in decline" (Van Creveld 1999) or even completely "dead" (Ohmae 1995), the announcement of the death of the state is, to this author, premature, and the rumors of its end a pure myth (Weiss 1998). Focusing on the state and its *modus operandi* could be a key for analyzing ethnic relations in the multinational setting. Unfortunately, "stateness" as a variable has been "undertheorized" (Linz and Stepan 1996b, 16). In the analysis offered in this volume, the state is considered central for the establishment of ethnic hegemony and, therefore, to the quality of societal democracy. If it is true that "without a state, no modern democracy is possible" (Linz and Stepan 1996, 17), the type of ethnic hegemony discussed in this study is also not possible without a state.

The modern state is, of course, a rather large and complex organization that could be, and in many ways must be, looked at very selectively. In examining ethnic relations within a multinational polity it is important to focus on the behavior of the dominant group's elite and to ask, pointedly, whether the fundamental political behavior of those elite could be characterized as a policy of the ethnicization of the state. In the context of analyzing the possible transformation of the state, it is important to ask whether the leading elite are even capable of conceiving such transformation and implementing it. The way members of the elite view the essence of their national project (Peleg 1998a) might be the key for the possible transformation of hegemonic states.

In a hegemonic situation, the state and all its agents – the elite, the bureaucracy, the armed forces, the police, and even the intellectuals – view themselves (although not necessarily with the same intensity) as acting on behalf of what Rogers Brubaker has called the "core nation" (1996). The interaction between hegemonic vision and a vigorous, purposeful state action on behalf of that vision is a crucial component in the phenomenon of hegemonism. Without the state, genuine hegemonism would hardly be possible in the contemporary world.

Following Theda Skocpol (1985, 21), the approach adopted in this volume emphasizes the power of the state to act, initiate, and adopt policies in crucial areas. Of special interest are the capacities of the contemporary nationalist, hegemonic polity. This approach is based on some of the now classic writings of Alexis de Tocqueville. The brilliant French analyst recognized by the middle of the nineteenth century the crucial role of the state within societies. States matter because they can encourage certain political actions (ibid.). Within the context of the present study, the hegemonic state's greatest power is in its ability to channel social resources of all types toward a particular goal in order to implement a certain vision. Hegemony is about converting societal resources into state action on behalf of the dominant ethnic group.

In the contemporary world, even more so than in the world known to de Tocqueville, the national state enjoys centralized control over enormous resources: large and often technologically sophisticated armed forces; police and other coercive security services; a sizeable economy that is governed by central institutions; mass media of previously unknown reach; an educational system with immediate impact on every member of society; and political influence over people's commitments and loyalties. As such, the modern state might be a political instrument of unprecedented power in human history.

When the state is monopolized by a dominant ethnic majority and used against an ethnic minority, within the context of a protracted intranational struggle, the power that it can bring to bear could be awesome. Such applied power, used on behalf of the ethnicized state and, eventually, the ethnic majority, could result in a powerful control system (Lustick 1980a, 1980b). Yet such a control system – hegemony, in the language of this study – may result in serious damage to democracy. The link between the hegemonic drive on behalf of a single ethnic group, the ethnicized state, and flawed democracy is almost inevitable.

The long tradition of emphasizing the centrality of the state in the process of achieving the vision of the nation – reflected in the now classical writings of the likes of Fichte and Mazzini, as well as in more contemporary analysts such as Hobsbawm and Tilly – is quite useful in the development of a theory of hegemonic statehood. Lumping *nations* and *states* together, however, especially in the commonly used term *nation-state*, could be greatly dysfunctional if it conceals the intrastate, internal relations between different nations that "happen" to inhabit the same state. It is the purpose of this study to avoid this problem.

Moreover, when the state is an instrument of domination in the hand of one nation against other nation(s) residing within the same political space, the concept of "nation-state" may lose its validity, explanatory power, and even meaning completely. There is, of course, an inherent historical logic behind this semantic confusion. The traditional model of nationalism, a European invention of the modern era, simply assumed that sooner or later internal national minorities within the state will disappear, that this process was desirable and simply part and parcel of "modernization" (Keating and McGarry 2001a, 2).

The "cunning" of history being what it is, however, the project of establishing the uni-national state, envisioned by so many as the inevitable result of the enlightenment process and of modernization has been only partially successful. Scots and Bretons, Basques and Catalans, Slovaks and Bosnians simply refused to melt into their respective "nation-states," some of them after hundreds of years of being dominated by others. By that refusal, these "minor nations" have created the alternative model of the nations-state (rather than *nation-states*) or the multinational state. These nations demanded sometimes their very own, independent state (e.g., Slovakia, Corsica, the Basque country).

There is, of course, an inevitable collision between hegemonism, carried out by the vision of the unified nation-state, and the multinational diversity that is often part of reality in numerous states. The multinational state has traditionally acted, in numerous ways, to create "unity" out of diversity. Several states (e.g., France and Italy) have invented or developed national languages and forced them down the throats of weaker, peripheral populations that spoke a variety of ancient dialects. They established compulsory educational systems to "modernize" their workforce (Gellner 1983, 1997) but also to uninationalize it. They promoted and invented symbols and myths (Anderson 1983) and forced them on reluctant and marginal groups (Weber 1976). The crucial fact to recognize is, however, that the national language, the unified educational system, and the "civic religion" were thoroughly ethnicized, not only ignoring a multinational reality but trying to actively erase it. These activities were, furthermore, merely elements in the broader, all-encompassing hegemonic vision of the dominant group. In some situations, the hegemonic project is not over yet; in others, it fights for its life.

Hegemonic, multinational states in the contemporary world (as compared with their nineteenth century predecessors) face, in principle, an identical, but inherently much more difficult, task. The creation of unity out of diversity is a monumental challenge in the contemporary world. When the ethnic divides in a society are truly deep – as they are in all hegemonic polities – the task of creating national unity is close to impossible.

One way to analyze the options open for the modern multinational state is through what could be called a Differential Citizenship Discourse (DCD). Within the context of this study, there are two opposing citizenship discourses: (1) the *civic state model*, which grants to all citizens equal and comprehensive citizenship rights, regardless of their ethnic origins; and (2) the *hegemonic state model*, which zealously maintains a distinction between those who are entitled to comprehensive citizenship rights and those who are entitled to basic but limited citizenship rights. The dividing line between these two groups in the multinational hegemonic state is determined in accordance with the ethnic identity of the individual: members of the dominant group are entitled to comprehensive citizenship, while members of subservient groups may be granted only limited rights.

In the civic state model, which is most often connected to the historical experiences of France and the United States, but that has now spread to numerous other countries, particularistic identities such as religion and language, ethnic descent, and cultural background, remain officially unrecognized by the state and its institutions. These particularistic "markers" are, at least ideally, privatized. The state claims to be ethnically neutral, even if it had arrived at this supposed neutrality through a process of coercive homogenization. Although it is often not entirely possible for the state to actually achieve such neutrality, as group-rights enthusiasts like to remind us (Kymlicka 1995) – thus, the majority's language and even religion might dominate the public sphere – the ideal of neutrality influences the discourse in the public square and pushes the polity toward inclusion. In some civil states, a special effort is carried out to respond to diversity by, for example, according equal status to several cultures or languages (Burg 1996).

In the hegemonic state model there are, officially or in practice, two types of citizenship, coexisting in considerable unease, side-by-side: (1) comprehensive citizenship, which gives its bearers all the rights, on an equal basis, including full access to "power loci" and the right to actively participate in the determination of the public good; and (2) limited citizenship, which gives its bearers some fundamental rights – especially individual-based rights – but pointedly prevents them from receiving collective rights, even if those are given to individuals belonging to other collectivities. The very essence of the hegemonic state and its hegemonizing project is an ongoing effort to maintain, strengthen, and perpetuate the fundamental distinction between full-fledged citizens and what might be called "partial citizens," although without necessarily admitting to it.

Smooha (1990) and Peled (1992) suggested that in what they have called "ethnic democracies" there are different packages of rights that are determined and awarded in accordance with a person's ethnicity. The main problem with such conceptualization is that if and when a Differential Citizenship Discourse is adopted, legally or in practice, a polity might cease being genuinely democratic. The very essence of the democratization process in multiethnic societies often involves a fundamental transformation of the citizenship discourse, as demonstrated in the case of recognizing the rights of historical minorities in post-Franco Spain (Moreno 1997, 2001), adding representatives of the Hungarian minority to the post-Mečiar government of Slovakia, or the expansion of voting rights to African Americans in the United States in the 1960s. Of all types of democracies, liberal democracies are particularly sensitive to the issue of differentiating between citizen rights, although their interest is especially in the formal, legal, and political equality and not in the social and economic one.

In defending themselves against the charge that they lack equality by maintaining Differential Citizenship Discourse, proponents of hegemonic states might argue that their governmental structures are based, in the final analysis, on the will of the majority. The difficulty with such an argument is that it ignores the principles of citizens' equality – which by Lockian philosophy cannot be eliminated even by the majority – and the principle of protecting minorities against the arbitrariness of the majority, a principle that has gained increasing validity particularly throughout the twentieth century. Already the Greek philosophers, and then America's Founding Fathers, recognized the danger inherent in the "tyranny of the majority," a danger that is fully reflected in the very essence of a hegemonic regime.

The democratization process in many parts of the world, particularly over the last fifteen years or so, creates special problems in terms of the relationships between hegemony and differential rights. Minorities in many polities are justifiably fearful that majorities might act hegemonially under the cover of majoritarian democracy. Thus the democratization process may become a path to hegemony, not democracy, as happened in several countries (e.g., Sri Lanka, Slovakia under Mečiar, Yugoslavia under Milosevic).

The danger noted in the preceding text is particularly acute in deeply divided societies. Thus in Georgia and in Serbia, for example, democratization has produced wars between rival nations and ethnic groups. The "engine" for such massive violence was frequently the hegemonic tendencies of the majority. In Rwanda and Burundi, the regime relied exclusively on ethnic kinsmen, leading the country down the path to eventual genocide, the largest in several decades. In numerous other multinational societies (e.g., Burma, Chad, Ethiopia, Iraq, Pakistan, Somalia), the use of the state as an oppressive, hegemonic tool had also led the polity in the direction of massive violence.

Hegemonic Behavior of Multinational States

The analytical focus of this study is the manner in which hegemonic states may democratize, particularly through a process of large-scale constitutional transformation, the type of process that occurred over the last several decades in Spain, South Africa, Northern Ireland, and other countries. Such a process, however, is extremely difficult to bring about, precisely because the hegemonic mode of thinking is so very deeply removed from the fundamental approach of liberal democracy and other forms of democratic regime.

Hegemonic states, by definition, are committed exclusively to the interests of their dominant ethnic groups. Their commitment is often metainstitutional, metahistorical, or even metaphysical: the state is supposed to represent the "people" as an organic unit, the essence of "history," "God" or other such transcendental Truth, and not merely the citizens as individual beings (as it is in liberal democracy). Spain under Franco saw itself as representing the true essence of Christianity and particularly Catholicism, as well as the ill-defined "Castilian Spirit." Many Afrikaaners in South Africa under apartheid justified their regime in explicit religious terms. Israel under David Ben-Gurion and his successors has viewed itself as representing Jewish history; therefore, Ben-Gurion thought that the Law of Return was not discriminatory but metaconstitutionally valid

(Peleg 1998a). The Soviet Union and other Communist polities saw themselves as representing the inevitable march of history toward Communism. Although their vision was nonethnic, it superseded the interests of the citizens as individual beings.

It is important to note that for its supporters, the hegemonic ethnic state is often not an end by itself, but merely a tool, an instrument for achieving the vision of national, ethnic grandeur. Such vision lives uneasily, if not in direct contradiction with not only democracy (in any of its versions, but especially in its liberal-democratic variant), but also with the concept of the modern state. The post-Enlightenment state strives to be, in most cases, a rational creature, a product of an imaginary contract among all her people as equal "citizens." The logic and the rationale of hegemonism, especially in its ethnic form, are antithetical to this nature of the modern state as rational and individualistic. In a genuinely democratic polity the state is, at least theoretically, a neutral arbiter, a content-free arena for the pursuit of conflicting interests within society. Although the neutrality of the state is an ideal that is rarely achieved in reality, as a supreme ideal within the modern democratic state it has enormous impact on the behavior of individuals and groups alike. That neutrality shapes the rules by which the state is governed.

In hegemonic ethnicities, neutrality does not exist, either as a reality or even as an ideal. Although in their sometimes desperate attempt to prove that they are democratic, ethnic hegemonies may create an elaborate democratic façade, and under it there is invariably uniethnic control. In hegemonic states, the public sphere, including all state institutions, are not neutral but expropriated for the exclusive use of the dominant ethnic majority. The "public good" in such polities is determined exclusively by those individuals and groups that belong to the dominant ethnic group (Peled 1992). The prevailing attitude toward the adjective *public* – whether it is the "public" good or the "public" sphere – is that it is the exclusive domain of the dominant ethnic group.

A hegemonic situation is invariably characterized by a deep gap and the incongruence between the sociopolitical reality of the polity, which is multiethnic, and the determination of the dominant ethnic group to maintain its exclusive hold on political power. This inherent contradiction within the system can continue for a long time, maybe even "forever," as long as the supremacy of the dominant group is accepted uncritically and maybe even subconsciously by the members of both the dominant and dominated groups. The notion of "Hegemonia," as developed by Antonio Gramsci and used by several other analysts, is extremely useful for analyzing this uncritical, unchallenged acceptance of reality. If and when the hegemonic control of the dominant group is challenged – thus losing its very "hegemoniality" – it might spell the beginning of the end for the hegemonic regime. Thus when the South African Dutch Reform Church deserted the notion of the religious choiceness of the Afrikaans, its deviation from the long-held theology of the group was a major blow to this group's "hegemonia." As long as the exclusive dominance of a single group goes unchallenged, its hegemony is assured. Hegemony exists as long as its content is regarded as an article of faith, a fundamental truth that ought not to be challenged.

But ideas have roots in reality. From the perspective of reality, an Ethnic Constitutional Order could enjoy a hegemonic status as long as the project promoted by it is seen as generally successful by those who might sustain it – the elite and the masses of the dominant ethnic group, members of subservient groups (who might come to believe that resistance to domination is useless), the international community (that might be inclined to ignore the incongruence between "hegemony" and "democracy"), and so forth.

Hegemonic condition is not merely an empirical reality; it is often a normative structure as well. Having been internalized by dominant and dominated alike, a hegemonic condition is eventually perceived as "given," "natural," the "way things are," and, therefore, the way things should be. The transformation from reality to norm, from what "is" to what "ought to be," and from the empirical to the normative, is a process that characterizes most hegemonic polities. It is not necessarily a permanent condition. A process that undermines and eventually reverses hegemony might occur, especially in a world that is increasingly dominated by the idea of "democracy." Once normative critique of hegemonism begins to gain momentum among dominated as well as dominant groups, it could easily lead to effective demands to change reality.

A hegemonic situation is invariably embedded in societal conditions. It is a situation where "a given cultural definition of reality dominates society at large" (Aronoff 1989, xiv). In such situations, the majority tends to view the state as a single-group entity, even if such political perception is historically and socially inaccurate and morally deficient. The formal existence of democracy is rarely an insurmountable barrier for such a distorted attitude.

As a political institution, the state in and of itself cannot be expected to break out of the condition of hegemonism. Although in the final analysis, the demise of hegemony requires changes in the way the state operates and even in the manner in which it is structured, the initiation of the change ought to be sought in other places within society. In this regard, the "state-in-society" perspective is extremely useful (Migdal 1988, 2001). The transformative development through which hegemonic polities change must be initiated by other forces within society. For example, the demise of South Africa's apartheid regime cannot possibly be understood without a careful examination of the economic interests of the white ruling elite. The analytical argument of this volume is that the ethnic force, which often reflects the deepest allegiances of most of society's members, is the foundation upon which the state institutions are built, but this force is impacted greatly by other societal forces. The modern state, in its bureaucratized, militarized, and organized power, is merely the instrument through which ethnic loyalties operate. It is these deep ethnic allegiances that must change if a genuine transformation is to occur in an ethnic, hegemonic state.

From a democratic perspective, ethnic hegemony is highly problematical. The relationship between hegemony and democracy completes the crucial triangle between hegemony, statehood, and democracy. The intersection of uni-lateral ethnically determined policy and the hegemonic power of the state (both described in some detail previously) is extremely dangerous from the perspective of genuine democracy. If and when these two forces unite in establishing a hegemonic ethnic state, genuine democracy is almost surely doomed, although flawed democracy may function.

The complete destruction or at least serious deterioration of democracy under conditions of hegemony is likely especially when several conditions prevail:

1. The core nation that is in control of the state enjoys multidimensional superiority in all-important socioeconomic areas (e.g., level of education, technological know-how, economic control); Israel is but one example for a situation of that sort.
2. The establishment of a hegemonic regime came about following deep, bitter, and violent conflict between the ethnic groups in the state (e.g., Serbia and Sri Lanka).
3. The state lacks a political culture and legal tradition that could be effectively used by proponents of change to bring about a transformation from within (as in Sunni-controlled Iraq under Saddam Hussein).
4. The ethnic majority that dominates the state is fundamentally intolerant toward "others," especially toward the rival ethnic minority (Shamir and Sullivan 1983, 1985).
5. There is no significant international pressure on the ethnic majority to treat the minority in accordance with acceptable international norms.

When these conditions or even only some of them exist in a hegemonic situation, one can expect, under the best of situations, an illiberal democracy to emerge, even if society has within it powerful forces that might work toward democracy. Yet a thoroughly ethnicized state can quite easily be transformed from illiberal democracy to a nondemocracy or a democracy carrying out nondemocratic policies (Serbia under Milosevic in the 1990s serves as a good example).

In an ethnically divided society, even more so than in other polities, the role of the political elite is crucial. The elite of the dominant ethnic group, in particular, may be able to pull the majority in the direction of instituting full equality and effective protection for the ethnic minority, thereby transforming the political system in a peaceful, orderly manner. Yet the temptation of using the "threat" of the minority to maintain power within the polity is often too great to resist for most majority ethnic elites, even in full-fledged democracies.

Within the political reality of interethnic conflict, one of the most effective ways of maintaining political power within the majority group is "scapegoating" the minority. Maintaining domination over the minority could easily become, for the majority politicians, the only game in town, the single currency of politics. That strategy has dominated Sri Lankan politics for decades (DeVotta 2005); it could equally become known as Meciarism or Milosevicism.

If and when the choice is perceived by majority politicians as between inherently dangerous democratic reform and remaining in power through minority scapegoating, the latter is likely to be the choice. Ethnic politicians in divided societies are not known for their inclination to commit political suicide. They invariably tend to jump on the nationalist train (and drive it to its destination) not under it.

The dimensions of the complete uniethnic control of the institutions of the state are as many as they are diverse. They most often include, but are not necessarily limited to, the following ten areas of public policy:

1. Maintaining and expanding the control of the majority over land as a means of physically marginalizing the minority and dominating areas initially in its possession by encouraging internal migration. States such as Greece, Indonesia, Israel, Malaysia, Sri Lanka, and the USSR have been involved in such efforts (Mitchell 1991; Murphy 1989; Taylor 1994; Yiftachel 1998, 2000a, 2001).

2. Establishing the primacy of the majority's language within the polity. Numerous ethnic hegemonies have established language policies designed to force their populations to speak the language of the dominant group: France (Weber 1976), Hungary, Italy, Spain under Franco, and Sri Lanka are but some examples (Laponce, 1987; Safran 1994).

3. Thoroughly dominating the educational system, both logistically and curricularly, as a way of transmitting the majority's culture.

4. Controlling all means of communications and the mass media within the political system.

5. Influencing the "demographic scene" in favor of the dominant ethnic group through citizenship and immigration policies and personal status issues, so as to maximize the majority's advantage.

6. Controlling all security services, the ultimate coercive arbiter between conflicting ethnic groups, in case all other means fail (e.g., Serb control over the "Yugoslav" armed forces, Hashemite control over Jordan's military).

7. Domination of public employment, including in particular the important political positions with the bureaucracy and the highly sensitive teaching profession.

8. Strict budgetary control to guarantee that the "hegemonic project" gets heavily funded while alternative projects do not.

9. Control over the state's iconography, symbols, and collective memory, including museums, monuments, and names of places (Azaryahu 1995; Benvenisti 2000; Friel 1981; Zerubavel 1995).

10. Domination over all the central governmental organizations, including the national courts (Barzilai in Kedar 2000; Lahav 1997; Peleg, 1998b).

Controlling thoroughly and in a coordinated fashion all aspects of public life and the public political space results, of course, in enormous damage to democracy, despite the fact that some ethnic states do all they can to appear democratic. Although modern democracy requires congruence between citizenship and rights (i.e., all citizens should have all and the same rights), the very *raison d'etre* of the hegemonic state is to give permanent advantage to the dominant ethnic group. As such, the hegemonic state can hardly be but marginally democratic.

The Consequences of Hegemony

Ethnic hegemony might be looked upon as one of several mechanisms for maintaining political stability and public order in a deeply divided society. It could be reasonably argued that a stable regime, and maybe even a stable democracy, could be established if and when the polity has a Staatsvolk, a national or ethnic people who are demographically dominant (O'Leary 2001a, 244–5). A normative argument on behalf of such a regime could also be made (Tamir 1993).

In general, it could be hypothesized that such arguments on behalf of a majoritarian ethnic regime are stronger for the short run than for the long run, that the larger the demographic dominance of the majority the more stable such a regime, and that the less hegemonic the regime the better its chances of survival. If this set of hypotheses is true, then in the longer run the results of such a hegemonic regime could be devastatingly negative, particularly if the relative size of the minority is substantial and the level of "hegemonism" high. While Chapters 4 and 5 will offer an analysis of several cases of ethnic hegemony in an effort to begin the empirical examination of the consequences of hegemony, here I will deal with the results of hegemonism in general terms.

First, ethnic hegemony must result, under the very best of circumstances, in low-quality, fundamentally flawed democracy. The very structure of "ethnic hegemony" is, in its essence, a gross deviation from the noble (if not always achievable) principles of democracy, a regime that aims at the inclusion of all citizens in the public life of the polity. Such deviations from the principles of democracy in hegemonic polities are rarely the result of personalities (although authoritarian leaders might exacerbate the problem). The deviations are inherent in the system. To democratize, ironically, hegemonic states have to work against their own nature. Lord Acton recognized, in the nineteenth century, that nationalism leads to oppression of minorities and absolutism (Lord Acton in Figgis 1907), a theme repeated by contemporary writers (Vincent 2002).

Second, it is important to realize that ethnic hegemony is fatal not merely to its "natural" victims – members of the minority group. Members of the dominant group, usually the majority, are also likely to be victimized (especially in the long run) by an ethnic regime, and so is the polity at large. Simply put, democracy is "indivisible," and if one destroys one aspect of it (i.e., majority-minority relations), one opens the gate for the destruction of other parts of the body politic. For example, the oppression of a minority is likely to lead, sooner or later, to the militarization of society to defend the status quo against inevitable challenges, to the emergence of unreasonable demands for unity within the majority to protect the hegemonic regime, to the identification of some members of the majority as "disloyal" minority sympathizers, and so forth. Each of these developments, in and of itself and particularly in their combination, is likely to harm considerably the democratic regime.

Third, ethnic hegemony is fundamentally an unstable regime, particularly in the contemporary world when it runs against the worldwide ideological order. Although the theory of hegemonic behavior cannot predict what might happen in any specific situation, on the whole the result of promoting ethnic hegemony is likely to be rather negative. In an increasingly democratic world, where close attention to human rights and civil rights dominates world public opinion, hegemonic behavior is likely to be self-defeating, counterproductive, and eventually unsuccessful, as learnt so very devastatingly by the leaders of white South Africa, Presidents Mečiar and Milosevic, and numerous other "ethnic hegemons."

The inherent instability of ethnic hegemonism is clear, especially when compared with liberal democracy or with any of the group-based democratic regimes. The tension between the self-proclaimed ethnic commitment of the hegemonic state and its adherence to democracy, however *pro forma*, is bound to invite instability and sustain it until that tension is resolved through genuine democratization.

Fourth, aggressive hegemonic behavior often results in massive bloodshed, as demonstrated by numerous writers (e.g., Byman and Van Evera 1998; Gurr 1993, 2000). The link between hegemony and violence is quite direct:

1. Hegemonic groups often "go for the jugular" and initiate action designed to finish "once and for all" their ethnic enemies. Examples include Pakistan's genocidal acts against the Bengalis in East Pakistan in the early 1970s, the 1994 Rwanda genocide, Milosevic's actions toward Serbia's rivals in the 1990s, and more. All of these cases resulted in untold suffering to millions of innocent people and are among the most horrific cases of massive violence since the end of World War II.

2. The mere definition of a political system in ethnic terms is likely to put those who do not belong to the dominant ethnic group on notice, threaten them with permanent marginality, and, possibly worse, encourage separatist movements on the part of the minority, and cause massive violence. Thus Franco's "hegemonic" behavior did more to encourage Basque and Catalan separatism than any other action by the Madrid government in recent memory. Similarly, Turkey's reluctance to accommodate the Kurds has been, altogether, a failed policy, and the same holds for Israel's policy toward the country's Arab minority. In brief, hegemonic ethnic behavior radicalizes its victims, politicizes them (often against their own natural inclination), forces them to organize politically and sometimes militarily to merely survive, and eventually use arms against "their" own state.

Despite the high stakes and the obvious dangers involved in maintaining hegemonism, states that have adopted that type of regime are not easily given to change. If the very essence of the polity is defined by its ethnicity, as often is the case, converting it to a multiethnic state (where rights are given to all major ethnic groups) or even to an ethnically neutral state (i.e., a liberal democracy where no group is recognized and rights are given equally to individuals only) would be, from the perspective of the hegemonic state, a form of a collective suicide. Although technical solutions for excessive ethnicization and unreasonable hegemony could be found (and many of these solutions are enumerated in this volume), the ethnic majority may not be able to fundamentally change "its" polity due to moral blindness, an unrealistic sense of power and invincibility, insensitivity to the needs of the minority, unreasonable fear of change, or other psycho-political reasons.

All things being equal, the ethnic majority is likely to insist on its hegemonic position within the polity, sometimes to the very bitter end and in spite of substantial evidence that hegemonism is simply untenable. Thus hegemonies such as Serbia and South Africa collapsed only after a long and bloody struggle, sometimes after a protracted period of legitimacy loss. If the state is ethnically defined, it could be expected that the membership of the majority ethnos would be fighting with all its might to sustain its privileged status.

The key for maintaining the exclusive control of the ethnic majority is in its ability to maintain the legitimacy of the hegemonic control in two rather different arenas, internal legitimacy within the polity and external legitimacy within the broader political system. Internal legitimacy is a function of "hegemony," the inability of members of the polity to conceive of a change in the situation. For achieving such a degree of psychological control, members of the majority should not only believe that it is beneficial for them to dominate the minority but also be convinced that it is absolutely necessary for them to do so. If and when most members of the majority believe that controlling the minority is a matter of survival, hegemony is at its peak. Although ethnic majorities rarely hesitate to use force for achieving their goals within their polities, establishing control through psychological means – by legitimizing the majority's control – is always preferred to brute force.

External legitimacy is substantially more difficult to achieve. It is legitimacy accorded to the ethnic majority and its hegemonic regime beyond the boundaries of the polity. The reason it is substantially more difficult to achieve and maintain such legitimacy is that the majority elite does not have the same degree of physical and psychological control over the outside world as it has over its own population. Yet if that elite succeeds in convincing outside forces that it is under attack by the minority and its allies and that it is merely defending itself against the ethnic minority, external legitimacy can be achieved as well.

An ethnic polity that desires to sustain its hegemony in face of the pressures to change might adopt policies that look as if they are democratic, even if in reality they are democratically problematical. Such means are many and diverse, and they include elections, referenda, complicated coalition building (in which the minority is automatically excluded or largely marginalized), parliamentary votes (which in a Westminsterian system have the final legitimizing power), and even supreme courts' decisions (the ultimate legitimizer in most democracies).

In ethnic polities with a clear-cut majority the Westminster model with parliamentary supremacy might be preferred by the majority to any alternative constitutional design. It is a democratic system with few political limitations on the parliamentary majority, which is controlled by the government. If a constitution and a bill of rights can be avoided in a Westminster democracy and if the courts are weak and noninterventionary or even render outright support to the ethnic majority, the rule of the majority is absolute, while appearing to be entirely democratic.

The ability to maintain that kind of democratic façade in a deeply divided society is of great importance for guaranteeing external legitimacy in a world where "democracy" is demanded of all. For that reason, any ethnic hegemonic regime is likely to devote substantial resources for maintaining their international reputation as a genuine democracy. Several of the governmental designs analyzed in this volume could be adopted, and it is the function of the analyst to examine whether they are compatible with the requirements of democratic regime (see Chapter 1).

Transforming the Hegemonic State

The most likely result of the collision between ethnic hegemony and the demands of democracy is violence, although violence in numerous hegemonic states may be postponed for a rather long time, especially when the ethnic dominance of the majority is absolute. Because the hegemonic state negates, *a priori* and by definition, the possibility of minority identification with it, and in many cases prevents even its assimilation, it invites endless conflict, political instability, and possibly even the eventual disintegration of the state. Although hiding behind the cover of democracy, sometimes with clever schemes, may postpone the demise of ethnic hegemonism, in most cases the contradictions inherent in the system are likely to deepen, evolve, and escalate.

One possible solution to the conflict generated by hegemonic, ethnic rule is the partial or complete transformation of hegemonism. Such transformation is, in the final analysis, the consequence of a struggle over the public sphere within society, including that part of the public sphere that is directly controlled, regulated, or influenced by the state. In an ethnic polity, the public sphere is constructed in a way that gives individual members of the majority and primarily the majority group unequal advantage in regard to the public sphere (Kymlicka 1995; Spinner 1994). Important resources at the public sphere such as land, which in some hegemonic states may be defined as a "national" resource, and governmental positions are limited to the regime's loyalists, which in an ethnic order must be members of the majority group. In a more benevolent, but equally consequential manner, the state's language (officially or in practice), religion, and public holidays and symbols are invariably those of the majority.

In democracies, even in *bona fide* liberal democracies, one can find all sorts of relatively benign inequalities, although these inequalities are often symbolic in nature rather than material. Thus it is the majority's language that dominates public discourse, and it is often the majority's religious holidays that are instituted as special days on the calendar. In the case of ethnic hegemonic regimes, however, the inequalities amount to material discrimination of the minority. Moreover, in democracies inequalities are often incidental, unintentional, and peripheral in their impact; in ethnic hegemonic regimes such inequalities amount to intentional, substantial, and material discrimination.

The policies of the ethnic state are aimed, specifically, at limiting the reasonable access of the minority, as a group, and its individual members to the public sphere. What might be such a "reasonable" access in a genuine democratic regime? There are, in principle, at least three possibilities:

1. Allowing *equal* access to the public sphere by the majority and the minority (as it is, e.g., in Belgium today or as it is proposed in the 1998 Northern Ireland deal). Such equal access could be given to individuals, a foundational principle of liberal democracy, and/or to groups, an idea inherent in consociational democracy.
2. Structuring access to the public sphere by the majority and the minority in a *proportional* manner, a principle that is highly compatible with consociational democracy. In a proportional system, access to the public sphere (e.g., monetary allocations, governmental positions) is divided in accordance with the demographic size of the ethnic group. Although such a system might be going a long way toward the resolution of the tensions inherent in ethnic hegemonism, it potentially violates some of the principles of liberal democracy insofar as such a democracy prefers to deal exclusively with individuals and, in particular, if it results in the unequal treatment of individuals.
3. Granting *preferential* access to the public sphere to members of the minority as individuals (as in affirmative action programs in the United States) or even as a group (as in the advantageous representation or overrepresentation in parliament given to the Turkish Cypriots in the early 1960s). Preferential access is in even more severe tension with liberal democracy than proportional access. Yet it is entirely compatible with asymmetrical federalism and other forms of consociationalism.

Although the granting of equal access to the public sphere to majority and minority as groups may violate (or at least be in tension with) liberal democracy, a regime that is based on the supremacy of individual equality, as long as such access does not violate directly individual equality or minimize such violation considerably, it could be democratically legitimate. Preferential access to the public sphere for the minority is in even greater tension with democratic principles than equal access to groups, although it might be necessary for reasons of historical justice, where past discrimination has left a minority in perpetual disadvantage, or for the creation of favorable conditions for political stability.

The most important fact to note from the perspective of this study is that in the hegemonic ethnic state, the minority does not enjoy equal, proportional, or preferential access to the public sphere. The minority in such a system is either denied access to the public sphere altogether (as was the case under the apartheid regime in South Africa), or its access is limited to a level that is considerably below its proportional share in the population. The limitations on minority access to the public sphere are often reflected in quantitative measures: the minority receives proportionately lower allocations of public funds for its collective activities (in areas such as religious or educational endeavors) or even on an individual basis (Kretzmer 1990), a proportionately small number of the minority members are appointed to governmental positions, and so forth. But the unequal access to the public sphere could also be reflected "qualitatively," by delegitimizing or preventing the participation of the minority in the determination of the polity's "public good" (Peled 1992), by excluding members of the minority from participation in major political bodies such as the government or the courts, and other such measures.

Patten believes that in federal and other systems, "a rough equality in the public sphere can be achieved between different national identities" (2001, 293). Thus a federal structure may facilitate access to different people on different levels of government. Such equality could transform a hegemonic polity and turn it into a much more inclusive system. The ethnic majority, however, might oppose such change for that very reason.

The key to real transformation of an ethnic hegemony might not be through a legally clever, differential access to the public sphere or through highly differentiated governmental structures that treat citizens in an unequal manner in accordance with their particular ethnicity. The key is, rather, in establishing genuine equality in access to the public sphere, regardless of ethnicity or similar factors, and guaranteeing that such equality is pedantically applied on both the individual and group level. The acceptance of such a formula – equal access to the public sphere – is probably conditioned, in the final analysis, on the emergence of some kind of common identity in ethnically diverse societies, a goal that might be judged to be a rather remote vision.

Although a true common identity might be a pipe dream in deeply divided societies, to make the polity minimally acceptable to all groups and avoid large-scale violence, the ethnic majority must give up its natural temptation to dominate the minority. In principle, the emergence of common identity is the most peaceful, permanent, and stable alternative to an endless ethnic conflict and separatist movements in divided societies. Other transformative options ought to be sought in the absence of such an alternative.

In terms of adopting transformative policies, an ethnic hegemony facing minority challenge may react in five analytically distinct manners, a distinction that will be further developed in the next chapter:

1. *Status Quo.* Despite the tension between the ethnic nature of the polity and democratic forces from within and without, the hegemonic state may be determined to maintain its ethnically unequal character.
2. *Moderate, "Cosmetic" Changes toward Increased Democratization.* In view of the pressures to liberalize, the ethnic state may agree to dismantle

the most flagrant forms of violations of civic equality but without genuinely changing the character of the hegemonic regime. Israel and Turkey, for example, seem to have adopted such a policy.

3. *Radical Revision toward Genuine Democracy.* A metaconstitutional transformation might be introduced, so as to change the character of the polity from ethnic hegemony to individual-based or group-based democracy. Examples include Spain after Franco (a change reflected in the 1978 constitution and other pieces of legislation), Northern Ireland's 1998 Good Friday Agreement, and South Africa constitutional changes in the 1990s.

4. *Mild Changes toward Further Ethnicization.* The hegemonic state might decide to move in the direction of strengthening its ethnic character but through relatively mild, moderate measures. Examples include post-Communist Russia (especially under Putin), India under the BJP, and so forth.

5. *Radical Action toward Full Ethnicization.* The ethnic majority and its elite might adopt radical initiatives to transform the multiethnic state to a purely ethnic state using harsh measures such as apartheid, expulsion, ethnic cleansing (large-scale killings), or even full-fledged genocide. Examples would include South Africa until the 1990s, Serbia under Milosevic, Rwanda in 1994, Pakistani action in Bangladesh in the early 1970s, and so forth.

Some of these transformative processes of hegemonic ethnicities are described in Chapters 4, 5, and 6, where they are applied to several historical cases that are arguably emblematic of the possibilities open to hegemonic regimes. The important fact to recognize is, however, that beyond the analyst's capacity to identify different results of transformative processes, such processes are rarely predetermined or known in advance. They are open to the complex interaction between countervailing political forces within an ethnic polity, forces that may push the system in diametrically conflicting directions.

The five "solutions" to an ethnic dilemma recognized by the analysis offered here are internal – they may all occur within the confines of the hegemonic state. There are, however, also possibilities for external solutions that go beyond the existing hegemonic state. Thus a hegemonic polity might split into several components (as happened in Czechoslovakia, Yugoslavia, or the USSR during the 1990s). Secession or separatism of the type that occurred in Pakistan in 1971 or the incorporation of the state (or part thereof) by other states (a possible solution for the Bosnian dilemma) are other possibilities for solving the dilemmas of hegemonic-ethnic regimes through the external route.

It is obvious by the analysis provided here that there are several important and distinct dimensions of the transformation of the ethnic state. Among the most important dimensions is the direction of the change, that is, whether the political elite of an ethnic-hegemonic polity decides to push toward enhanced democratization or increased ethnicization. A second dimension is the size of the change adopted by the polity, that is, whether the transformation is mild or radical in nature. A third dimension deals with the mechanisms of the change, that is, whether transformation is brought about through violent or constitutional process and whether the change is internally or internationally induced. A matrix of theoretically possible cases of transformation could be constructed usefully to distinguish between the different dimensions of transformation.

Despite the importance of identifying the various dimensions of systemic transformation of hegemonic polities, one of the most fundamental questions that ought to be asked is whether transformation of a deeply hegemonic system is possible at all? This volume is written with the fundamental assertion, which it examines theoretically and empirically, that the transformation of a hegemonic state is not only possible (as proven by a series of cases discussed in Chapters 4 and 5) but that in most situations it is necessary as well. Such transformation is essential from both the perspective of democratic norms and perspective of political stability. Put differently, it seems that in the contemporary world ethnic hegemony in deeply divided societies is hardly sustainable, particularly in view of the unprecedented, accelerated spread of democratic norms and the demand for equality of all individuals and groups.

Even in Western Europe, possibly the most genuinely democratic region of the globe today, many societies are actively reexamining their governmental structures and, as a result, restructure their polities so as to better reflect their ethnic diversity. Not only has the previously authoritarian Spain renegotiated its union (a process not yet completed) but also old democracies, such as the United Kingdom and France, have come to adopt what might be considered a kinder and gentler approach toward the idea of their own diversity.

The direction of political change in the vast majority of contemporary democracies today is clear. They tend to move toward greater recognition of the diversity of their population, accept an enhanced representativeness of their ethnic subunits, and actively affect the transfer of power from their center to their periphery. In view of this reality in the democratic world, one of the most important questions of our time is the following: "Can traditionally hegemonic states become part of this process?"

One way of answering this question is by noting that the hegemonic state (like most if not all other states) is, in the final analysis, but an invention, an intellectual construct with as much viability in the "real world" as political actors choose to give it. The hegemonic ethnic state, as an invention, is a political creature "imagined" to represent one group of people residing in the state and not others who live in the same political space. This imagined community (Anderson 1983) believes itself to be a nation, created by common ethnic descent, shared history or destiny, common religion and language, and so forth. This community might also believe that a certain territory belongs to it exclusively. Although hegemonic states present themselves to the world as ideologically, historically and culturally uniform entities, their minorities – those who, by definition, do not belong and cannot belong – are constant reminders of the inherent artificiality, as well as instability, of the polity within which they are considered a foreign body.

If the hegemonic state is, as argued, quite undemocratic by definition and empirically unstable, one of the ways in which it could improve its democratic performance and enhance its stability is by deconstructing itself and, then, "reimagine" itself in a more realistic, just, and democratic manner. The issue of democratic transformation, thus, could be a matter of creative imagination, leading to restructuring the ethnicized polity in a more inclusive manner. Constructive change of multinational but hegemonic polities is, in the final analysis, about transforming them in a manner that makes them fit better the needs, interests, and values of all their citizens, not merely the needs of those who imagine themselves to be members of the core nation.

The reconstruction of the multinational (or multiethnic) hegemonic state, in a manner that would make it more stable and more democratic, could proceed in several different directions. First, the multinational state, viewing itself as the sole sovereign entity within a given political space, might decide to grant, if it so desires, rights to "its" constituent nations (or ethnicities), as a Spanish conservative would argue was done by the sovereign Spanish state when it granted recognition to several of the Peninsular nations, notably the Basques and the Catalans. Second, the multinational hegemonic state could reconstitute itself as a confederation among several equal nations, as many Quebecois would like Canada to do. Third, a multinational hegemonic state could transform itself into the state of all of its citizens, as individuals, and cease to define itself in a collective manner or associate itself with any particular group.

It is difficult for any truly *hegemonic-ethnic state* to accept any of these positions, although it prefers the first option to the third, and the third to the second. In regard to the first position, although the hegemonic state might grant some of its ethnic components collective rights, it refuses to grant minority nations equal collective rights or even recognize that they have – as groups – any inherent rights. The hegemonic state views itself as the exclusive province of a single dominant "nation" and as such it can grant other groups within it limited rights only and reserve to itself the right to revoke those rights. The hegemonic state would reject the second option, forming a confederation of equal nations and do so in even stronger terms: such a constitutional arrangement would negate the very essence of ethnic hegemonism. The third model, that of equality of all citizens on an individual basis, is incompatible with the philosophy of hegemonic rule, but if the dominant group in society is confident enough in its sociopolitical dominance within the polity, it may agree to a constitutional deal based on individual equality.

To affect a genuine transformation and move toward stability and democracy, the traditional hegemonic state must change in the direction of one of the three options identified here or possibly some kind of combination of these options. While the second alternative is genuinely unattractive for hegemonic majorities because it negates the very essence of hegemonism, a transformative solution could be implemented through the first option (where the dominant group grants rights to subservient groups) or via the third alternative, where the dominant group establishes a genuine liberal democracy. The first solution reflects a classic group-based approach to conflict management while the third option reflects an individual-based approach to political organization. In the vast majority of cases, neither of these approaches represents a real danger to the existence of the polity; in many cases, these approaches represent a measurable improvement in the stability, let alone the democratic character, of the polity in question.

Hegemonic states have traditionally taken the position that they belong exclusively to the core nation. The sovereignty, as in the first approach, is to be found in the majority people and only there. So although minorities might possibly be recognized, it is up to the dominant nation, and it alone, to grant such recognition. Moreover, inherent in such hegemonic attitude is the idea that minorities – representing an alien element within the polity – can neither expect to receive equal recognition within the hegemonic state nor should they demand such recognition. This exclusivist position, it is hypothesized (see Chapter 3), has become less and less sustainable in the contemporary world.

In our time, characterized by accelerated globalization, the nature of political organizations is changing quickly and dramatically. In many ways, the very concept of a "nation-state" has become an anachronistic misnomer. In a world where the state is challenged, the hegemonic ethnic state might be the last bastion to crumble. If external boundaries between states are falling (a process that is the very essence of globalization), can internal boundaries between ethnicities, boundaries that sustain the hegemonic state, fall as well? Could the essence of hegemony wither away, a relic of the past whose time has come and gone? Whether the end of sovereignty is real or not (Camilleri and Falk 1992), the end of unilateral ethnic control within a multinational setting might come sooner than later.

The dual globalizing process of the weakening of the state from above and from below, through the establishment of transnational institutions and the emergence of multiple ethnoterritorial claims, is also likely to weaken the hegemonic state, a political creature that negates in its very essence the contemporary Zeitgeist. The processes associated with globalization, let alone with the spread of democracy and human-rights, call for greater equality among all citizens, thus negating the very logic of hegemonism. The erosion of state power, feared by hegemonic elites and their following "ethnics," could be good news for democrats, human rights activists, and others. Hegemonic states could learn to adjust to this change, transform themselves accordingly, and flourish in a new and changed world. The alternative might be too sad and too threatening to contemplate.

The transformation of the hegemonic state could possibly impact majorities, traditionally dominant ethnic groups, and minorities, groups that have traditionally been alienated from the polity, its institutions, and its policies. Ironically, a reformed hegemonic order does not even have to be fully deethnicized to achieve a higher quality of democracy or enhanced stability. Even if transformed, such political order could still be structured around the multiethnic reality from which it has emerged. Moreover, it could achieve simultaneously several goals by offering all citizens of the polity equal rights, as individuals, and regardless of their ethnicity, or by allowing all groups within the polity to live side-by-side, in equality, and without losing their distinctiveness.

The contemporary hegemonic, ethnic state does not do either of these. To achieve these goals, it ought to guarantee both individual and group rights, in a balanced fashion, so that the one does not harm the other. A system based on pure individualistic justice (Rawls 1971), or one based on pure communitarian justice (Sandel 1982), is likely to prove insufficient. What could be called "national communitarianism," built around the dominant ethnic group (Tamir 1993), is particularly unjust in a multinational setting, because it excludes, by definition, those who do not belong to the "nation."

In deeply divided societies – exactly the type of societies that give rise to ethnic hegemonies – justice requires not merely equal treatment under the law for individuals but also the recognition of the special needs of groups, especially ethnic minorities. The meaning of that requirement is that along with the granting of equal rights to all individuals, and the creation of genuinely shared citizenship of all citizens, the polity ought to recognize the unique, special needs of its major constituent groups. In a complex but necessary manner, the shared civic culture of the polity should be complemented by public recognition of diverse ethnic cultures, all under the same and equal "roof" of the state. The transformation of the hegemonic state to the multiethnic state does not mean that ethnicity is dead or that cultural divisions are bridged; it means that gross inequality is replaced with equality for all, individuals and groups alike.

The thesis offered in this book is, then, a direct challenge to two dominant philosophies: (1) *nationalism*, an idea that a divided society often leads to what this volume calls "hegemonism," and (2) *liberalism*, especially the idea of pure individualistic citizenship. Although the notion of straightforward individual equality is highly attractive, laudable, and necessary, it is simply an insufficient remedy for the problems of societies that are already deeply divided.

Although passionate nationalism in a multinational setting is, almost unfailingly, a recipe for true disaster, liberalism in its unadulterated, pure form can be a just and stable solution only in relatively homogenous societies, societies that ironically have often achieved such homogeneity through ethnic cleansing or the marginalization of minority groups. Liberalism has inherent difficulties in responding to the challenge of nation-building projects in multinational societies (Patten 2001); it could and should be part of a solution to the problems encountered by deeply divided societies but only a part.

John Stuart Mill's point that the presence of two or more nationalities within the same polity leads to "mutual antipathies" and prevents liberty is probably altogether too pessimistic, although it surely has some empirical validity. Antipathies can be dealt with, although evidently not easily, and liberty could be established if a careful balance is struck between individual and group rights.

What is, however, most important to realize, is that multiethnicity is simply an unavoidable fact of life in most contemporary societies, and, even if Mill's observation is entirely valid, it forces upon the political analyst the obligation of devising effective means for dealing with that given reality.

The hope of some analysts that larger historical forces would eventually overwhelm the destructiveness of nationalism is, in all likelihood, invalid. Thus although the forces of worldwide globalization and democratization could theoretically weaken the nationalist passion on the part of domineering majorities or embittered minorities alike, there is no convincing proof or unfailing logical rationale that such a link is inevitable or even likely. Globalization is hardly an alternative to nationalism; on the contrary, in numerous situations it encourages nationalism as an antidote to its very essence. In general, the way to deal with nationalism is neither to fight directly against it nor to ignore it but to recognize it for what it is and try to steer it, channel it in acceptable directions. Nationalism is a natural human force (Tamir 1993) that must be somehow structured in a positive or at least acceptable manner. The same could be said about democratization. In many situations democratization encourages nationalism and does so destructively (Snyder 2000).

The transformation of ethnic hegemony faces today, specifically, the emergence of ethnic nationalism on the substate level, often in countries that seem to have solved their national problems centuries ago (e.g., France, the United Kingdom). It is a phenomenon that established states and humanity at large can ignore only at their peril. Subnational groups should be directed toward the achievement of positive, realistic goals within the broader regional and world community and taking into account globalizing processes (Keating 2001b). Equally, however, their bone of contention with their mother-nations can easily deteriorate toward full-blown confrontation.

One way of approaching ethnic relations within deeply divided societies, as well as the potentialities of solving ethnic antagonisms in such a setting, is through the psycho-attitudinal prism linked to the notion of the "other." Societies characterized by deep sociopolitical cleavages often witness a strong, almost permanent tendency on the part of majorities and minorities alike to negate each other's claims to legitimate rights. What might be called "otherization" (Peleg 1994) occurs when someone perceives someone else as the complete negation of himself, a phenomenon that is not limited to individuals and often characterizes groups.

Hegemonic conditions are invariably about intergroup relations in which antagonism and hostility have escalated and crystallized into an attitude of extreme and possibly even total negation. The process of establishing hegemony might begin with the differentiation between various members of society on the basis of ethnic origin, religion, language, culture, race, or any other socially significant attribute. This initial, "objectivist" differentiation among individuals and groups could easily become, especially in deeply divided societies, a dominant sociopsychological reality that controls the entire milieu and particularly the public life of the polity.

The most important fact to realize is that "otherness" – the perception of other individuals and groups as fundamentally different and highly negative – is organically linked to the social status of various groups in society. Within a hegemonic setting, minorities are often the "other," and their political status is, equivalently, low. Moreover, those who perceive minorities as others and assign them low status often have an interest in sustaining and even perpetuating the resulting sociopolitical hierarchy within society. Otherness is, therefore, not merely a device for maintaining the integrity of a long-held worldview but also an instrument for sustaining a hegemonic sociopolitical order.

To the extent to which a minority-perceived-as-the-other is a victimized social group within society, it is a source of potential political instability as well as a violation of some of democracy's most fundamental tenets. One of the central questions from the perspective of this study is whether such condition could be changed as a means of affecting sociopolitical transformation, and how it can be changed. There are several variables that might impact significantly the level of antagonism and otherization and possibly result in its decline: (1) the type of education given to the younger members of the antagonistic groups, the majority and minority alike. Although there is a natural tendency to perpetuate the biases on which otherization rests, countervailing factors could intentionally be introduced into the educational system; (2) economic well-being: in time of economic stress, interethnic relations are likely to deteriorate; and (3) actions taken by the political elites of the rival groups – particularly the elite of the majority group – in the context of alleviating the prevalent ethnic hostility.

In the final analysis, the possibility for transforming a hegemonic polity to a more democratically inclusive system depends on the ability of the majority group and its political elite to affect these types of factors in a positive manner. Only by convincing the members of the majority to change their attitude toward the out-group can transformation occur. The intensity of the negativity toward the minority is a key factor to work on in an effort to bring about a transformation.

The process of trying to transform a hegemonic system is, obviously, deeply political, and the main stage for this political drama is within the majority group (rather than in the relations between the majority and the minority). In an entrenched hegemonic situation, members of the majority working toward transformation of the system are likely to become targets of intimidation, accusation, and even oppression by those who see themselves as the guardians of the true nature of the polity.

3

Classifying Multinational States

> Peace is not the absence of conflict but the presence of creative alternatives to
> conflict, alternatives to passive or aggressive responses, alternatives to violence.
> (Dorothy Thompson, 1893–1961, an American journalist)

This volume attempts to understand the process through which a hegemonic, ethnic state might become a more inclusive polity: it focuses on the transformation of Ethnic Constitutional Orders to regimes that meet more fully the requirements of contemporary democracy as described in Chapter 2. The hegemonic ethnic state, however, is not a separate planet unto its own. It is part of a larger galaxy of states that includes different types of political systems. To understand the very essence of the hegemonic ethnic state, its *raison d'etre*, and its typical behavior as a political actor, one must be able to compare it to other types of polities, both theoretically and empirically.

The function of this chapter is to offer a classificatory system, reflected graphically in Figure 1 that will enable us to systematically analyze hegemonic states and, more specifically, study their potential for transformation. The classificatory system could be looked upon as an analytical framework that includes both static and dynamic components. Although it statically identifies a series of alternative political systems in deeply divided societies (e.g., liberal democracy, federal state, or consociational government), it also identifies (dynamically) five modes of reaction adopted by states in deeply divided societies, trying to resolve the ethnic tensions within their existing political space (as well as two additional modes of reaction in which the ethnic hegemonic state tries to resolve its dilemmas in an external fashion).

The Logic of Classification

Several general issues ought to be dealt with in approaching an ambitious classificatory system of the type presented here:

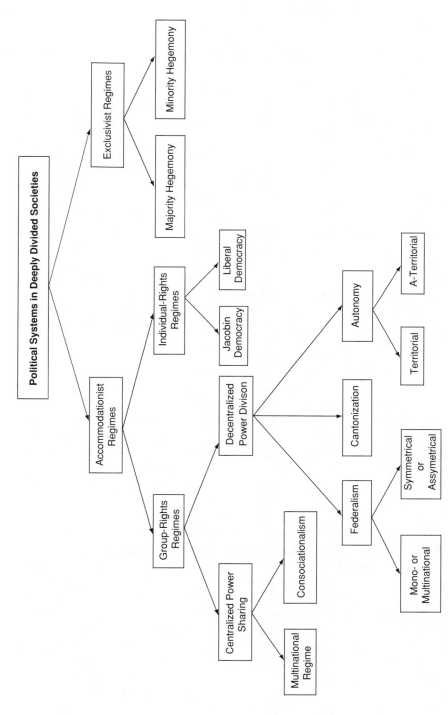

FIGURE 1. Classification of Ethnically Divided Polities.

1. What exactly are the units that are being classified?
2. What is the basic logic of the classification?
3. Why is it important to classify, especially in terms of the current project?
4. What would make a useful classificatory system?

This chapter will first address these questions and then proceed with the exposition of the classificatory system of this volume, a system that includes the *majority-hegemonic system* and large number of systems into which such a hegemonic system might evolve in the process of transformation.

The classified units that are the subject of my interest are societies that are deeply divided ethnically (or even nationally). By focusing on "ethnic" (or "national") divisions, the chapter dwells on societies in which there are at least two distinct groups – in terms of their own collective identity and/or the way they are perceived by others – living within the same political space. The ethnic distinction between the groups could be based on seemingly objective characteristics such as common descent, shared experience, or cultural traits (Gurr 2000, 4) or on even more essentialist, primordial markers such as race, language, or religion. Often, however, the ethnic distinctions are a matter of subjective self-identification (Coakley 1992, 356) where a group is differentiated from another group within a state due to "enduring social constructs" (Gurr 2000, 4). Such constructs might be desired by members of the distinct group or imposed on them by others.

One of the most important aspects to examine in any political system, a sort of a litmus test for the classification of a polity, is whether it allows members of a minority within it *dual identity* amounting to full acceptance by the larger political community as well as within their own particular ethnic community. In some countries – mostly those that are defined in my classification as *accommodationist* – a dual or hyphenated status presents no problem. One can be a Scot and a Brit in the United Kingdom, a Jew and an American in the United States, an Ibo and a Nigerian in Nigeria, thus being "recognized as a member of the larger nation" (Safran 1994, 65). Yet there are countries, those that are defined in my classification as *ethnohegemonies*, where this duality is not easily accepted or rejected altogether. One might find it hard to be a Slovak and a Hungarian, an Arab and an Israeli, a Breton and a Frenchman.

Be that as it may, the goal of the classification offered here is to develop an analytically useful way for distinguishing between states that face deeply divided societies in terms of the ethnic origin or even the national identity of their citizens (i.e., numerous states in today's world). Although others have offered classifications of democratic systems (e.g., Smooha 2002), the classification offered here is quite different and, in general, significantly broader. It deals with all political systems in deeply divided societies, democratic and non-democratic alike. One of the main goals of this classification is to call attention to and facilitate comparison between exclusivist systems that are democratically flawed and accommodationist systems that are inherently democratic.

The analytical framework presented in this chapter is a combination of taxonomy and typology. It includes the classification of entities by logical types (e.g., "exclusivist" vs. "accommodationist" regimes or group-based polities vs. individual-based polities), but it also codifies existing knowledge (by distinguishing, e.g., between power-sharing and power-division regimes, and between such decentralized governmental methods as federalism, cantonization, and autonomy, as well as their subcategories). What this means, specifically, is that each of the regime types identified in the classification offered in this chapter is both logically possible and empirically identifiable. At the same time, certain "cells" within my classificatory system remain underdeveloped in this volume for lack of knowledge (at this time) or, more often, lack of theoretical interest within the framework of the present study. Thus this volume does not have a particular interest in offering a detailed analysis of apartheid (or minority hegemonic regimes in the language of this study). The work is concerned mainly with the transformation of majority hegemonic regimes into inclusive, accommodationist systems. So within the framework of the classification offered here, minority hegemony (apartheid) as a regime type is merely recognized but without offering a detailed analysis of it.

Like all classifications, the one offered here, although intended to be useful for the purpose of analyzing politics in deeply divided societies, is imperfect in several ways:

1. The classification is oversimplified by including, in most cases, only two outcomes, although more outcomes might be logically identifiable or empirically found. Thus under "centralized power-sharing" regimes the classification recognizes, on the one hand, bi- or multinational systems (where the polity is officially defined as "belonging" to two or more groups) and, on the other hand, a "consociational" system, where the majority-minority roles are more distinct and less equal. It might be that more than merely two outcomes are possible. No classification could possibly be entirely exhaustive nor should it try to be, lest it loses its parsimony.

2. A classification, which is necessarily based on distinction between types of institutions and behaviors, must by its very nature "ignore the great complexity of the real political world" (Coakley 1992, 345). Thus although the classification of regimes in deeply divided societies offered here starts with a distinction between "exclusivist" and "accommodationist" polities, it is clear that in many cases states adopt a *mixture* of policies, rather than pursuing exclusively one type of position. The function of the dichotomous approach adopted here is to bring into sharper relief underlying uniformities of seemingly different political systems. This approach is not necessarily capable of explaining why a specific polity behaves the way it does in every instance.

3. The classification offered here is not exhaustive (i.e., there might be regime types that are not included) nor does it achieve perfect discreetness. Some of the regimes might be "found in combination" (McGarry and O'Leary 1993, 5). In reality, that is, a regime might be a primarily

individual-based liberal democracy but in certain respects it might be also capable of recognizing group rights. Similarly, a regime might be pursuing a hegemonic policy and an accommodationist policy at one and the same time toward different parts of its population. For example, "contemporary Israel practices consociationalism amongst Jews of different ethnic origin but control over Palestinians" (ibid.). The point is, simply, that regime types are not always, in reality, entirely mutually exclusive. While Spain and Britain are both unitary states, the first has become semifederal and the other has "devolved" over the last several decades.

Despite those limitations, which are inherent in any broad classificatory system (particularly in the social sciences), comprehensive classification of regimes in deeply divided societies is essential as a stage toward understanding and explaining the behavior of such regimes. In this particular study, the functions of the classificatory system are several and closely related:

1. To recognize and highlight significant differences between different political regimes established in deeply divided societies, where distinct ethnic or national groups live within a single polity.
2. To describe those differences, especially in terms of the regime's approach for solving majority-minority tensions through the establishment of political institutions and the adoption of public policies.
3. To explain the differences between the various regimes in terms of their behavior by identifying a set of variables such as the relative size and strength of the minority, the ideology and determination of the majority, international pressures put on the regime, and so forth, a topic more fully developed in the final chapter of this study.
4. To offer at least some prescriptions regarding the possible transformation of "hegemonic regimes" (especially majority hegemonic regimes) to more "accommodationist regimes," based on either individual equality or group rights, or preferably some combination of both.

A serious scholarly effort to produce a classification of some kind is necessary for any and all of these tasks. Yet several conditions must be met to produce a useful classification for a specific study. To be beneficial, a classificatory system must meet at least three conditions:

1. Be *empirical*: related to actual identifiable cases rather than being merely theoretical in nature. The classification offered here is specifically applied to a large number of cases, particularly in Chapters 4–7.
2. Be *broad*: offer a comprehensive perspective on the phenomenon it is suggesting to study or offer a "tour d'horizon" of that phenomenon (Safran 1994, 61). Thus, for example, the otherwise useful study of power sharing by Timothy Sisk offers a typology of conflict-regulating practices (1996, 47–48) that is too confined.
3. Be *explicit*: be as clear as possible for the reader. Numerous analyses of complex social phenomena include implicit theoretical notions,

conceptual classifications, and the like. The purpose of this study, and this chapter in particular, is to avoid such an approach and clarify all elements of the analytical framework as much as possible.

Accommodationist vs. Exclusivist Multinational States

The first, and most fundamental distinction offered by this study and by the classificatory framework in this chapter (Figure 1), is the one between a multinational state that tries to accommodate at least the most important ethnic groups within its borders and a multinational state that adopts an exclusivist approach in face of and despite its multiethnic reality. The ultimate purpose of this study is to inquire into the conditions that might facilitate the transformation of one type of exclusivist state, the majority hegemonic state, to accommodationism (of which there are many variants).

The theoretical distinction between the exclusivist and the accommodationist state is fairly simple and straightforward, much more so than the distinction between the variants of those two basic models. The exclusivist multinational (or multiethnic) state strives by all the means at its disposal to maintain, enhance, and perpetuate the dominance of one ethnic group over all others. The state becomes the tool of such exclusivity and genuine democracy becomes its victim (see Chapter 2). For the core nation the state is its national possession, and its alone. The state is merely the institutional reflection of the nation; it is certainly not a neutral zone for interethnic competition (as it might be, e.g., in the liberal-democratic state).

The accommodationist state readily recognizes its own diversity. Although it might strive for unity and integration as means for establishing a stable political order, the accommodationist state will do so through the recognition of its ethnic components. Such recognition could be translated into numerous institutional arrangements, some very different than others, but the fundamental purpose of the state remains to balance the interests of the different ethnic groups. It is important to note that for a state to be "accommodationist," it must recognize its ethnic group(s) as legitimate and give this recognition institutional expression (Safran 1994, 72).

One way to distinguish between exclusivism and accommodationism in a multiethnic setting is to describe the former as ethnocentric and the latter as state-centric. The deeply ingrained ethnocentric position of the exclusivist state is reflected in the classical position of nineteenth-century European nationalism, a set of ideas that tended to equate the state and the nation, and that eventually led to the adoption of the concept of the nation-state (Cobban 1969). In that tradition the state is often considered the highest achievement of the nation and, as such, the single-minded promoter of the interests of the nation. At the same time, it is important to note that although some exclusivist states might adopt a tough, Jacobin position toward the minorities within them (Schnapper 2004), others may try to "melt" them into the majority culture using softer assimilatory and integrative mechanisms (see the following text).

The accommodationist position, when compared to all forms of exclusivism, is inherently more sympathetic to diversity – including ethnic diversity – within the state. Such diversity might be recognized, albeit indirectly, either by the state conscious decision to pay no attention whatsoever to ethnicity (Van der Berghe 1981a, 353–4) or, alternatively, by the state adoption of a group-right approach in which various ethnic collectivities are politically recognized. Either way, the purpose of the accommodationist political regime is to publicly accept the "other" rather than to dominate it (Peleg 1994).

The accommodationist approach is inherently and significantly more democratic than the exclusivist one, particularly because it is willing to recognize the equality of all ethnic groups within society or, alternatively, to privatize ethnicity altogether. While J. S. Mill and others have maintained that "united public opinion" – that is, uniethnicity – is necessary for democracy, and that democracy is incompatible with multiethnic society ([1861] 1958, 230), an accommodationist approach at least attempts to prove this pessimistic thesis wrong, given that multiethnicity is a powerful fact of life in most countries.

Like others, this author doubts that there are "viable alternatives to democracy as a system of just and stable conflict management" (Sisk 1996, 29). Although an exclusivist system could be legitimately recognized as effective in "managing" conflict, it is by definition nondemocratic or democratically flawed. At the same time, it is also unjust and, in most (although not all) cases, unstable. The denial of the legitimacy and possibly even the very existence of an ethnic minority (e.g., Turkey's traditional position toward the Kurds) is not a recipe for democracy, justice, or stability.

Exclusivist states, even relatively democratic ones, are inevitably led on the path of denying their minorities' very existence or at least their right for a legitimate independent voice. Thus many in Jacobin France have traditionally dismissed the Breton identity and others as "folkloric," Romanian politicians have often denied the "Hungarianess" of most people in Transylvania, and Turks have tended to deny the existence of an independent Kurdish identity.

In contrast to the exclusivist approach, in accommodationist situations the "central" authorities, who by definition primarily represent the ethnic majority, typically respond favorably to at least some of the concerns of the ethnic minority. Such a response could take the form of public recognition of the minority, but it is often institutionalized through either the "neutralization" of the state as the exclusive arena of the majority or some form of majority-minority power sharing or power division (see the following text).

Although exclusivist regimes start with the assumption that there is only one legitimate nation in the state, accommodationist regimes are ready to acknowledge diversity. The assumption of unity-despite-diversity leads exclusivist regimes almost inevitably down the path of coercion, forced assimilation, denial of linguistic rights, and even population transfer and other modes of ethnic cleansing. Such hegemonic behavior is, simply put, inherent in an exclusivist regime (Bocock 1986).

Despite the sharp differentiation drawn here between exclusivist and accommodationist regimes, it is essential to recognize that, in reality, exclusivist and accommodationist ideas often live side-by-side within one political system. Rogers Smith, for example, has shown that in the United States "liberalism" (an accommodationist regime par excellence) has lived together with the more exclusivist "republicanism" and the thoroughly hegemonic "ethnocentrism" for generations, and Shafir and Peled have shown it in the case of Israel (Shafir and Peled 2002). It is clear that "states often pursue a mixture of policies, not all of them consciously chosen or explicitly put into effect" (Coakley 1992, 345). Yet the classification is useful if it facilitates or promotes our understanding and ability to explain reality.

In principle, however, as accommodationism takes over as a characteristic of a regime, the identification of the state with any single ethnic or national group weakens, and it becomes more and more committed to either complete neutrality in the relations between ethnic groups or an explicit reconciliation between its major ethnic constituents. Through this transformative process the differentiation between exclusivism and accommodationism becomes clearer.

Exclusivist Regimes: Minority vs. Majority Hegemony

An *exclusivist regime*, within my classificatory system, is one that privileges one ethnic or national group over all others, often by making its preferential status a permanent feature of the polity and by establishing multiple institutions designed to perpetuate the ethnic hegemony of the privileged group over all other groups.

The institutionalization of the dominance of one ethnic group is the distinguishing trait of an exclusivist regime. The assumption of the regime is that although the state belongs to the dominant group, other groups have, fundamentally and inalterably, a lesser claim to the state and, consequently, lesser rights. At the same time, it is important to understand that in most exclusive regimes, the nation is clearly more central than the state, which is merely an institutionalized instrument for achieving the national goals. The significance of this fact is that although the national goals as defined by the majority or the elite can hardly be revised (let alone abandoned), the form or design of the state may be transformed, a central concern of this study.

There are two different types of hegemonic exclusivist regimes, a majority-based hegemonic regime (of which an Ethnic Constitutional Order is the most common) and a minority-based hegemonic regime (of which apartheid is an example). There are several important differences between them, although both are thoroughly nonaccommodationist:

1. *Who governs*. As the designation of these two variants of hegemonic exclusivist regimes indicate, in one of them an ethnic minority rules over a majority. South Africa under apartheid, Ian Smith's Rhodesia, Iraq

under Saddam Hussein and the Sunni minority, and Syria of the Ale-wite Asads are but several examples of a minority-led hegemonic regime, which is by definition nondemocratic and sometimes outright racist. In a majority-based hegemony, the largest ethnic group governs, but it does so exclusively on its own behalf. Because the majority rules, such a regime might be, mistakenly, identified as a perfect democracy, especially if it assumes the appearance of a democracy by adopting some of its prac-tices (e.g., regular elections) or institutions (e.g., parliaments).

2. *Targets of discrimination.* In minority-based hegemonies, both the major-ity group and individual members of the majority are actively discrim-inated. The regime keeps a zealous eye on challenges to its segregatory guidelines that are the *sine qua non* of its existence, whether these chal-lenges come from majority groups as such (a very likely situation) or from individual members of that group. In majority hegemonies the tar-get of discrimination, for the most part, is the minority groups. Because the state belongs, by its very own definition, to a single ethnic group, such a group will surely prevent any and all competitors (i.e, other eth-nic groups) from making an effective claim on it, especially a claim for equality. Exclusivist majority hegemonies might not discriminate directly, actively, and blatantly against individuals, especially if the majority feels secure in its position and if members of the minority do not chal-lenge directly the existing exclusivist order. Yet it is important to note that the discrimination against minority groups in majority hegemonies is very likely to impact negatively on the rights of their members as individuals.

3. *Modes of discrimination.* The two types of exclusivist regimes differ also in regard to the way in which they deal with members of the minority. In a minority hegemony such as South Africa's apartheid regime, discrimi-nation was formal, official, explicit, and public. In majority hegemonies, particularly democracies, the modes of discrimination toward members of the minority are, in the main, less formal. Although some legislation may be part of the inequality structure imposed on the minority, discrim-ination more often is part of less formal, even if governmental, policy. It is often present in widespread practices (public and private alike). The "authorities" in such a regime, however, often do not act aggressively against such discriminatory practices.

Sammy Smooha, in a series of remarkable publications (e.g., 1990, 1997, or Smooha and Hanf 1992), developed a model that he called "ethnic democ-racy," a model in which all citizens are granted basic political rights (e.g., the right to vote and be elected) and civil liberties (e.g., assembly, association, and expression), but a single ethnic or national group maintains institutionalized dominance in the state. In a seminal article, Peled added the distinction between liberal and republican rights, adopting Smooha's basic notion of ethnic democ-racy (Peled 1992).

The distinction offered here between two different variants of exclusivist regimes differs from the Smooha formula in several respects:

1. It is much more general in character and, therefore, could be applied to many more situations. What Smooha calls "Herrnvolk democracy" (or apartheid) is, within my typology, only one type of minority hegemonism, one based on race. Similarly, what Smooha terms "ethnic democracy" (a term that should be rejected as misleading) is just a specific type of majority hegemonic regime.

2. As indicated in the preceding text, the distinction offered in this book puts significant emphasis on the sharp difference between majority and minority hegemonic rule in terms of the identity of the governing group, the targets of its discrimination, and the discriminatory modes that it adopts, all important aspects of both variants of exclusivism.

3. Although Smooha describes majority dominance accompanied by individual rights as democratic (this type of regime is, for him, ethnic democracy), within the classification offered in the current volume, it is exclusivist and hegemonic. Institutionalized discrimination against minorities, as groups or individuals, is in terms of my definition of democracy, a negation of one of democracy's most fundamental principles, that of equality of all citizens.

Despite certain similarities between the two forms of exclusivism (minority based and majority based) they are often quite different in terms of the overall character of the regime and, most importantly from this study's perspective, their capacity for transformation into nonhegemonic forms. Minority hegemonism is entirely incompatible with pluralism of any kind, individual liberties, or recognition of any group rights (save the prerogatives of the majority, of course). It is a regime based on brute force – as in the case of Rhodesia, South Africa in the past or Saddam Hussein's Iraq – and the willingness to use this force indiscriminately against an oppressed majority.

Majority hegemonism often is based on adopting some democratic principles (e.g., the government tends to reflect the will of the majority), while ignoring others (e.g., violation of the principle of equality and, especially, group equality). It is a regime with a significantly softer edge and more benign character than minority hegemonism. Because the majority is presumably supportive of the hegemonic structure erected by the elite on its behalf, the resort to brute force toward the minority could be minimized, even if the minority is, in reality, marginalized. Parliamentary majorities, watchful executives, and respectable courts can effectively replace brute force in keeping the majority in a hegemonic position. Moreover, in a majoritarian hegemony, semiconsociational arrangements, although not real consociational provisions, could be and often are adopted, giving the minority a sense of participation in (if not real influence over) the political game.

Some majority hegemonies can even move gradually toward a form of liberal, majoritarian democracy, although it is much more difficult for them to move toward any of the group-rights regime types. A confident, numerically safe majority can, and often does, offer minority leaders "deals," co-opting them into the existing hegemonic structure, and establish other assimilatory techniques to blunt the knife of hegemonic control.

A pragmatic, clever leadership of a hegemonic majority can "manage" an active or potential ethnic conflict for a long time, prolonging hegemony in a remarkably "civilized" manner. Although it is the thesis of this study that this could not be done "forever" in today's emerging world with its emphasis on genuine equality, the transformation from exclusivism to accommodationism in a "soft" majority hegemonism is possible, albeit difficult (see Chapter 4).

One of the difficulties in transforming a majority hegemonism to any type of accommodationism is that "the problem of ethnic overbidding is pervasive" (DeVotta 2005; Sisk 1996, 17). Ethnic leaders often outbid moderates, describing any and all compromise moves as a sellout of group interests. Ironically, the more democratic the state is, the greater the problem might be.

An even more serious problem is the inherent perception within the majority population in exclusivist regimes that the state belongs to it and it alone. The intensity of the sense of possession that the majority has toward the state is a key determinant of the capacity of that state to shift from exclusivism to accommodationism. Because in an exclusivist situation the state on all of its resources and symbols has been "expropriated," conflict is almost entirely inevitable.

Although "hegemonic control" (Lustick 1979) has been used frequently in history, maybe more so than any other exclusivist method, the conditions for its perpetuation in today's world are far from ideal. This is particularly the case within deeply divided societies and especially when the divide is ethnic. In such an exclusivist system, the elite do not have the capacity to develop a transcendent, overarching identity that would deal effectively with ethnic differences. In the past, countries were able to establish such an all-state identity (the United Kingdom, France, the United States, Italy, and Germany are but some examples); now it is significantly more difficult to do it in the contemporary world of self-determination. Even the authoritarian Communist regimes of the USSR, Czechoslovakia, and Yugoslavia, armed with a cosmopolitan and nonethnic ideology, were unable to "invent" a new identity for their states and populations.

The more democratic a state is, the more difficult it is to maintain and justify ethnic exclusivity, a notion that runs against the grain of democracy's very essence. Democratization breeds opposition to ethnic exclusivity, as shown in the several cases of Communist regimes mentioned previously, as well as in many other cases (e.g. post-Franco Spain). In deeply divided societies, the existence of democracy is not a guarantee that a system of control would not emerge (Chapter 5).

Historically speaking, hegemonic exclusivism has a track record of some success, however it is likely to be overthrown in the long run. In today's world, the system breeds radicalism because it stands in such stark, fundamental contradiction to the worldwide dominant values of democracy, equality, and self-determination. Although exclusivist hegemony is then doomed, it might result in an intense conflict that makes genuine accommodation rather difficult. Through subjugation, isolation, avoidance, and displacement of ethnic groups (Rothchild and Olurunsola 1986, 240–1), hegemonic majorities might be able to postpone the decline of their exclusivist regimes but only for a limited time. Even electoral contests that result in hegemonism (be that in Sri Lanka or Northern Ireland) are often merely stopgap measures adopted by exclusivist regimes, not real, long-term solutions to exclusivism.

Accommodationist Regimes: Individual- vs. Group-Based

Unlike exclusivist systems, *accommodationist regimes* are polities committed to the peaceful resolution of their ethnic conflicts by granting equal rights to all their citizens and, in some cases, the public recognition of all their major ethnic groups. To be sure, the task of the accommodationist regime is never an easy one. The conditions for democratic solutions in multiethnic societies are rarely promising. What might make an accommodationist regime successful, however, is the dual belief that (1) accommodation between ethnic groups is preferred to the domination of one group over the other(s), and (2) interethnic conflict ought to be resolved exclusively through democratic means. There is an intimate link between accommodation and democracy, just as there is a link between exclusivist hegemonic conditions and nondemocracy or, at best, flawed democracy. Although the record of nondemocratic regimes in solving ethnic problems is miserable (e.g., the USSR, the former Yugoslavia, Czechoslovakia, Iraq, and Franco's Spain), the record of democracies is mixed and by no means perfect (Peleg 2000).

Accommodationist solutions adopted by ethnically divided societies tend to be based on several ideas, regardless of the specific institutionalized arrangements established by those societies:

1. The belief that social problems, including ethnic conflicts, could benefit significantly from "political engineering" (Sartori 1968; Russell 1994). What this means is that the political regime institutionalized in a multiethnic state and the rules of the game in the political arena in accommodationist orders, should encourage moderation and try to control the destructive ethnic forces within the polity. The "trick" of successful political engineering in a multiethnic setting is to maintain democracy while channelling the popular forces on which it is built in constructive, accommodationist directions.
2. The belief in human equality as a foundation for the political order. Although the exclusivist formula for interethnic conflict assumes the inherent superiority of one ethnic group over all others (e.g., due to its numerical advantage, historical rights, higher worth), accommodationism assumes equality as a supreme value, a desired goal, and a preferred public policy.

The classification of regimes offered in this volume recognizes two types of accommodationism:

1. *Individual-rights regimes.* These are polities in which all citizens, as individuals, are equal before the law. These regimes tend to be either neutral toward social groups (as is the case of liberal democracy) or possibly disapproving if not openly hostile toward them (as is the case of Jacobin democracy, given in this study a different interpretation than the usual one that equates it with totalitarianism).

2. *Group-rights regimes.* There are many more variants of regimes recognizing group rights than those based on individual rights. Importantly, some of these regimes are based on power sharing while others are based on power division. These forms are dealt with in the next section of this chapter; they hold great significance for the overall argument of this volume.

The granting of equal individual rights to all citizens has been at the very center of the modernization of the Western state. This process, although resulting in human equality on an individual basis, has contained within itself the seeds of the tension between individual equality and group rights. This tension continues to have major impact on most of today's multiethnic states (e.g., Canada, Spain). Individual equality, as a universal philosophy and as a regime type, is often inherently unfriendly toward the very notion of group rights, which it views as, potentially at least, dangerous to its most basic principles.

A dynamic, historical outlook may bring this tension into sharper relief. The old European order was based on monarchical, nondemocratic societies where certain groups had special rights that were clearly differentiated from the rights granted to other groups. The French Revolution changed all of that: in the new, Jacobin conception, all citizens were equal as individuals and no group within society had any special rights. The notion of equality before the law has meant both individual equality and the negation of special rights or privileges for any group.

But here lies the problem. The uneasiness of the modern, individual-centered state toward the rights of ethnic groups is often a source of conflict, especially when such groups perceive themselves as entitled to special recognition due to historical precedents, cultural uniqueness, or other reasons. The historical process of transformation from a corporate, group-based state to an individual-centered polity could make this incompatibility rather serious.

Interestingly, the tension between individual rights and group rights exists both in a Jacobin state like France and many other states that have adopted the French model, a model that views the nation as united and indivisible in pursuing its ideals and interests (Schnapper 2004), and in liberal polities like the United States and many polities that adopted its model, a system that views the rights of the individuals as paramount and the interests of any and all ethnic groups as private. Because most Western countries today reflect some kind of combination of unitary Jacobinism and enhanced liberalism – the United

Kingdom is a good example – the tension between the state and assertive ethnic groups of all types is almost inevitable.

At the same time, this volume asserts that the tension between individual-based statehood and group rights could be reduced, if never fully resolved, as long as the fundamental principle of liberal democracy, individual equality protected by law and adhered to in practice, is maintained. Fully developed liberal democracies, more so than democratizing states, can afford the recognition of some group rights in the interest of equity and stability. Thus if the principle of majority rule is accepted, as it is in all liberal democracies, the recognition of some group rights could be accepted without the immobilization of the state.

The problem of group rights versus individual rights is well reflected in an example given by Sisk (1996, 68). The Canadian Charter of Rights and Freedoms (1982) sought to protect the individual rights of all citizens, including members of distinctive groups, against all forms of discrimination. Several years later, the Meech Lake Accord sought to constitutionally designate Quebec a "distinct society." In doing so, Meech Lake undermined or was perceived as undermining the liberal tradition by granting Quebec's group rights. It failed, along with the Charlottetown process that followed it, and brought about a larger crisis (Welsh, 1993, 51) that continues, at least potentially, to date.

In terms of ethnicity and its place in the political order, the position of individual-based regimes is straightforward: ethnicity ought to be privatized. While the individual is the cornerstone of these regimes, ethnic affiliations are often formally unrecognized, although not necessarily discouraged (especially in liberal democracy). So although ethnic groups may form separate social organizations and associations (including schools), they are generally not entitled to state support. If, however, one ethnic or religious organization is entitled to such support, all are; thus, equality between all groups is maintained zealously. In the United States, for example, all charities, including those run by ethnic groups, are entitled to tax exemption on the basis of equality.

Although individual-based democracies, for the most part, do not adopt a position against ethnic affiliations as such, they often try to foster an overarching identity, citizens' identification with the polity as a whole, over and above the particularistic ethnic identities found within them. Although the term *assimilation* may be politically incorrect in many liberal democracies today, they certainly have a clear preference for integration, a process in which minority ethnicities "melt" and minorities adopt, in effect, the majority culture. Integration is traditionally more successful when used toward immigrant groups than toward "natives," ethnic groups living in their ancestral homes (e.g., Native American). Minorities in contested homelands are particularly opposed to any and all forms of assimilation or integration (McGarry and O'Leary 1993, 19).

Although all individual-based democracies promote mainly individual liberties, they tend to be equally committed to the nondiscrimination of minority ethnic groups even though such groups are technically private associations of individual citizens. Moreover, such polities often adopt administrative, legislative, and judicial positions designed to equalize the conditions of historically disadvantaged ethnic groups.

Individual-based regimes may not be the preferred governmental option for powerful minorities. Such groups might believe in their chances of benefiting more from a group-rights regime. Yet individual-based polity, and especially liberal democracy, is surely a desirable choice for weaker minorities. The neutral, nonethnic institutional design of most liberal democracies, and the ethnically "blind" policies of such regimes may allow some ethnic groups to flourish.

In several deeply divided societies, such as Canada or Spain, individual-based liberal democracy is often perceived by minority groups as insufficiently responsive to their concerns. Although liberal democracies might be committed to accommodation, many minorities have taken the position that genuine accommodation could be achieved only through group rights and never through pure liberal (let alone Jacobin) democracy.

When it comes to political accommodation within deeply divided societies, the picture is substantially more complex when we shift from the individual to the group level. We can identify at least five different variants of group-rights regime. Moreover, it is inherently impossible to argue that any of these variants is invariably better than all others. Accommodationist regimes often combine different group-based methods, as one can see in the case of Canada or Belgium (Coakley 1992, 348). The selection of an appropriate model for a particular polity might come to an *ad hoc* choice based on the specific political problems faced by that system.

The thesis developed by this volume is that *although individual-based democracy is altogether a very attractive regime, it often does not respond to the needs of all ethnic groups within a deeply divided society*. In such situations, unless a satisfactory group-rights solution could be found, serious conflicts might develop. A process that could be called the "dynamics of ethnic rights" often leads ethnic groups to demand equality as individuals and then group rights – cultural rights (e.g., use of language in public and in the educational system), institutional political recognition, and so forth (Coakley 1993, 4–7).

The move from individual to group rights is, however, highly problematical. The problem with group rights (especially when compared to individual rights) is that they have "never been coherently codified in a package that has attracted general agreement" (ibid., 5). Although individual rights are based on the relatively simple principle of citizens' equality before the law, it is not easy to define precisely and impossible to define authoritatively which group is entitled to group rights and to what rights they are entitled. Although this inherent difficulty could add yet another argument in favor of individual rights regime, when there is a serious and deep ethnic division the state might have to respond to it by granting group rights to certain groups.

It is interesting and important to note that although in the interwar period (1919–39), group rights were developed to the fullest under the auspices of the League of Nations Minorities Treaties, they have somewhat declined in the postwar era, possibly reflecting the ascendance of the United States, with its strong preference to individual rights and liberal democracy. It is also important to recognize that not all group rights are clearly distinguishable from individual rights (Laponce 1987, 160–4).

Some of the tensions associated with both individual-based rights and group-based rights are reflected in the fierce debate over affirmative action. Although it is a policy designed to correct past discrimination based on racial traits, affirmative action is perceived by many analysts as establishing new type of discrimination (so-called reverse discrimination), thus violating the most fundamental principles of individual-based regimes. At the same time, in a regime based on group rights, affirmative action may be (or at least be perceived as) favoring some groups over other groups, thus violating the ethos of that regime.

Several countries have, nevertheless, made commitments to assist historically disadvantaged groups in the interest of justice and stability. Thus the Indian constitution of 1949 committed the new state to "promote with special care the educational economic interests of the weaker sections of the people, and in particular of the Scheduled Castes and Scheduled Tribes" (Article 46). Despite the pervasive effects of past discrimination, affirmative action in India led not only to criticisms but even to violence.

In the United States, affirmative action has been initially adopted as a means for dealing with the exclusion of minorities. It then became a major bone of contention within the political system, and it is now being, generally if not decisively, rolled back. As a method for dealing with the exclusion of minorities, affirmative action is expanding in some countries such as South Africa. In several countries, it was found that although historically disadvantaged groups must be given opportunity through special programs, the use of inflexible quotas for such groups rarely works. It often reinforces the separation of ethnic groups and their hostility toward each other, and it is widely perceived as a violation of individual equality.

The widespread debate over affirmative action in all types of societies, those based on individual rights and those based on group rights, brings into focus the inherent tension between those different foundations for building an acceptable order in ethnically deeply divided societies.

The theoretical framework introduced in this study makes a distinction between two types of individual-based regimes, liberal democracies and Jacobin democracy. The distinction between those two ideal types brings into a sharper relief the issues that this study confronts: the tension between individual-based and group-based rights and the tension between social groups, particularly ethnic groups, and the national state.

The models for liberal democracy are the United States and the United Kingdom, although other Anglo-Saxon states, as well as Scandinavian countries, could qualify. As a matter of principle, in the United States all rights are given to the individual and none to groups of any kind (including ethnic or religious ones). In reality there are deviations from the fundamentals of the model – thus, Native Americans have rights based on agreements with the U.S. government, affirmative action programs have been established for the benefit of traditionally discriminated groups, and so forth – however, the essence of the American system is the maximization of individual rights, granted on an equal basis. Moreover, the American federal structure creates decentralization intended to weaken the central authorities (i.e., the sovereign state), although not necessarily the American nation.

The second individual-based model is Jacobin democracy. It is used in this study in a very different sense than the usual one where it connotes nondemocratic totalitarianism. This model grants extensive individual rights to all citizens, but it is different than liberal democracy because of its militant attitude against any and all separate ethnic groups and its decisive promotion of Statist and cultural centralism. Theoretically at least, this type of system has dominated France since the revolution (Hazareesingh 2002) and, in some ways (although not in others), long before the revolution. Moreover, this system was "borrowed" by other countries such as Italy after its unification, Spain in the nineteenth century, and Ataturk's Turkey. Most contemporary West European countries are greatly influenced by the French design. The Jacobin model shares with the American model at least two fundamental principles: all citizens are equal before the law as individuals, and no group is entitled to particularistic recognition or special rights. At the same time, the French model differs from the American one in two respects: the centralization of all power in the hands of the state (rather than the division of power between different levels of government built into the American constitution) and the strong emphasis on a unified culture and language that reflect the "national character." Most interestingly, the American model had to make relatively few concessions to nonliberal pressures (e.g., limited affirmative action that violates individual equality), and the highly principled Jacobin model had to make even more profound concessions.

Throughout the long history of France, sometimes hundreds of years before the revolution, emphasis has been put on the unity of the polity. Religious unity was reinforced by the expulsion of the Jews during the fourteenth century and later the exodus of the Protestants. Although the country expanded continuously by the annexation of diverse provinces, by the sixteenth century the French language was imposed as the official language on the entire land and enforced at the expense of local languages. Relatively early "the dominant ethnie was so widely dominant that it thought of itself in national terms" (Schnapper 2004, 105). After the revolution the trend toward centralization and homogenizing continued and intensified. The ideal of the French model was that people may maintain separate identities in private, and that they must conform to the French logic in the public sphere. The Republican state saw itself as neutral; ethnic identity was denied entirely as a relevant criterion in public life. Accordingly, immigrants could easily become French citizens, but the assumption was that they must quickly assimilate (a concept softened later into "integrate") into the French polity.

This ideal-type French model of complete national unity on the political level had to adapt to the reality of an increasingly differentiated French society. This adaptation was achieved in different ways, all strengthening the particularistic over the universalistic logic, and indirectly legitimizing the group over the individual approach (even though, in general, the French system remains less group-based than most democratic societies). First, the establishment of an extensive welfare state in France, as in all West European countries, has benefited individuals and even groups in different ways and on different levels. And although such programs could and have been justified in terms of guaranteeing national unity, they are not unrelated to ethnic (and other social) differences.

Second, over the last two decades ethnic associations have received financial aid from governmental agencies. Although on an ideological basis France does not accept the notion of multiculturalism, as this concept is used in such Anglo-Saxon countries as Canada and Australia, the state recognizes that it has to act "ethnically" by channeling public resources to distinct groups. When the National Assembly recognized the Armenian genocide in 1998, influenced by the 300,000 French citizens of Armenian descent, some saw it as a broader "symbolic ethnicization" of the French polity.

Third, a larger number of children in France study today "regional" languages in a country where the centrality and even the exclusivity of the French language has been a fundamental principle for generations. Radio and television programs in languages that have not been used publicly and heavily for a long time (e.g., Occitan, Breton, Alsatian, Corsican) are also growing in popularity. In 2001 Jack Lang, France's minister of education, admitted publicly that for more than two hundred years the government had repressed regional languages. More importantly, he announced that bilingual education would, for the first time, be recognized. The government continues to recognize today, to a limited extent, regional and minority languages.

It thus seems that Jacobinism, in the sense of a centralized national state completely controlling all aspects of life and eliminating any trace of group identity in its way, is declining in France, as well as in other societies. Assimilation is perceived as oppressive and even "colonial," and significant integration is extremely difficult to achieve. The centralized state has to compete against ancient regional identities, as well as against the identities of newcomers. Once in a while, the State feels that it has to "put its foot down" in the name of its sacred principles, such as the ethnic "neutrality" of the public sphere. The 2004 legislation prohibiting the wearing of religious symbols, including head scarves, in French schools has to be looked upon as reflecting this statist sentiment (Killian 2003; Harding 2004).

It remains to be seen whether the fundamentals of the French Republic and its Constitution – French as the language of the republic, the principle of strict secularism, cultural unity, and other such notions – can withstand the "ethnic assault." In general, it seems as if France might be moving gradually toward the acceptance of some kind of a *de facto* group-rights regime.

Group-Rights Regimes: Power-Sharing vs. Power Division

The thesis of this study is that in deeply divided societies the principles of liberal democracy, based on individual rights, while important and even crucial, are insufficient for creating a stable and just polity. These principles must be complemented by group rights, as long as these rights do not violate the "fundamentals" of the individual-based regime (i.e., equality of all citizens before the law).

The translation of this principled position to political reality is, however, quite complex. Different societies have different histories and traditions, a variety of pressures and needs to cope with, and uneven capabilities and tendencies. The argument could be made, therefore, that when it comes to group rights the *principle of diversification* has to be adopted. To put it in the colloquial, as far as group rights are concerned "one size does not fit all."

Several important distinctions are offered here in terms of group-rights regimes, so as to facilitate the analysis of interethnic relations within multiethnic polities. The first distinction is between centralized power-sharing regimes and decentralized power-division regimes, two fundamentally different methods for dealing with ethnic tensions within deeply divided societies. The second distinction is within power-sharing polities, and it is a distinction between consociational regimes (a model developed by Arend Lijphart and others) and binational or multinational regimes. Although in some situations binationalism or multinationalism might be perceived as a form of consociationalism, it will be argued in this chapter that from the perspective of analyzing interethnic relations within a multiethnic setting, it makes sense, at least potentially, to view those regime forms as qualitatively different from consociationalism: they represent a higher order of power sharing than most consociational modes. The third distinction, within the category of power-division systems, is between several governmental approaches, all reflecting the idea of dividing power as a means for establishing interethnic peace. In this chapter, three such approaches will be identified: *Autonomy* (where a further distinction between territorial antonomy and non-territorial autonomy is essential for analyzing interethnic relations); *federalism* (where a further distinction between symmetrical and asymmetrical variants is offered as an important and highly controversial issue in today's world of deeply divided societies); and *cantonization*, as a unique hybrid between territorial autonomy and federalism but nevertheless substantially and sufficiently different from both to warrant differentiation.

Because all of the regimes will be discussed and analyzed empirically in Chapters 4 and 5, with concrete examples given to each of them, only general comments about these regimes' *modus operandi* will be offered here, especially as governmental structures for resolving interethnic relations in deeply divided societies.

The distinction offered here between centralized power-sharing regimes and decentralized power-division regimes is theoretically very important. Yet it is essential to understand that power-sharing and power-division models could both serve as modes for establishing stable interethnic regimes, reflecting the interests of several ethnic or national groups living within the same political space.

Nevertheless, there are several important distinctions between the two group-rights regimes identified in this study. First, there is a fundamental difference between sharing power, which requires a measure of trust and ability to cooperate, and dividing power, which requires only that the parties to a political deal avoid each other. Ethnically mixed societies could and have adopted either of these paths or a combination of both. Power-sharing modes include, for example, the establishment of grand coalitions, where political leaders of various ethnic groups may decide, together, on all or the most important issues affecting the polity as a whole. Power division focuses on the clear distribution or allocation of power so as not to share it. Territorial autonomy, cantonization, and especially what could be called *robust ethnic federalism* where the federal units are ethnically defined and very strong, are examples of power division.

Second, there is a fundamental distinction between a centralized and a decentralized regime, a distinction that is intimately linked to power sharing and power division. Power sharing in deeply divided societies requires centralization of power. Authority in such regimes could be found at the polity's capital and it rests in the hands of the most powerful political leaders in the land, those who in deeply divided societies are also the leaders of the competing, rival ethnic groups. Thus in Belgium, especially prior to the further federalization of that country, power was centralized in Brussels in the hands of the Flemish and Walloon political leaders, and centralization characterized other power-sharing regimes as well. Power division usually means decentralization, no matter what specific governmental design is adopted. Thus territorial autonomy (see the following text) and ethnically based federalism are by definition decentralized. Although the units in cantonized polities are invariably small, the spirit of the regime is also thoroughly decentralized.

Third, while power-sharing arrangements often reflect a more or less even distribution of power between the ethnic groups, or at least a situation in which all groups participating in the power sharing have substantial resources, power division is often reflective of a condition in which one dominant "nation" grants limited power to considerably weaker "ethnicities." In most of the classical consociational polities, power was truly shared by different groups, albeit not necessarily ethnic ones (Belgium was an exception). In power-division situations, the inequality between the parties is much clearer and the traditional divides rather deep. Canada and Spain are good examples of that inequality resulting in power-division structures.

Among the centralized power-sharing regimes, it is important to distinguish between binational or multinational states and consociational systems. The level of power sharing between these two is quite different. The multinational state (of which the binational state is but a variant) is, at least in theory, a regime entirely shared by several different nations, a situation that J. S. Mill thought was nonconducive to democracy, but that Lord Acton saw as "a condition of civilized life" (Mill in Spencer and Wollman 2002, 7).

The truth of the matter is that, whatever theoretical arguments are made for or against a multinational state, there are very few genuine examples of such polities, a fact that is, in and of itself, an indication of some of the difficulties involved in establishing it. The Austro-Hungarian Empire after 1867 was, at least in theory, a multinational creature, but several nations within it did not share power and the state was clearly nondemocratic. Czechoslovakia in the interwar period was established as a binational state, and democratic at that, but the relationships between its constituent nations were somewhat strained. Several Communist regimes – notably the USSR, Yugoslavia, and Czechoslovakia – also constituted themselves as multinational states, defining their "republics" in ethnic terms. Yet Communist federalism was a sham and when it declined the multinational state fell with it. The fate of the Cypriot Republic was not better.

There is, then, an irony in regard to multinationalism in all its forms, including binationalism. While a multinational regime might form the perfect arena for power sharing among distinct ethnicities and on a basis of group rights, in reality it is unlikely to be successful as a regime form in the contemporary world. In the few countries where a binational formula may work, due to favorable balance of power, empirically it does not. Thus Belgium, a "consociational" state for Lijphart but in fact a binational polity with a promising balance of power between its constituent groups has become a rather robust federal state since the early 1990s. It crossed over from being a power-sharing polity to becoming a power-division polity.

Consociationalism has been researched in much more depth as a power-sharing method on the central government level (Coakley 1992, 347) than multinationalism, possibly due to the fact that in today's world it has been perceived as a more realistic form of government. As an analytical concept, consociationalism is primarily the product of the creative mind of the political comparativist Arend Lijphart (1968, 1984, 1997, among others). Lijphart assumes that deep social divisions – including ethnic ones – cannot be eliminated. Therefore, they ought to be "managed" (McGarry and O'Leary 1993, intro.) or, in the language of this volume, politically "engineered" so they could be controlled. To avoid uni-ethnic rule, even if democratic (i.e., a Westminsterian or majoritarian democracy), Lijphart describes, analyzes, and endorses a regime that he terms "consociational." In such a polity the government is a coalition of all of society's major groups, every group has veto power over issues of importance to it, proportional representation divides the national "pie" in a fair manner, and all groups enjoy autonomy. The agreement between the groups in society is the product of elite cooperation (Nordlinger 1972, 73).

Smooha and Hanf (1992) view Belgium, Canada, and Switzerland as "Western consociational democracies" and describe them as polities that "have coped with their internal divisions and conflicts through the polities of accommodation and reconciliation between the different ethnic groups" (33). Other cases mentioned by analysts include the Netherlands, Austria, India (Lijphart 1996), Malaysia (1955–69), Lebanon (1943–75), and, more recently, Northern Ireland under the Good Friday Agreement (O'Leary 2001b).

Some analysts believe that in certain polities where ethnic conflict is prevalent, there is "a simple choice between creating consociational democratic institutions or having no meaningful democracy at all" (McGarry and O'Leary 1993, 36). Moreover, consociationalism is better than most of its alternatives, including the hegemonic control on which this volume focuses. Consociationalism could potentially work in situations where no single ethnic group dominates all others (ibid.). In the absence of the balance of power, where one group is heavily favored, the rationale for a consociational compromise is simply nonexistent.

The empirical track record of consociationalism has been mixed at best, although in theory it might look more promising. The "assertion that elites can effectively regulate conflict in divided societies" has been challenged (Sisk 1996, 38). The experience of post–Meech Lake Canada, post–Good Friday Ireland, and the shift of Belgium into an increasingly federal structure, not to mention Lebanon, Cyprus, Malaysia, and India, suggests that consociationalism has its limits.

Although in the political world consociationalism might be challenged as unlikely to satisfy the nationalist claims of the majority group, from a normative perspective many liberal democrats, in particular, view consociationalism as "reinforcing and entrenching ethnicity in the political system" (ibid., 39) and establishing an undynamic model for conflict management (Barry 1975). This is true especially, argue some analysts, in the transition time of democratization (Snyder 2000).

In an era of unprecedented media attention to ethnic conflict, it is especially difficult to reach and then maintain a consociational deal. The grass roots push the leaders toward tough, noncompromising positions rather than toward quiet, behind-the-scene deals of power sharing. The future of Northern Ireland, for example, is decisively impacted by these types of factors.

All in all, the chances of creating effective centralized power-sharing arrangements in an ethnically conflictual polity (particularly one lacking a balance of power) are quite low, and the chances of maintaining it for a considerable period of time in a stable condition are even lower.

The poor track record of power sharing (in both its consociational and multinational forms) leads me to discuss, with a slightly more optimistic manner, several power-division ideas. The best-known conflict regulating power-division technique (although it is rarely presented as such) is federalism. From the perspective of this study, it is important to keep in mind two distinctions in regard to federal systems:

1. *Mononational vs. multinational federalism.* Mononational federalism is a federal system established within the political space of one nation, however diverse it might be ethnically or religiously. The numerous rationales for mononational federalism include the arguments that it creates a governmental structure that is closer to "the people," is more effective, is reflective of local interests, and might represent regional differences. Multinational federalism is a federal system erected in a society where there are several nations and where the established federal division has ethnoterritorial character (i.e., it takes into account historical and demographic considerations, attempting to establish territorial division that

closely reflects such considerations). The former USSR, Burma, and the former Czechoslovakia were multinational federations or polycommunal federal structures (Duchacek 1973, 166; 1987), while the American federal system has no ethnic base whatsoever. There are also mixed federations that combine both rationales (Canada, India, the former Yugoslavia).

2. *Symmetrical vs. asymmetrical federalism.* In a symmetrical system, all units within the federal structure have the same relations with the central government and the state. In an asymmetrical system the units might have different and unique linkages to the center, an issue of great importance for some minorities. Spain in the post-Franco era is a prime example for the emergence of at least a semifederal system in a polity that is clearly multinational and in a form that is clearly asymmetrical. Moreover, that system emerged side-by-side and in close interaction with the democratization of the Spanish state (Horowitz 1985, 623; Moreno 1997, 2001a, 2001b; Share 1986).

3. The interesting feature of federalism is that it could be structured in a variety of ways, so as to meet different goals. Thus, for example, federalism could have a consociational character and assume the face of genuine power sharing. Within the context of the present study, my interest is primarily in emphasizing the ways in which federalism could be used to establish territorial units that match the ethnic aspirations of certain groups (Walker and Stern 1993, quoted in Sisk 1995, 49) and thus enhance the likelihood of transforming a hegemonic situation to an accommodationist one.

In order for ethnoterritorial federalism to be maximally useful as a tool for resolving ethnic conflict, it must be based on the understanding that the federal agreement cannot be revised without the mutual consent of the center and the federal units (or at least the majority of them, deciding either directly or through their representatives). If such a unilateral action is banned by a written constitution, and the ethnic, territorial units receive substantial and independent powers, federalism can go a long way toward the resolution of conflict and toward the establishment of a genuine democracy in a multiethnic setting.

One of the major issues in designing a federation is how exactly to divide the power between the center and the units. The emergence of supranational bodies (such as the European Union) and the decline of the state as the sole power holder, may give support to federal solutions to ethnic problems, allowing the development of more creative power-sharing schemes in the future.

Like all methods of conflict management, ethnically based federalism is not free of problems. The most fundamental problem is that such federalism could easily lead to the evolvement of a separatist movement and, eventually, to secession. Once an ethnic unit is created within a polity, it could become (even if initially it is not intended to become) a focal point of diversity, conflict, and finally withdrawal from the union (a move that usually results in war). The post–Cold War history of the USSR, Czechoslovakia, and Yugoslavia are quite instructive in this regard.

Several analysts have suggested that India is a counterexample for successful federalism, combining heterogeneous states with linguistic boundaries, strong public support for accommodation, and, on occasion, the use of force against separatists. Analytically, however, while some see India as a majoritarian democracy (e.g., Brass 1999), others see it as consociational (Lijphart 1996). The increasing ethnic conflict in India points out the difficulties of any governmental design in dealing with social division.

In an era of nationalism, the political dynamics in any ethnically based federation may push the polity toward eventual dismemberment. This is especially the situation if the ethnic minorities feel underrepresented at the federal level, being economically exploited by the center (Basques and Catalans), and underappreciated as an important and distinct nation within the federation. McGarry and O'Leary found that biethnic federations are especially fragile (1993, 34).

One way of reducing minorities' frustrations in such federations is to offer them special conditions. Such special conditions are known now as "asymmetrical federalism" (Coakley 1993, 17; Tarlton 1965) and are often demanded by Quebecois (despite the clear indications that the rest of Canada is vehemently opposed), as well as the Basques and the Catalans in Spain (where special provisions have been agreed to, albeit not always to the full satisfaction of all concerned). Asymmetry "rests on the assumption that . . . peripheral ethnic dissent can be undermined by concession of some kind of special status to peripheral areas" (ibid.). Asymmetrical federalism is a highly contentious issue in several federal democracies today, including Canada and Spain. It is perceived by some analysts, although by no means by all analysts, as a direct challenge to the relations between group rights and individual rights.

Cantonization and autonomy are in certain ways similar to federalism but in other ways quite different. It could be useful, within the context of a study of resolving ethnic conflict, to devote some attention to these governmental forms. Although cantonization is strongly linked in most people's minds to one particular country (Switzerland), it should be thought of as a general model, a design with an increasing usefulness and important role in resolving ethnic conflicts.

The basis of power division in cantonization is invariably ethnic and territorial. In Switzerland, for example, there are twenty-one German-speaking cantons, seven French-speaking cantons, and one predominantly Italian-speaking canton. As a method of managing ethnic differences, cantonization is clearly a mode of decentralized power division where power is devolved to the smallest possible units. Moreover, the relationships between the cantons and the central government are asymmetrical and generally accepted as such.

From the perspective of ethnic relations, the idea behind cantonization is to create highly homogeneous units to minimize ethnic conflict and maximize coherence. If and when homogeneity is lost, it could be quickly restored, as happened in the case of the Swiss Canton Jura (see Chapter 4). Within the individual cantons, the principle is self-government on the most localized basis possible.

It is rather difficult to judge to what extent the Swiss model, "a super local option" (Sisk 1995, 50), can work in other places, especially because it evolved in Switzerland over a very long time and might reflect the special circumstances and unique character of that country. Yet McGarry and O'Leary speculate that in Bosnia cantonization "may have made a great deal of sense," despite the obvious difficulties. They also mention Canada as moving in the direction of cantonization (1993, 31–2).

The third regime under the rubric of power division is autonomy, a governmental design that shares several characteristics with federalism and cantonization but that has several unique characteristics. Autonomy is "a device to allow ethnic or other groups claiming a distinct identity to exercise direct control over affairs of special concern to them, while allowing the larger entity those powers which cover common interests" (Ghai 2000, 8). Sisk views autonomy as a type of consociationalism; I tend to see most autonomies primarily not as power-sharing arrangements but as power-division ones.

While *autonomy* might mean different things to different people, it could be yet another governmental structure for solving interethnic conflict. Moreover, there are also various types of autonomy (e.g., very importantly, territorial and nonterritorial), and some autonomies are substantially more robust than others in terms of the powers they grant to the autonomous group. When an ethnic group is geographically concentrated, it can demand territorial autonomy and control over all or most of its affairs. The state toward which the claim is made, however, is likely to resist this demand, fearing that in the long run it can lead to secession.

Weak and dispersed ethnic groups may be satisfied with mere non-territorial autonomy, sometimes referred to as personal autonomy (because it is granted to individuals and not to territories), or cultural autonomy (because it might cover areas such as language and religion but not politics). States might feel somewhat easier about granting such autonomy, because secession is less likely to become an option in the absence of ethnic concentration.

Although territorial autonomy has much in common with other types of "deals" between majority and minority (Lapidoth 1996), it is still differentiated from them. Autonomy is generally less powerful than a federal system in a multiethnic state, where the units are fully or even partially defined by ethnicity, and it is a great deal less localized than cantonization. The reason I do not see autonomy as consociational is that it is definitely not a centralized power-sharing regime.

Territorial autonomy and NTA can live side-by-side, as argued by Coakley (1994, 308), although in the contemporary world NTA is, generally, on the decline. Several indigenous peoples enjoy a measure of NTA: the Maori of New Zealand, Indians in Canada, and the Saami in Norway are examples of populations that do not threaten the dominance of the majority and, therefore, have been "able to secure institutional recognition of certain privileges" through NTA. There are a few other cases of nonterritorial devolution, which Coakley tends to see as consociational (1994, 309–10): Cyprus (1960–3), Lebanon (1973–5), and Belgium today are but some examples.

Types of System Transformation

The main interest of this study is in the transformation of hegemonic regimes (especially of the majority hegemonic type) to either individual-based or group-based accommodationism. The real interest is in the dynamic process through which such regimes might change. In terms of the dynamics of change, it is important to distinguish between the direction of the transformation (i.e., whether an already hegemonic system is moving toward further ethnicization or turns toward increasing democratization), its intensity (i.e., whether the change in the system is moderate or radical), and whether the transformation is internal or external (i.e., implemented within the existing polity or outside the polity). Accordingly, the analytical framework offers a classification of transformation based on the distinction between seven types of transformation, five of which are internal and two external.

The following are the seven types of potential transformation modes in multinational states:

1. *Status quo*. Despite the tension between its own ethnic nature and pressures to democratize from internal and external sources, the hegemonic state and its ruling elite may choose to maintain the hegemonic structure intact. Examples are many and diverse and include Malaysia and the People's Republic of China. Given that changes are invariably dangerous by generating unpredictable processes, maintaining the status quo is a rather attractive option, particularly when the hegemonic ethnic group is in control and the threat on its rule is not severe or immediate.

2. *Moderate democratization*. The ethnicized state and its ruling elite may decide to gradually end the most flagrant violations of the democratic credo inherent in its hegemonic regime, so as to ease the pressure for change, generate stability, enhance its legitimacy, and so forth. Israel and Turkey are two recent examples of countries that have somewhat improved their collective attitudes toward their minorities, and the United States in the 1960s is yet another historical example. The United Kingdom under "devolution" goes through a similar process today, although English domination there has not amounted to hegemony in recent generations. Canada has acted similarly in the past in dismantling discrimination against the French-speaking minority.

3. *Radical ("mega-constitutional") democratization*. In this situation, a fundamental change is implemented by transforming the hegemonic polity. Such transformation might be introduced by either a minority regime (such as postapartheid South Africa or Belgium in the early part of the

twentieth century) or by a majority regime (e.g., post-Franco Spain or the attempt to transform Northern Ireland over the last ten to twenty years and especially since 1998). Such radical democratization is, of course, a primary interest of this study.

4. *Moderate ("benign") ethnicization.* The direction in such a change is toward emphasizing further the ethnic character of the hegemonic state but doing so in a relatively moderate and restrained manner. The already hegemonic state strengthens its hegemonic nature but does so with relative moderation (e.g., India under the BJP, as well as postcommunism Russia).

5. *Radical ("malignant") ethnicization.* This situation is one in which a hegemonic ethnic state takes drastic action to purify itself from nonethnic elements within it through ethnic marginalization, expulsion of minorities (ethnic cleansing), genocides, and other such actions (e.g., Mečiar's Slovakia, Milosevic's Serbia, and Rwanda in 1994).

6. *Peaceful separation.* This solution to an ethnic conflict involves the agreed-upon division of the territory of an existing state into its ethnic components. This is a rather radical mode of transformation and therefore not very common. Nevertheless, since the early 1990s several multinational countries have seen that type of resolution to an ethnic conflict. Chapter 5 deals with one of the most interesting cases of peaceful separation of a multinational state, the case of Czechoslovakia.

7. *Forced partition.* An ethnic conflict within a multiethnic society could be "resolved" by a forced partition, a solution somewhat different than peaceful separation (e.g., in terms of the amount of violence involved). Chapter 5 deals with the case of the Republic of Cyprus, a case that involved not only a conflict between the ethnic groups on the island but also the landing of foreign forces on its shores and its eventual partition.

Chapters 4, 5, and 6 will cover in some detail and in an empirical fashion these types of transformations in multiethnic states. The cases will be detailed within the context of the theory presented in the opening chapters of this book.

4

Transforming Uni-national Hegemony in Divided Societies

The Gradual Option

> We can only hope to "manage", not to solve, conflicts arising from ethnocultural diversity. People who seek a "solution" to ethnocultural conflicts are either hopelessly idealistic or murderously genocidal.
>
> Will Kymlicka, 1998, 3

A Set of Empirical Questions: Comparing Transformative Experiences

In previous chapters, particularly in the last sections of Chapters 2 and 3, the theoretical foundations for dealing with the transformation of hegemonic states were laid down. These foundations will enable us to examine empirically this transformation in the next three chapters. The goal is to use the distinctions introduced in the previous chapters as a guide for examining a series of cases included in these chapters.

There are several major theoretical questions, observations, and distinctions that must be given special attention in examining specific historical and contemporary cases of transformation from hegemonic to pluralistic systems. First, there are two questions in regard to the factors producing the transformation of the system:

1. From an internal perspective, to what extent has systemic transformation occurred in the political system as a result of violence or as a result of nonviolent pressures? If significant violence or the threat of violence did not play a role in transforming a political system, what factors (e.g., public opinion, economic trends) have?
2. From an external perspective, to what extent has systemic transformation occurred due to outside pressures (e.g., international sanctions and threats, globalizing economic developments, the expectations of world public opinion)? Have pressures from the broader environment been crucial in producing a change?

Second, there are at least five important questions in regard to the essence of the systemic change and for its consequences:

1. Has the systemic transformation been partial or complete? Namely, has it been affected through moderate and gradual change or through a meta-constitutional and profound transformation, a transition from one type of regime to another, or a restructuring of the political system through a major historical constitutional act that transcends the existing legal order? In the case of metaconstitutional change the system can imagine itself as new and different than the old one. This chapter will deal with several cases of gradual transformation; the next chapter (Chapter 5) will analyze several metaconstitutional cases where a process of mental reconstruction occurs.

2. Has the transformation of a system affected control of and access to the public sphere so as to facilitate such control and access to groups previously unable to enjoy it? As for the new situation, one must ask what kind of access is enjoyed by minorities under the transformed regime – equal, proportional, or preferential. This is a critical issue because hegemonic regimes, by definition, severely restrict the access of minorities into the public sphere.

3. Has the systemic transformation created, produced, or promoted a common, overarching identity within the political system, and what is the shape or content of that identity? Do all groups and individuals share in this identity?

4. What has been the overall direction of the transformation? Most important, has the transformation led toward a higher degree of democratization, integration, and inclusion within the polity, or has it led to a higher degree of hegemonic control, ethnicization, and exclusion? The five-point scale offered will be applied to each case to identify both the direction and the intensity of the transformation. Specifically, it needs to be assessed whether the status quo has been maintained, or whether the system has adopted a moderate form of democratization, radical (metaconstitutional) form of democratization, mild (or benign) form of ethnicization, or radical (or malignant) form of ethnicization.

5. One needs to focus on the substance of the transformation. Has the systemic transformation taken the form of internal or external change and what specific form(s) has it taken? By *internal change* I mean systemic transformation through the adoption of new federal or semifederal institutions, the social and political recognition of the minority's distinctiveness, the establishment of a consociational regime, revisions in the direction of liberal pluralism, the granting of autonomy rights to minorities, and so forth. By *external change* I mean the partition of the national territory into separate national states (as in the case of several previously communist countries in the 1990s) or even consociationalism affected

through the involvement of outside powers (e.g., Northern Ireland), as well as conquest of parts of the national territory by an outside party (e.g., Cyprus).

These seven dimensions of systemic transformation could be applied to any hegemonic system. They could teach us valuable lessons regarding any transformative change.

Alternative Variants of Gradual Modes of Transformation

In contemplating a change in their character, a series of diverse options are available to hegemonic polities. Four cases of meaningful but relatively mild change (Spain, Canada, the United Kingdom, and Switzerland) will be analyzed in this section, demonstrating the variety of routes available for hegemonic polities (or subpolities, as in the case of Switzerland) that are determined to achieve better relationships between their dominant majorities and minorities that would not assimilate (or "melt") or that actively oppose the dominance of the majority.

Semifederalism: The Case of Post-Franco Spain

Since the eighteenth century, the Spanish state has followed traditionally the French model of a highly centralized political system (Requejo in Gagnon and Tully 2001b). Even though modern Spain has never achieved the ethnic homogeneity of its northern neighbor, that country's centralized, Jacobin tradition was adopted for the most part. Thus one author saw Spain's liberal constitution of 1812 as an "attempt to bypass historic regions" in favor of a unitary and centralized government, resulting in the control of the center over the periphery (Carrillo 1997, 40–1). Fifty administrative provinces were created as "a means of controlling the territory from the center" (Colomer 1998, 42), reflecting the influence of Napoleonic France.

In opposition to these long-held traditions, Spain's Second Republic (1931–9), an elected and democratic regime, believed in the decentralization of the state and in the explicit recognition of the various national groups within the Spanish society. The political process initiated by the republic to implement this vision, however, "was interpreted by the right as a precursor to the disintegration of the nation-state" (Coates 1998, 259).

During the long dictatorship of General Francisco Franco (1939–75), following the fall of the Second Republic, authoritarian centralization was reinstituted and doubly emphasized. The unity of Spain was at the center of the dictatorship's political and rhetorical program. But this program was not neutral or contentfree. The ideal of Franco's state was an authoritarian, ethnically Castilian, Catholic Spain. The regime saw its mission as the eradication of any trace of regional, ethnic, or national independence or even autonomy, focusing its energy on suppressing Spain's historic national groups, most specifically the Catalans and the Basques. Political, linguistic, and cultural oppression were widely and systematically adopted. Thus, the Institut d'Estudis Catalans (Institute for Catalan Studies) changed its name to Instituto de Estudios Mediterraneos (Institute for Mediterranean Studies).

The main goal of the Francoist regime was political: the fortification of a centralized, conservative, and authoritarian regime located in Madrid. The aims were frequently reflected in heavy ideological language and imagery. The centralized state of Franco was designed to protect what one analyst called "the old and unpolluted Castilian spirit" from the country's ethnoterritorial peculiarities (Moreno 1997, 67). Spokesmen for the regime argued that Spain was Castile and that only the Castilians had the ability to lead the country. In the language of this volume, the Francoist goal was to maintain a hegemonic Spanish-Castilian order in a country characterized by significant ethnic diversity.

Interestingly, in pursuit of its political goals, the Franco regime resorted to rather active invention of traditions (Hobsbawm 1990, 1–14; Ortiz 1999). The regime presented itself as representing "Eternal Spain," its people, and their supposed spiritual values. Areas that were particularly republican during the deposed Second Republic, such as Catalonia, were singled out for an extra dosage of the predominant dogma of National Catholicism. These regions that were subjugated in the past were now relegated, politically and ideologically, to a second-rate status.

One line of defense for the Franco regime and its lack of democracy, within the context of the almost universally democratizing Western Europe, was the idea of Spanish exceptionalism, the argument that Spain was different (Carr 2000, 1, 9). It is important to note that for instrumental and ideological reasons, most hegemonic regimes emphasize their uniqueness, especially when fighting off arguments that they are nondemocratic. Nevertheless, the belief in uniqueness is often sincerely and deeply held.

Juan Linz identifies two political transitions in post-Franco Spain: the first was the transition from authoritarianism to democracy, and the second was the transition from centralization to decentralization (Linz 1985). Within the context of this study it is important to note that both transitions were not content-free, neutral processes: both of them amounted to the transition of Spain from a hegemonic uninational regime (Castilian-Spanish) to a semifederal regime willing to recognize the diverse ethnic legacies of the country.

One of the most interesting questions in regard to the transformation of Spain (as well as political transformation in general) is the reason behind it. Although historically such transformation is often the result of a defeat in war (e.g., Germany and Japan after 1945) or at least a serious threat of defeat (e.g., Portugal in the 1970s), Linz and Stepan believe that post-Franco Spain did not change as a result of such external factors. Their view is that in the case of Spain we had what they call a *regime-initiated transition*: those who were in power following Franco's death knew that they could not stay in power without excessive repression, while those who were in opposition did not have sufficient power to overthrow the regime (1996a, 88). The result was what might be characterized, within the context of this study, as a *deliberate, megaconstitutional transformation* through compromise on all sides, where the polity changed due to internal, societal pressures. The strongest societal desire was to avoid at all cost the type of clashes that led to the Spanish civil war of 1936–9: this desire led the politicians to a negotiated agreement.

Although the primary transformative act – the adoption of the 1978 constitution – was embraced by the people of Spain, international factors were not insignificant in their influence on those involved in the process. Many individuals and groups, especially the business community, "felt an increasing need and desire to become integrated into European economic structures" (Bonime-Blanc 1987), a process that would not have been possible without democratization and pluralization.

The restructuring of the Spanish state came about through an agreement (Colomer 1991, 1995). It is a prime contemporary example for the power of political engineering on a grand scale, in other words, megaconstitutional transformation. The essence of this transformation was the replacement of the artificially imposed unitary structure by a pluralistic regime that accepted the diversity of the Spanish society and polity as a given. None of the parties negotiating the 1978 Spanish constitution was entirely satisfied with the result, however, the consensual document was perceived as a reasonable compromise and was supported by the overwhelming majority of the citizens of Spain and by their representatives. Not only did the four major parties of Spain support the constitution but so did 258 of the 274 members casting their vote in parliament and 87.8 percent of the voters in the referendum conducted on December 1, 1978 (Linz and Stepan 1996a, 100).

In reviewing the Spanish transformation, it is interesting to note (in response to the first question formulated in the preceding text) that it did not come as a result of violence, as, for example, was the case with the 1998 proposed transformation in Northern Ireland. Yet it could be argued that Spanish politicians knew after the death of Franco that unless they initiated some kind of serious reform in a democratic direction, the instability of the country would eventually lead to violence. After all, two years prior to Franco's death his prime minister and heir apparent were gunned down by Basque nationalists. It is reasonable to assume that the vast majority of the people wanted change and that Spain's politicians knew that change was necessary and inevitable, and possibly even an action needed to prevent a return to violence.

One should realize, however, that despite the commitment to change on the part of most Spaniards, and the magnitude of the transformative action taken, the constitution of 1978 and the reforms that followed it to date have not necessarily been the final end result of the reform process. A certain amount of flexibility was built into the new system, facilitating a continuous process of reexamination and change. The Spanish system could be regarded as a work in progress, a regime that is still evolving like other federal systems in the world.

By and large, the Spanish transformation represents a real change in terms of regime type. The old, highly authoritarian and considerably ethnicized polity was eliminated, and a new political system has emerged as a result of a deliberative constitutional process. The new system was not merely a fully democratic society but a political system recognizing its own diversity and willing to incorporate it into the design of its institutions.

Different individuals, groups, and social forces came into the reform process with different agendas, but, quite remarkably, they were able to resolve their differences through compromise and without significant violence. Thus, although many moderate reformers wanted a federal state, the conservatives (or unionists) demanded a unitary state with no regional autonomy or, at most, autonomous areas that are recognized by the sovereign Spanish people. Some of the nationalists (especially in Catalonia and the Basque Country) demanded self-determination.

The constitutional result of the struggle was, pointedly, "a mixed bag of unitarian and quasi-federalistic elements" (Bonime-Blanc 1987, 84). Thus the important Article 2 of the 1978 constitution emphasized "the indissoluble unity of the Spanish people" but hastened to recognize and guarantee "the right to autonomy of the nationalities and regions," while Article 6 spoke of "political pluralism." All in all, although Spain has not declared itself a full-fledged federal state, it has adopted numerous federal features (although not necessarily federal institutions) and thus made the continuous federalization of the system possible and likely. The net result has been that the regional and cultural distinctions that were eliminated forcibly by the Franco dictatorship reemerged in full force over the last quarter century but without tearing the country apart. Moreno calls the Estado de las Autonomias that emerged, and the following developments, "an example of 'devolutionary federalism'" (2001b, 25).

One can legitimately call contemporary Spain a quasi-federal or semifederal state, based on the explicit recognition of both the regional and the ethnic (or national) diversity of the country. Although many of the demands of the three historic nationalities were accommodated, they received limited autonomy, and the parameters of this autonomy are still determined exclusively by the center. Moreover, when autonomy was given to other regions, some among the historic nationalists felt that their claims were banalized (not unlike the reaction of the Quebecois to the universalization of rights within Canada). Therefore, some nationalists in Catalonia, and even more so among the Basques, have continued to criticize the constitutional arrangement of contemporary Spain as insufficient. Requejo, for example, has argued extensively not merely for the establishment of federalism in Spain but also for asymmetrical federalism. Such an arrangement would establish cultural equality in Spain (e.g., equal status to the languages), give minorities veto power over certain issues in a more powerful senate, and so forth. The chances of Spain adopting such a program are quite slim.

In transforming Francoist Spain into a democracy, decentralization became an essential tool. Yet as was the case on other issues, the decentralization formula reflected a political compromise. To maintain the unity of Spain, a main concern for the conservatives, the fifty nineteenth-century administrative provinces were maintained, reflecting the idea that the center controls the entire national territory. Responding to the demands for recognizing diversity, mechanisms for achieving autonomy were established for the three "historic nationalities" – Catalonia, the Basque Country, and Galicia – and for other regions (Colomer 1998).

From the perspective of this book it is essential to note that the hegemony (although not the influence) of the dominant ethnic group withered away in a process in which a real negotiating process has transpired. Both the process and its result indicate the dramatic shift from heavy-handed Francoist domination and coercion to a dynamic and open "exchange" process. The autonomy given to the historic nations, and later to fourteen additional regions, has continued to grow over the last two decades, although not always to the full satisfaction of all the autonomous people.

All in all, we witness in Spain a genuine transformation in the direction of democratization and inclusion. Although full-fledged federalization, with a powerful senate representing the constituent units, would have given diversity a stronger presence in the system, in the absence of such an institution, the minorities have developed alternative mechanisms for promoting their interests. Thus the regional parties, represented in the central parliament, have been able to expand the power of the regional governments. Although the largest Spanish parties were trying to halt the decentralization using the 1981 Organic Law for Harmonization of the Autonomous Process (LOAPA), in 1983 the Constitutional Court revoked the key provisions of the law, recognizing the capacity of the regional governments to make their own decisions in certain areas.

Colomer has argued that the collection of taxes has moved "increasingly in favor of the autonomies," the Statues of the Autonomy has been implemented, and the autonomies have received new powers in areas such as police and health services (1998, 48). Changes in the initial legislation have been invariably in favor of the autonomies and not in favor of the central government, and the distribution of funds is also moving their way. Thus Moreno and Tielles have reported that in terms of the distribution of public expenditure, the share of the central government declined between 1981 and 2002 from 87.3 to 48.7 percent, while the share of the regional governments increased from 3 to 35.5 percent (2005, 522).

The interesting dynamics of the Spanish case indicate that a formal change in the definition of the state, such as declaring the country as "federal" (which the Spanish constitution refuses to do), is not absolutely essential for the promotion of the interests of the minorities. A determined minority can achieve significant power within a nonfederal setting by acting politically on the central government level, as has been done, for example, by the Catalans since 1978. In 2006 the Zapatero government accepted the right of the Catalans to define themselves as a "nation." Although, institutionally speaking, a powerful senate would have helped the minorities, they have been able to promote their agenda even in its absence by means of bilateral negotiations with the central government.

In terms of access to the public sphere by all Spanish citizens, including those who see themselves as belonging to nations distinct from the Castilians of central Spain, there is no denial that the situation today is significantly more inclusive than in Franco's time. The essence of Spanish politics is often now the struggle between center and periphery, and ethnoterritorial autonomous areas have a loud voice in that struggle, probably proportional to their size in the overall population. Although the minorities surely do not have an equal voice in a polity that is not consociational and do not enjoy preferential weight, their representation in deliberation on significant political issues is assured.

An example of the access of Spain's minorities to the public sphere is the sensitive and important area of language. Since the defeat of the Catalans in the eighteenth century, Castilian has become the dominant language in the region, particularly in the public sphere. Only the short-lived Second Republic recognized the equality of Castilian (Spanish) and Catalan, but the Francoist regime reversed course dramatically. As part of the overall repression of Catalonia, which included an end of Catalan autonomy, the use of the native language was prohibited in the public sphere.

The 1978 constitution adopted, as on other matters, a compromise position between those who spoke in terms of the unity of Spain and those who emphasized its diversity. While Spanish (i.e., Castilian) was maintained as the sole official language of the country as a whole, it was agreed that regional languages might be recognized as equal to Spanish in their region. All Spaniards today must know Spanish; however, Catalan is now a co-official tongue in Catalonia, side-by-side with Castilian.

This theoretical linguistic equality is, however, not yet complete. For example, Catalan could be used in dealings with the local Catalan authorities, and Castilian is used in the dealings with agencies of the central government. Although there is unilingualism on the statewide level, there is multilingualism on the regional level. From the perspective of the minorities the language situation is not as favorable as it is in Canada or in Israel, but it is a remarkable improvement if compared to the Francoist situation (Greenwood 1985).

As for the evolvement of a common identity among the citizens of Spain in the wake of the dramatic constitutional changes of the last quarter century, several general points could be made. First, a common Spanish identity seems to have emerged. Second, there are still significant differences between people, and the differences are correlated to their individual ethnicity. Relating to both generalizations, Linz and Stepan have found that "in the new democratic Spain, complementary multiple identities persist," and that "Catalans, to a greater extent than ever before, accept their identity as members of the Spanish state," while, at the same time, "the overwhelming percentage of Catalans are proud to be Catalan" (1996a, 102–3). The situation among the Basques is significantly worse in terms of identification with the Spanish state.

In effect, contemporary Spain has witnessed the emergence of "dual identity or compound nationality" (Moreno 2001b, 5) in which more than two-thirds of the citizens feel loyalty to the state but also to their regional autonomy.

All in all, people who live in the historic nationalities' regions express lower levels of belonging to Spain and being attached to it than do people from other regions (Bollen and Medrano 1998, 612), but "there is a degree of duality which tempers the viability of secessionist options" (Moreno 2001b, 5).

Despite the uneven development of an all-Spanish identity, a phenomenon to be expected in such a diverse land, there is no question that the country has moved decisively toward democracy, inclusion, and recognition of diversity. In terms of the classification developed in Chapter 3, post-Franco Spain represents the radical, metaconstitutional pole. It is a country that transformed its regime in a multidimensional manner, not merely in terms of moving from authoritarianism to democracy, but also in moving from uninational, hegemonic centralism to multinational, cooperative decentralization. While the debate on the exact form of that decentralization continues, it is remarkable that other than Euskadi ta Askatasuna (ETA) terrorists, Spanish citizens of all stripes and national background have accepted the process of restructuring the regime through peaceful and democratic means.

As explained previously, the democratization process has been influenced by a combination of internal and external factors. The death of Franco found the vast majority of Spaniards determined to move forward through badly needed reform. There was general recognition that Spain would never be accepted in Europe and the West unless it democratized, liberalized, and recognized its own historically based diversity. The political class responded to these internal and external sentiments creatively and produced a document – the 1978 Constitution – that, while not perfect, genuinely tries to reconcile the deep differences within the Spanish polity and, importantly, is flexible enough to allow further changes in the future. The emergence of Spain as a member of the European Union has helped in furthering the democratization process that started in the mid-1970s, and the same is true about globalization processes in general.

The lessons of the Spanish case are many and far-reaching, although one has to remember that each historical and political case is, in the final analysis, somewhat unique and that "borrowing" from one milieu to another is always dangerous. Nevertheless, several lessons ought to be formulated:

1. Although the past is an important guide for what might be politically possible, it is never a fool-proof determinant of all political options. In the Spanish case, there was an all-system determination to avoid the bloody past and to move away from a system – Franco's regime – that, while apparently stable was fundamentally unsustainable in the long run. Thus the tragic past fulfilled a useful role in Spain's democratization.

2. The Spanish example has some possible implications for the possibilities of political engineering on a large scale, even on a metaconstitutional scale. In the mid-1970s Spaniards, Europeans, and the world at large hoped and expected the democratization that was soon to follow; however, the process could have evolved in numerous ways.

3. The Spanish example demonstrates the crucial role of practical and moderate (i.e., compromise oriented) leadership in "producing" an acceptable political solution to highly complex dilemmas. It also demonstrates the importance of popular support to elites' initiatives.

4. The Spanish case demonstrates the importance of maintaining flexibility even after a constitutional compromise has been hammered out. Since 1978 several components of the Spanish constitution have been changed. It is important not to close off options that could enhance the effectiveness and stability of the system.

Recognizing Distinctiveness: The Canadian Case

The case of Canada is significantly less dramatic than the case of Spain in terms of the "size" of the change introduced in the political system, although the direction of the change – enhancing the quality of democracy and minority inclusion – is generally similar. With Francoist authoritarianism as its legacy, Spain started in the mid-1970s in a rather low place on the democracy scale. Democratization alone was a significant achievement for the Spanish polity; democratization based on explicit ethnic recognition, built into the very basis of the system, was huge leap forward, a project of true historic proportions.

As for Canada, the country had a long democratic tradition, and, therefore, the challenge to its government, in terms of developing more inclusive policies, was significantly less profound than in the case of Spain. Nevertheless, like Spain, Canada is a good example of the power of constitutional processes to transform the character of an existing polity. It is also a unique case of using full-fledged federalism to deal with a relatively large minority that is regionally concentrated and has a significantly distinct historical and cultural identity.

Historically, Canada has been the product of one colonialist settler society, the British, defeating another colonialist settler society, the French, and giving birth to a polity made in its own image or, at least, significantly influenced by it. In other words, in the case of Canada we deal with a country that has been a pluralistic "mosaic" (Kivisto 2002, 85) from the beginning but also a case of hegemony, albeit significantly moderated by the country's democratic traditions. Moreover, in contrast with the United States or Australia, the English hegemony in Canada was always somewhat limited by the "French factor." It was unable to marginalize, let alone completely eliminate its historical rival and had to devise complex mechanisms that enable it to live with that rival while still maintaining dominance. For example, while the Anglican Church had an official status as the established Church in Canada as a British colony, the Catholic Church was granted official status in Quebec in 1774 (Laczko 1994, 31).

The overall pattern of political relationships between the two national groups has been that of British primacy, accompanied by the accommodation of French-Canadian interests. Thus the Quebec Act of 1774 and the Constitutional Act of 1791 recognized the distinct way of life of the French minority, protecting formally not merely the status of Catholicism but maintaining New France's *code civil* as a basis for the civil law in Quebec. Kivisto (2002, 87) sums the British-French relations as "a non-assimilative and asymmetric policy of inclusion of the French into Canadian society – one that officially recognized difference and at the same time the hegemonic status of British Canada." This relatively liberal policy enabled the British to gain the allegiance of many leaders of the French population (Brooks 1996; Kivisto 2002, 87). Yet the French legislature of Lower Canada (Quebec), where most French speakers resided, was subordinated to an English executive (Schmid 2001, 102). In terms of the historical process, side-by-side with British hegemony there has been a development in Canada toward increasing inclusiveness and pluralism on a basis of equality, although not necessarily reaching the level of recognition desired by the French-speaking or other minorities.

Following the British victory over the French in 1759, Canada witnessed the emergence of a predominant British rule. Although the special status of the French language was recognized, "francophones were excluded from Canada's economic elite" (ibid., 104). There were even some attempts to assimilate the French speakers in Lower Canada by reuniting this region with Upper Canada or even eliminating the French schools (McRoberts 1997). These hegemonic policies led to the Rebellion of 1837, a French protest against the dominant British economic class. Some believe that the rebellion resulted in the intensification of British oppression; thus, Lower Canada and Upper Canada joined in the Act of Union of 1840. English became the sole official language and an effort to assimilate the French was launched, albeit unsuccessfully (Craig 1963). The two "national" communities became increasingly exclusive (Karmis and Gagnon in Gagnon and Tully, ed. 2001a).

Once Canada became independent in 1867, the English majority, and particularly its political and economic elite, quickly established control over most aspects of public life. To reinforce the connection to Britain, the national flag adopted was that of a modified Union Jack. Previous consociational arrangements, dividing political power between the English and the French, declined in importance, although the Canadian constitution continued to protect both English and French cultures (Page 2000, 35). Cannon views 1867 as marking the "ascendancy of the English elite segment" in Canada and the period that followed (1867–1960) as resembling Lustick's control model (Lustick 1979; Cannon 1982, 55). A bifurcated system was established and the British North America Act of 1867 officially recognized the bilingual character of Canada. The duality of the situation is noted by Carol Schmid when she states that "while there was some recognition of the French fact, at the national level the lingua franca of the state was clearly English" (Schmid 2001, 104).

At the same time and despite English domination, the 1867 British North America Act created a federation to deal with and reflect the reality of two distinct national groups. It is important to note, however, that while the French enjoyed a high degree of autonomy (especially in areas such as religion, culture, and education), the English maintained complete control over the central Canadian government. Policy-making positions within the central government, for example, were allocated by the dominant British elite. Thus the Canadian "experiment" (Burgess 2001, 258) reflected from the very beginning the inherent contradictions and tensions that are part of the Canadian reality even today.

There are several examples of how the post-1867 period reflects the English dominance, especially in comparison to the pre-1867 period that was semi-consociational (Cannon 1982). The English-French copremier structure of pre-1867 was replaced by a single prime minister after 1867, and the cabinet changed from a bicultural institution to a majoritarian (i.e., English-controlled) body. The Quebecois were relegated to giving symbolic support to the regime but were clearly not coequal political players. The English hegemony was reflected in numerous areas: resource allocation, economic domination, immigration, and so forth. Thus English migrants to Canada "were not always called or considered immigrants," and they gained immediate voting rights. British immigrants were permitted or even expected to "remain British" (Laczko 1994, 29–30). Don Page, a defender of the Canadian experiment, states resolutely that until the 1950s, Canadians of British origin – the majority – viewed their culture as a mere "extension" of the culture of the "mother country," thus turning Canadian patriotism into "simply a quiet loyalty to the monarch" (Page 2000, 44).

The large number of non-British immigrants that arrived in Canada, particularly from Eastern Europe, "was expected to conform to the dominant Anglo-Saxon culture as quickly and as thoroughly as possible" (Sheridan 1987, 2). In this sense, to become a "Canadian" meant, traditionally, to become "English," emphasizing the hegemonic position of "Englishness." Prior to the 1960s, observes Kymlicka (1998, 44), immigrants to Canada were expected to "shed their distinctive heritage and assimilate to existing norms," that is, go along with "Anglo conformity." Only in the 1970s was the well-established assimilationist model rejected in favor of policies encouraging immigrants to "maintain various aspects of their ethnic heritage" (ibid.). A real transformation occurred in the field of immigration and in the area of language.

In broad historical terms, it seems that developments after World War II have begun to transform the "essence" of Canada, a transformation that might not be completed as of yet. The decline of Britain as a world power meant the significant weakening of Canadian links to the United Kingdom. The economic and political dependence on the United States increased. Changes in immigration patterns increased the non-British element in the Canadian population.

Maybe the most critical factor in producing the transformation of the Canadian polity was not external, the loosening of the link to the "mother country," but internal. The single most important internal change, notable especially in the 1960s, was the rise of Quebecois secular nationalism and its dual intent of achieving liberation from the control of both the English business community and that of the Catholic Church. The Quiet Revolution that followed – Quebec's economic development and secularization – facilitated the emergence of a more open and inclusive Canadian polity.

The rise of Quebecois nationalism in the 1960s forced the Canadian government to rethink its policies in regard to the relations between the two dominant ethnic groups. Royal Commission on Bilingualism and Biculturalism (B and B) was established (1963). A new Canadian symbolic order emerged; a more neutral flag (featuring a red maple leaf), a new national anthem, and new stamps and coins were adopted. In no other area has the change been as dramatic as in that of the status of the French language, reflected in the adoption of the Official Language Act (1969). This was a serious attempt to equalize the status of English and French at the federal level. Until 1969 immigrants had to learn English, and only English, before they could obtain Canadian citizenship. The important 1969 language legislation was designed to convince the Quebecois that Canada was also their country. It gave federal institutions "a resolutely bilingual face" (Burgess 2001, 259), recognizing the legitimacy of the French language in Canada's public sphere.

It is interesting to note that in regard to language, the Canadian polity today is extraordinarily inclusive. It incorporates the *personality principle* (accepted also in South Africa and to some extent in Finland): language rights are given to individuals and may be exercised wherever these individuals may reside within the country. Significantly more limited is the *territorial principle* (e.g., accepted in Belgium and in Switzerland), where language rights are tied to a particular part of the country.

The personality principle allows French speakers who reside out of the province of Quebec to educate their children in French schools, and it allows English speakers who reside in the province of Quebec to educate their children in English schools. Nevertheless, many French speakers have viewed the law as favoring the English language because of the strength of the English-speaking majority in Canada and the overwhelmingly dominant position of the English language in North America.

In response to these concerns, the parliament of Quebec passed Bill 101 (1977), which declared French as the exclusive official language in Quebec and required that children, with few exceptions, were required to attend French-language schools in Quebec. The English minority in Quebec and others viewed Bill 101 as discriminatory and in violation of the federal law. The opponents of the bill succeeded in rolling back some of its provisions by appealing to the Supreme Court of Canada.

It is important to note in the context of dealing with systemic transformation from hegemony that in the 1960s Canada began to shift toward a more open, inclusive society, accepting the French language as equal, at least theoretically, to English. The polity has become fully bilingual in a way that Spain, for example, has not.

Moreover, in 1971 a far-reaching (although controversial) policy of multiculturalism was adopted. This policy became part of Canada's permanent political landscape with the adoption of the 1988 Multiculturalism Act. Although numerous Canadians continue to criticize multiculturalism as divisive (e.g., Bissoondath 1994; Gwyn 1995), reflecting the thinking of some American writers (e.g., Schlesinger 1992), it is possible that in the absence of multiculturalism the Canadian polity could have experienced greater instability. Some of the most serious reservations about multiculturalism came from the French Canadians;

their understanding of the special status of Canada's founding nations – the English and the French – is, to them, incompatible with multiculturalism. The main force behind multiculturalism was Prime Minister Trudeau; he rejected the B and B Commission's conception of biculturalism in favor of multiculturalism, reducing Canada's dualism to language alone.

In general, several analysts have interpreted the traditional Canadian model as consociational (McRae 1974; Noel 1971b; Presthus 1973; Smiley 1979). Yet Arend Lijphart, the high priest of consociationalism, views Canada as semi-consociational (1977, 119–28). The Canadian case is altogether difficult to classify because side-by-side with Westminsterian elements (i.e., straightforward majority rule), there are consociational and, a great deal more important, federal elements.

Cannon (1982) tends to see historical Canada, the one in existence during the years 1867–1960, as reflecting a control model (Lustick 1979), and his argument is quite convincing. I would add to that the argument that over the last forty years or so Canada has changed significantly in the direction of opening its system and becoming less hegemonic than it chose to be in the past.

The control system, in place (with variations) during the years 1867–1960, declined by the 1960s, due to a large extent to Quebec's economic development and the assumption of power in the French-speaking province by the Quebec Liberal Party, the modernizing elite of the Quebecois. While the roots of the change could be found in the 1940s and 1950s, with the development of an ideology of modernization, it came to fruition with the "Quiet Revolution" of 1960–6 and the rise of the French middle class. This period saw the decline of the Catholic Church and the ascendancy of the secular intelligentsia in Quebec.

Cannon maintains (1992, 59–60) that at this period "the control relationship between the English and the French became strained, and by the early 1970s had collapsed entirely." As a result, a semiconsociational model has emerged. It could be argued that this semiconsociationalism has characterized the Canadian system ever since, facilitating the transformation of the polity from a largely hegemonic to a largely inclusive system.

The emergence of a semiconsociational system did not mean that the Quebecois became entirely equal in a country with a clear English majority or that their claims were fulfilled in full. English Canada has resisted many of the demands and the Quebecois suffered from fundamental internal disagreement.

Looking at the Canadian case in a broad historical perspective, it seems that Canada had a variety of possible options to follow and that in many ways it has adopted a model mixing several of these options, reflecting the country's tradition of tolerance and compromise:

1. *English hegemony.* Throughout much of its history, Canada has lived under the hegemony of the English settlers, their offspring, and the culture that they brought with them and maintained. This model has characterized Canadian history especially between 1867 and the early 1960s, but it has generally disappeared today or at least declined significantly.

2. *Biculturalism or the two-nations model.* There has always been recognition by English Canada of the uniqueness and special status of French Canada, especially within the borders of Quebec Province. While this recognition never rose to the level of establishing a full-fledged binational state with equal status to the English and the French, Canada has shown openness, albeit belatedly, in accepting the French language as an official tongue in all Canadian institutions. Although some Quebecers continue to demand an even stronger form of recognition that is offered them today (Kymlicka 1995; Taylor 1994), in relative terms their status as a minority has been rather strong. Many Quebecers continue to be deeply attached to their provincial government (Laczko 1994, 27).

3. *Liberalism.* Since the 1960s the Canadian polity has liberalized in the sense of giving all Canadian citizens, as individuals, equal rights and protections under the law. One of Prime Minister Pierre Elliot Trudeau's most important "projects" was the 1982 Canadian Charter of Rights and Freedoms, reflecting this approach. This liberal initiative was perceived by some Quebec nationalists as undermining their own national project, precisely because it negated the group-rights approach that they had endorsed.

4. *Multiculturalism.* Beginning in the early 1970s, Canada adopted (also under the leadership of Trudeau) an official policy of multiculturalism, recognizing, in addition to its two historic nations (the English and the French) and its native population, additional minorities. Canada was the first country in the world to adopt multiculturalism (in spite of the opposition of both liberal purists and French-speaking nationalists).

Once Canada deserted English hegemony, the path toward enhanced inclusiveness through other policies – liberalism, bi- and multiculturalism – was open. Although not all Canadians perceived the process as being that of increased equality, it was. It should be noted that the country adopted a nondiscriminatory policy on the immigration of non-Europeans only in 1967. The desertion of Anglo-conformity meant "an expanded conceptions of Canadian society" (Abu-Laban and Stasiulis 1992, 365–6).

The multiculturalism of the last three decades has generated strong opposition from a variety of quarters within the Canadian society. First, multiculturalism was perceived by some as a negation of the two-nation concept, according to which Canada was a union of two founding nations, English and French. Many Quebecois have refused to see their status reduced to that of just another ethnic or "cultural" group in Canada (Kymlicka 1995). The argument has been made that, in general, multiculturalism injures collectivities that view themselves as nations, and this argument has to be given some credibility in the case of Canada. Moreover, there might be a qualitative difference between a "nation" living in its own ancestral land and an immigrant group moving into a country where another national culture has been formed already. While the former is likely to see multiculturalism as an active negation of its "nationhood," the latter is likely to cherish the opportunities that multiculturalism might offer it in terms of maintaining its separate identity.

Within the Canadian context, many French Canadians have viewed multiculturalism as "an opportunity for English Canada to ... reaffirm its superior tolerance at Quebec's expense" (Mackey 1999, 14), that is, to demonstrate openness while, in reality, strengthening the dominance of the majority's culture. A similar reaction has been registered on behalf of Catalans, for example, when the Spanish government recognized the right of autonomy of seventeen different areas in Spain. This type of approach – recognizing the rights of all groups – tends to hurt the groups that view themselves as deserving of special recognition while strengthening the position of the dominant group.

A second opposing attitude toward Canadian multiculturalism comes not from Quebec nationalists but from those who opt for a sense of Canadian national unity. Such opponents of multiculturalism view it as dangerously dividing the Canadian society into rivaling ethnic components and, thus, threatening the existence of "one Canada." They would like to see a Canada that has a unified, overarching concept of itself. Although this desire for a unifying national concept is natural, members of minorities are likely to look at it as designed to assimilate them and homogenize the society at their expense. One official Canadian report on multiculturalism, the Spicer Report, argued that diversity could be achieved only when individuals have commonalities. Most supporters of multiculturalism view this formula as rejecting the ideal of pluralism and recognition. Above all, in terms of the concepts used in the current study, a call for any type of all-Canadian unifying concept is likely to be perceived by members of minorities as a return to a British-rooted, old Canada, "unspoiled" by the impact on non-British immigrants.

A third argument against multiculturalism is that the granting of group rights might damage the polity's liberal traditions. Multiculturalism has been perceived as not merely politically divisive but also as resulting in the differentiated, discriminatory treatment of individuals. The latter critique of multiculturalism is particularly common among American writers when they deal with ethnic problems (e.g., Schlesinger 1992; Snyder 2000). They tend to see any group rights as divisive and, therefore, dangerous for the integration of a free society on the basis of individual civil rights.

Will Kymlicka has noted (1998, especially Chapter 3) that most of the Canadian multicultural policies "are clearly integrationist in their aim" (43) and that "none promotes either ethnonationalism or marginalization" on behalf of the various ethnic groups (52). He disagrees with the argument that multiculturalism promotes disunity or that it endangers individual rights.

A final opposition to multiculturalism comes from those who have argued that it is a policy that "implicitly constructs the idea of a core English Canadian culture" (Mackey 1999, 2), thus discriminating against non-English cultures. Within this prism, non-English cultures become "multicultural" and are marginalized in comparison to the dominant Anglo-Canadian core culture (Moodley 1983). Although this critique is not invalid, it must be viewed in relation to what Canadian culture was originally (i.e., totally dominated by the English tradition) and what it would be without multiculturalism. It should be pointed out that the Canadian polity and culture is significantly less hegemonic today than at any time in the past. Even Mackey, a critic of Canadian policies, admits that in Canada today "power and dominance function through more liberal, inclusionary, pluralistic, multiple and fragmented formulations and practices concerning culture and difference" (5). In other words, although multiculturalism does not create full equality, it could help in making the system more open and egalitarian.

It is interesting to note, within the context of this book, that the American approach to ethnic diversity has differed from the Canadian approach. The Canadian polity has recognized from the very beginning its fundamental diversity, even in the height of "Anglo-conformity." As Canadian history progressed, there has been increasing willingness to recognize this diversity, first in terms of biculturalism and then in the form of multiculturalism. The American approach to diversity has been remarkably different. It has been marked by a commitment to uniculturalism, reflected by an insistence on a single official language (English), as well as by a determined effort to inculcate in all Americans an overarching attitude to a unified national, patriotic culture. This American approach emphasized such symbols as the American flag, the Fourth of July celebrations (as well as Flag Day), patriotic parades, the pledge of allegiance, and so forth. Although the Americans adopted an "English-only" policy, the symbols were surely non-British. At the same time, the American approach, also in contrast to the Canadian attitude, has been to privatize ethnicity.

Over the last forty years or so, with the decline of English domination of any type in Canada, the competition for redesigning the polity has been between those who would like to see Canada as a liberal society (represented above all by the late Pierre Elliot Trudeau), those who would like to see the strengthening of a binational English-French Canada, and multiculturalists, who see themselves as representing ethnic groups left out by the traditional formulas (English hegemony or English-French power sharing). While multiculturalism and Quebecois nationalism might be perceived as being in direct competition with each other, many English-Canadians view multiculturalism with suspicion equal to that of the Quebecers.

It is easy to view ethnic multiculturalism in Canada as the opponent of English-French biculturalism (or binationalism); however, it can also be looked upon as a continuation of it. Both bi- and multiculturalism amount to the transformation of Canada to a more open, inclusive society, and they are ideologically connected. The 1969 law regarding languages was a major move toward the equalization of French and English cultures. The multicultural move, which came two years later, further expanded the policy of recognition on behalf of the Canadian government. Either of these policies could have gone even further; they both undermined the old model of unilateral English dominance. In combination, the acts of 1969 and 1971 meant that the previous policy of assimilating those susceptible to assimilation (i.e., new immigrants) to English

Canada was no more the policy of Canada's central government. It was surely a legislative program for moving away from hegemony and toward cultural openness.

Thus, I would argue, although Canada of 1950 was still essentially an Anglo-polity in numerous ways, contemporary Canada had become a multicultural, multiracial, poly-ethnic state, where the English and French languages are privileged, but where all minorities receive at least some recognition. Efforts to grant Quebec special recognition as a "distinct society" have failed due to opposition by Anglo Canada and are unlikely to succeed any time soon. Ironically, the hostility toward that recognition might fuel demands for Quebec independence (McRoberts 1997). At the same time, the collective identity of the French speakers is recognized not merely through their majority status within the province of Quebec but also through the equal status of French and English in Canada as a whole. This policy reaffirms the Canadian tradition of recognizing group rights (Paltiel 1987).

In terms of the questions introduced in the opening sections of this chapter, it is clear that some violence, and a threat of even more violence on the part of militant Quebec separatists, as well as peaceful but forceful political demands, forced the Canadian federal government to introduce changes. At one stage of the process Prime Minister Trudeau had to invoke the War Measures Act to quell the militant insurgency (Kivisto 2002, 93).

Nevertheless, the changes eventually introduced by the government were relatively modest, although not insignificant: symbolic changes were accompanied by a new linguistic order, and a multicultural policy was adopted. At the same time, English has remained the dominant language, and the basic federal structure has remained intact. Now there is probably more of an overarching identity in Canada than in 1950, and despite the critique of Quebec nationalists the system is more inclusionary. Without a doubt, the change was produced by an internal mechanism not by international pressures.

Devolution: The Case of the United Kingdom

The policy of devolution in the United Kingdom over the last few years has been a rather interesting process of responding to an increasing attention to multinational reality (although not always explicit reality) in one of Europe's oldest unitary states. Some commentators have seen the devolution program as "a profound process of transformation taking place in the British state" (Bogdanor 1999b, 287–98) amounting eventually to a form of federalism; even those emphasizing the great impact of devolution often noted its limits. Thus Vernon Bogdanor, one of the more prolific writers on devolution in the United Kingdom, reminds us that the newly established Scottish parliament is still "a constitutionally subordinate parliament" (1999a, 185), that is, it does not have sovereign powers. Others also have seen the process as less meaningful, emphasizing the continuing supremacy of the parliament in Westminster (Bradbury and Mitchell 2002, 299). It remains to be seen whether devolution in the United Kingdom will evolve into full-fledged federalism. The emphasis in this section will be on the potentialities of devolution as a method of alleviating ethnic conflict.

In traditional British thinking, the unitary British state has reflected the belief that the non-English sections of the country – Scotland, Wales, and Northern Ireland – constitute but parts of a single British nation. Devolution represents somewhat of a departure from this thinking. The devolutionary framework emphasizes that Britain is a multinational entity that accommodates several different nations. If so, the United Kingdom has to go through a regime change, leading to the emergence of a new governmental design that reflects that reality. This change cannot possibly be anything but controversial. While the Conservatives have traditionally opposed the transformation of the unitary state, both Labor and the Liberals have endorsed it.

The long history of the British Isles suggests to the prodevolution advocates that the United Kingdom is a union among nations rather than a single nation. This is particularly the case in relation to Scotland (Keating in Gagnon and Tully 2001, 48–9), where the union among the English and Scottish crowns occurred in 1603 and the union between the two parliaments not until 1707. Although the English have always been the dominant group, analysts have noted that "in the United Kingdom no Jacobin project of national socialization" has occurred (ibid., 50). Thus a national educational curriculum was never established in the United Kingdom, separating it clearly from France and other continental entities.

Although the Scots and the English share a common language, important differences between them have been maintained in terms of the legal system, the education system, and religious institutions. Most importantly, separate identities have survived through the ages (Miller in Gagnon and Tully 2001, 307–12). It is possible to argue that the devolution program initiated in 1997 is an explicit recognition by the dominant group, the English, of the separateness of the Scots, as well as other groups.

The devolutionary scheme negates the unitary idea, an idea that dominated European political thought for a long time. Yet it can be implemented and possibly create a more stable political system, especially if the special conditions of the different units and their relations to the center are taken into account. In the case of the United Kingdom it is important to note that different groups have received different levels of recognition, resulting in asymmetrical political arrangements (similar to post-Franco Spain).

In 1999 the Scots elected the first Scottish parliament in almost three hundred years. The old-new body can legislate on all issues but foreign and defense policy, immigration, fiscal and monetary policies, and social security. The revived parliament has primary legislative powers and the authority to impose an income tax. The tendency of the Scots has been to focus on policy areas that made Scotland different than England over the millennia and follow the British lead on other issues.

Although Scots have benefited from their link to England, their nationalism also reflects resentment toward English hegemony, as well as other factors.

For example, in the 1970s Scotland declined economically in comparison to England. The Conservative governments of Thatcher and Major were viewed as unfriendly toward the Scots. The British political tradition, to which the Tories subscribed, emphasized "Westminster's sovereignty as absolute and indivisible" (Simeon and Conway 2001, 357).

Elections were also conducted in Wales, although the powers given to the Welsh parliament were substantially more limited in comparison to the ones given to the Scottish parliament. Thus the Welsh assembly received only secondary legislative powers, and it still must submit proposals to Westminster for primary legislation. Many in Wales have come to believe that the assembly was not given sufficient powers. It is possible, maybe even likely, that this frustration would eventually lead to the granting of more powers to the Welsh assembly in the future.

Northern Ireland is somewhat more complex. A power-sharing assembly was established in 1998 as part of the Good Friday agreement. The ongoing conflict between Republicans and Unionists impacts, however, the devolutionary process.

The idea of devolution in England remains open but underdeveloped and inherently problematical. Some have called it "the hole in the center of devolution" (Pilkington 2002, 184). The reluctance to proceed with that devolution project in England indicates a lack of political will and possible fear of dividing England (Hazell 2000). There is fear that if an English parliament is established it could become "a real rival to Westminster" (Bogdanor 1999b, 293). The huge demographic advantage of the English over all others – there are about fifty million English in a country of about sixty million – makes devolution in a newly constituted English parliament unlikely.

Interestingly, although devolution could eventually lead to the independence of the smaller nations, particularly Scotland, it could also result in the strengthening of the union by reducing the tensions between the constituent nations or regions of the United Kingdom. Bradbury and Mitchell (2002, 314) believe that "before devolution, territorial politics in the UK was strongly characterized by varying degrees of political instability," that "a culture of oppositionalism developed as a result of being out of power and perceiving that this was likely to remain the natural order of things," and that "in Scotland, Wales and Northern Ireland, sizeable sections of the population questioned the legitimacy of the constitutional order pre-devolution." Although there are still debates on the constitutional future of the various groups, "a remarkable degree of legitimacy is now attached to the existing arrangements" (ibid.). Also Bogdanor (1999a, 193) notes that devolution could lead to the weakening of the demand for independence rather than encourage separatism as some have feared.

The future of devolution as an instrument for political stability might be determined by the way in which different national groups in Britain identify themselves. In the past, Scottishness, Welshness, and Irishness were "formed in opposition to Englishness" (Bogdanor 1999b, 292). For the English, the terms

British and *English* have been used interchangeably; however, they were clearly distinguished by the other inhabitants of the British Isles. It is not entirely clear what would be the future relationships between the various components of the British population under a devolutionary regime. There are several options: (1) *complete integration*: this is unlikely to happen in view of the strong identities of the various nations; (2) *full-fledged federalism*: this solution is also unlikely in a country that has seen itself traditionally as unitary, led by national institutions such as the Westminster parliament. Moreover, a federation among England, Scotland, Wales, and Northern Ireland would be entirely unbalanced in view of the huge demographic advantage of England; (3) *devolution*: this could be looked upon as an intermediate solution between integration and federalism, the continuation of the unitary tradition and complete independence.

Bogdanor believes (1999a, 187) that, at least insofar as the balance between England and Scotland is concerned, "the relationships between Westminster and Edinburgh will be quasi-federal in normal times and unitary only in crisis times." By *quasi-federalism* he means, for example, the division of legislative powers between the two parliaments. He thus equates devolution with quasi-federalism. He sees Westminster as having theoretical primacy; in reality, it will allow full domestic legislative power to Edinburgh.

One interesting point introduced by Bogdanor (1999a, 189) is that devolution will inject the spirit of federalism into the deliberation of Westminster, a spirit that has been traditionally absent in the British parliament. Another interesting result of the devolutionary process has been that, despite some observers' expectations, the devolved assemblies in Scotland and Wales did not become "mere microcosms of Westminster" (Pilkington 2002, 181). The parties in these two regions "have learned to work together" in a significantly less adversarial manner than at Westminster, and the executives have often developed independent positions in regard to matters relating to their regions (ibid., 182).

Bogdanor, in an authoritative and comprehensive analysis of devolution in the United Kingdom, suggests that "the United Kingdom is becoming a union of nations, each with its own identity and institutions" (1999b; 2001, 287). He distinguishes between the constitutional and the political meaning of devolution. Constitutionally, devolution is merely the transfer of power from the traditionally superior body – the Westminster Parliament – to the newly established but clearly inferior Scottish Parliament and Welsh Assembly. Politically, however, devolution places a powerful weapon in the hands of the Scots and the Welsh.

The assumption of devolution is that there is a separate, independent political will, especially in Scotland. If Scotland is a nation, it follows that it has the right to self-determination and, eventually, secession from the United Kingdom. Bogdanor believes that eventually the relationships between the United Kingdom (Westminster) and Scotland would become quasi-federal where the Scottish Parliament will be "the supreme authority over Scottish domestic affairs" (ibid., 290). Power would be transferred from London to Edinburgh, although more as a fact of political life than in constitutional theory.

The real change would be enormous. For hundreds of years Westminster was able to determine Scotland's domestic affairs not merely in theory but in reality. Under the new, devolutionary circumstances, Westminster would be theoretically superior but in reality it would be marginal in determining Scottish internal matters. But the change, according to Bogdanor (1999b; 2001, 293), would be a great deal deeper and far-reaching than merely rearranging English-Scottish relations. It would create "a new constitution for Britain as a whole."

The key question from the perspective of this study is whether the English hegemony within the British setting will be better balanced and more justly mitigated within the newly emerging quasi-federal structure. Devolution in the United Kingdom may lead to full-fledged federalism in which the different regions enjoy greater powers in relation to the center. Moreover, devolution may even lead to the inconceivable – separatism and eventual secession. At the same time, devolution could result in increasing solidarity among the distinct "components" of the United Kingdom.

In several European countries devolution has led to the significant weakening of the pressures to break up. In Catalonia, for example, the increase in the power of the province has led to a decrease in the demands for independence. Devolution can fuel the desire for independence or, alternatively, lead to mutually satisfying power sharing. Separatism is not inevitable.

The quasi-federal model that is evolving in the United Kingdom, just like the one emerging in Spain, could prove an effective antidote to the traditional hegemonialism in both polities and to the hegemonic model in general. The traditional hegemonic model, practiced in the United Kingdom and in Spain (as well as in France and other European countries) for hundreds of years, was based on the assumption that stability and political well-being meant the concentration of all power, responsibility, and authority in one hand, that of the "national" government. This model might work in a situation where there is one national identity within the territorial confines of the state; however, it is doubtful that it can work when there are several national groups within this territory. This is particularly the case when several of the "subservient" nations are concentrated in a particular and well-defined but peripheral region. Such a condition is as sure a recipe for the evolvement or sustaining of nationalist sentiments as any.

Under these conditions, the dominant group – like the English in the United Kingdom – is probably wise in devising an inclusionary strategy as an antidote for separatism. Devolution might be an effective medicine to the resentment that many Scots and Welsh harbor toward the English.

From the perspective of the questions introduced in the opening section of this chapter, it is clear that the changes introduced in the United Kingdom came about, quite typically, not as a result of violence or even a threat thereof but from a recognition that something had to be done in response to the increase in identity politics, particularly among the Scots. The rise to power of the Labor Party facilitated this internal change. In terms of the substance of the transformation, it is a relatively small change that could strengthen the polity.

Cantonization: The Case of Switzerland and the Jura

The cantonal, federal system of Switzerland has several quite unique features that evolved over many centuries. In some ways Switzerland has remained "a pre-modern political entity, often referred to as a 'special case Switzerland' (Sonderfall Schweiz)" (Erk 2003, 56). It has never emerged as a unitary nation-state based on homogenous unity of the type established in Europe during the nineteenth century.

Nevertheless, and particularly because of this uniqueness, the Swiss case is worthy of examination. Some features of the Swiss model, which is the quintessential antithesis of the Jacobinistic model, could potentially be transferred to (or at least examined and learned from by) other polities confronting ethnic conflicts. The recognition of diversity built into the Swiss governmental scheme is impressive. Not only is the small country divided into twenty-three cantons, but also three of these are further split into "half-cantons" (thus forming, in effect, twenty-six cantons), and "there are more than 3,000 communes which enjoy a wide range of powers" (ibid.). The Swiss state grew from below rather than being imposed on from above, a fact that might explain its decentralized, diversity-recognizing essence until today.

Although the uniqueness of this medieval, pre-French Revolution structure (Steinberg 1996, 88) cannot be denied, several analysts believe that the Swiss model can be exported to other multicultural countries (e.g., Basta and Fleiner 1996; Beaufays 1995). My own position is that the model as a whole might not be exportable, however, some elements of it hold promise for easing conflict in certain parts of the world. An examination of the Swiss political system as a model for conflict resolution in deeply divided societies is in order.

The democratic Swiss system devolved for a very long time and eventually crystallized during the nineteenth century as "a compromise between traditional federalism and the centralized form of government" that some people desired. Within the new system, sovereignty was divided between the central government and the cantons (Jenkins 1986, 86). The overall design of the nineteenth-century constitution remains intact today despite some revisions throughout the years.

The most interesting phenomenon to note in the context of the present study is that despite its overall stability, the Swiss system has proven capable of changing in response to newly emerging challenges. It can be argued that a particular combination of factors that does not exist anywhere else in the world resulted in the unique Swiss form of government (ibid., 162); however, other countries facing ethnic conflict and separatist movements might want to evaluate the way in which the Swiss have dealt with deep sociopolitical divides and, in particular, the way in which they have responded to new challenges.

In general, the Swiss tradition, evolving for over seven hundred years, is based on respect for the diversity of local communities, allowing the linguistic mosaic of the country to flourish, and accepting the religious differences that exist in addition to the cultural, linguistic divides. Nevertheless, despite its image to the contrary, Switzerland did experience some serious ethnic conflicts over the last two centuries or so. World War I created interethnic tensions due to the cultural-linguistic affinities between certain ethnic groups in Switzerland and some of the countries engaged in the war (Kohn 1956, 127). After the war, irredentist Italian propaganda (1920–40) generated some tensions in the Italian-speaking Swiss canton of Ticino. Nevertheless, on the whole, some scholars believe that ethnic conflicts "have been minor and far less divisive than issues of religion, economy and class" (Bohn 1980, 176).

Not only has Switzerland in general experienced internal challenges of an ethnic nature, but specific challenges emerged in certain cantons. Possibly the most severe challenge of all arose as a result of the incorporation of the Jura into the Bernese canton following the defeat of Napoleon Bonaparte. The 1815 Act of Union between the bishopric of Basle and the canton of Bern brought into Bernese control not only the town of Biel, which was German speaking, Protestant, and located in the Mittleland (sharing all these characteristics with Bern), but also a peripheral mountainous region in northwestern Switzerland that became known as the "Berenese Jura." The region was quite different than the rest of the Canton Berne. It was Catholic and "had no historic link with Berne whatsoever" (Jenkins 1986, 92). No wonder that a few separatist movements emerged in the region between the early nineteenth century and the middle of the twentieth century, generating considerable tensions within the Canton Berne and the country as a whole. The demand of these ethnically based movements differed. Some of them supported the formation of a new canton (a demand that was eventually accepted), others endorsed regional autonomy for the Jura within the Canton Berne, and some demanded union with France.

The causes for the separatist movements were several. During the nineteenth century the primary cause for conflict was religion, namely the Catholic-Protestant divide (although, meaningfully, the Swiss confederation managed to stay out of the previously fought Thirty Year War between Protestants and Catholics despite its divided population). In the twentieth century language became more important than religion. When some cantonal officials in Bern showed inclination to Germanize the Bernese Jura and when the pre–World War I pan-German propaganda became dominant, the French-speaking population responded with increasing demands for separation from the canton. Jenkins believes (98) that the threat of Germanization united the French-speaking population, Catholic and Protestant alike. Moreover, World War I, and later World War II, further strengthened the mutual suspicion between Switzerland's two major linguistic groups, and this tension was reflected in the uneasy relations within Canton Berne.

Despite the inherent problem in attaching the Jura to Bern, in disregard to differences between them in terms of language, culture, religion, and history, it is important to note that until the 1940s the separatist movements of the North Jurassians tended to be short-lived phenomena. But the so-called Moeckli affair of 1947 gave birth to a more profound separatist movement that eventually led to the establishment of a new canton. In September 1947 the members of the legislature of the Bernese canton rejected the nomination of Georges Moeckli, a French-speaking Jurassian as the canton's director of public works and railways on the ground that "the office was too important to be filled by a francophone member of the Council." This decision generated significant anger among the French-speaking public in the Jura, leading to a movement that called for the establishment of an independent Jurassian canton. Despite some concessions by the cantonal government in response to these emerging demands, the separatist idea caught fire. To the amazement of many in and out of Switzerland, some Jurassians even resorted to violent attacks on railways, army installations, and other targets.

After two decades of considerable agitation, by late 1968 the cantonal government in Bern decided to allow the electorate of the Bernese Jura to determine its political future. This began the process that led eventually to the establishment of the new canton, a truly remarkable result achieved with a relatively limited amount of violence.

In some ways, however, the response of the Bernese government to the Jurassian challenge can be viewed as "typically Swiss," reflecting a long-standing tradition and a deeply ingrained political culture. The overall approach to governmental structure in the deeply divided Swiss society has been that of combining a high degree of local autonomy on practically all issues with a relatively weak, loose federal system. In this regard, the Swiss model has been as non-Jacobinistic and decentralized as possible. There has never been an assumption in Switzerland that all citizens must share the same culture by forcing them, for example, to speak the same language.

The eventual establishment of the Canton Jura (on January 1, 1979), merely a decade after the cantonal government began the constitutional process facilitating that meaningful change, serves as an example of the impressive capability of the Swiss system to respond to ethnic pressures and settle conflicts in a peaceful and democratic manner. The Jura case is interesting particularly because it was a situation where, atypically, integration of a cultural minority (i.e., French-speaking Catholics) failed. Nevertheless, it is a case in which the political system found a constitutional solution to the serious problems this failure produced.

Part of the failure of integrating the North Jura was due to the fact that the differences between it and the rest of the Canton Berne were overlapping to a large extent. Thus the North Jura was Catholic and French speaking, while the rest of the canton was mostly Protestant and German speaking (with a minority of French-speaking Protestants). In addition, the North Jura was significantly less developed economically than the rest of the canton, and many of its inhabitants felt discriminated not only politically but also economically (Linder 1994, 65). More specifically, the South Jura benefited much more from the watch industry than the North Jura; moreover, the northern region suffered from unfertile mountain soil (Bohn 1980, 177).

In that context it is interesting to note that when the referendum on the separation of the Jura was held, the three southern Jura districts – French speaking but Protestant since the sixteenth century – decided to remain as part of the Canton Berne; these areas were also economically more prosperous than the north. In other words, when differences between the majority (German speakers) and the minority (French speakers) were not overlapping (i.e., when French speakers were Protestant and better off than their French-speaking Catholic "brethren") they chose to stay within the German-speaking, Protestant Canton Berne.

It is important to note, in historical terms, that the Jura "problem" came to a head only after World War II. Its emergence as a primarily political issue may reflect the new European political environment. For the first time in a long time Switzerland's security was not threatened by the overall unstable European situation, and this might have given the Swiss an opportunity to deal with some of their internal problems, primarily the Jura. The local elite of the North Jura had a long-standing, hostile attitude toward the relatively centralist Bernese government, and it could be argued that the new post–World War II milieu enabled them to act upon their long-term agenda.

Despite the propaganda campaign of the Jurassian separatists, and what was perceived by some as their eventual "major victory," in pure ethnic terms they did not fully succeed in achieving their goals because not only did the southern Jurassian districts choose to remain part of Canton Berne, but so did the German-speaking but Catholic district of Laufen (Jenkins 1986, 149). Some Jurassians defined themselves as "separatists" and demanded independence from Bern; others were "loyalists" and interested in maintaining the status quo. The final result confirmed this difference, with the separatists achieving only partial victory.

The establishment of the new canton followed agreed-upon democratic procedures approved specifically for dealing with the Jura problem. What is truly impressive is that the system was capable of inventing and adopting complicated procedures, approving them through the highly democratic means of referenda (a governmental method often used in Switzerland), and then going through a lengthy process that produced a result endorsed by the vast majority of the people involved. The people of the Jura region, Canton Berne, and the citizens of the entire Swiss federation (as well as the separate cantons) were all given a say in the matter and actively participated in the resolution of a problem that could easily have been prolonged and then escalated.

First, the Bernese people accepted the proposed set of procedures for deciding the future of the Jura (1970). The 6:1 majority legitimized the process, including the possible outcome of Jura separation. Several years later (1974–5) the inhabitants of all Jura districts voted by a small majority (37,000 to 34,000) for independence. It was clear, however, that while the majority in North Jura was for separation (by a 3:1 margin), the majority of South Jura citizens wanted to stay within Canton Berne (if by only a 2:1 ratio). A constitution drafted by a constituent assembly dealing with the future of the Canton Jura was then adopted, and the Swiss people approved the new arrangement in a countrywide referendum in 1978.

Few political systems have shown the capacity of doing what the Swiss system has done – implementing peacefully an ethnically based separation, a process that more often than not has led to bloodshed. The impact of this orderly and democratic procedure could be seen when a similar process was used fifteen years later (in 1993). One district, the German-speaking but Catholic Laufenthal, joined Canton Baselland. Thus a "new" tradition was born in Switzerland, although a tradition reflecting the old political culture of the country.

In the final nationwide referendum regarding the Jura, the people of Switzerland as a whole voted in favor of the new canton's creation. Only 41.5 percent of the eligible voters took part in the referendum; however, 82.3 percent of those voters supported the move, separating the new political unit from Berne Canton of which it was a reluctant limb since 1815. This decisive majority legitimated the move, although future challenges to the outcome (particularly the rejection of separation by three districts) are not entirely out of the question.

Although the resolution of the Jura problem could be celebrated as a victory for diversity and the ability to recognize it through democratic means, the resolution was not easy or automatic. It followed a struggle that lasted for more than forty years. The Jurassian minority that felt discriminated for generations resorted to riots and violence, behaviors that were considered by many in the prosperous and democratic country as "un-Swiss" (Jenkins 1986, 151).

What is particularly remarkable about the solution is not only that Jura is the first truly new canton to be established since 1815, but also that this constitutional step added a sixth French-speaking canton to a federation where a clear majority, about 75 percent of the people, are German speakers. In other words, this development strengthened the hand of the French minority in a country where both economics and demography favor the German-speaking majority and where, therefore, the majority could have been expected to resist the pressure of the minority.

It is possible, and even likely, that had the Swiss system as a whole, and Canton Berne in particular, refused to take a bold initiative on the establishment of the new canton, the ethnic tension in the canton and in the country at large would have escalated. There are numerous significant religious and linguistic divides within Switzerland that could have been deepened as a result of a long-term confrontation with the Jurassian separatists. During the nineteenth century the country has witnessed severe conflicts such as the 1847 civil war (the Sonderbundskrieg) in which twelve Protestant cantons defeated seven Catholic cantons. This intense if brief war left a mark: it alienated the Catholic, North Jurassian population from the inhabitants of South Jura (French speakers but Protestants) as well as the rest of Canton Berne (Bohn 1980, 177). This war led to the constitution of 1848 that laid down the basis for the unique Swiss governmental design of today (although several important changes have occurred since 1848).

In solving the Jura problem, the Swiss recognized that they had a unique problem in the important Canton Berne. With the exception of the Canton Graubuenden, Berne was "the only Swiss canton within whose boundaries conflicting loyalties of language and religion exist" (Jenkins 1986, 14). That is, the language of the majority of the inhabitants of the former Bernese Jura was French, while the majority of the inhabitants of the Canton Berne as a whole spoke German. Moreover, there was a religious divide between the mostly Catholic population of North Jura and the Protestantism that is followed by the vast majority of the Canton Berne. Under such circumstances, the German-speaking, Protestant majority could have insisted on keeping the North Jura within Canton Berne. The fact that 69.6 percent of the voters in Canton Berne cast a vote in favor of establishing Canton Jura is a testimony to the political maturity of the country and its population.

The resolution of the Jura question in Switzerland, as well as the efforts to resolve similar questions in Canada, Spain, and the United Kingdom, ought to be considered from a constructivist perspective: it could and should be examined by "paying due attention to the way cultural differences are assumed by the protagonists" (Voutat 1996; 2000). Thus during the interwar period, Jurassian intellectuals were primarily interested in preserving the historical awareness on the Suisse Romande (French-speaking Swiss) identity in the French-speaking Jura as against the dominance of the Swiss Germans. After World War II, this emphasis evolved into a more specific and more limited "Jurassian" identity.

Similarly, it has been persuasively argued that contemporary Switzerland "has come to reflect the underlying ethno-linguistic divide between the French Swiss and German Swiss despite the formal federal system based on 26 cantons" (Erk 2003, 50). Assuming that this is a correct depiction of a long-term process, it still remains to be proven that this is a negative development from the perspective of either stability or democracy. The new Swiss constitution, which came into force in 2000, allows cantons to form associations among themselves and even form common institutions (Article 34–1); the old constitution banned such initiatives. This could and probably would mean that the divide between the two main linguistic groups in Switzerland will deepen and that the linguistic cleavage will be exacerbated, strengthening the sense that "essentially Switzerland is divided into two large public spaces, that of French-Switzerland and German-Switzerland" (ibid., 61).

Yet as long as the decision on links between the cantons is left in these cantons, and as long as the cantonal form of government allows maximal political participation in the decision-making process to every citizen, these new developments ought not to be looked upon negatively. Although they allow identity politics to come into focus, this is part of a worldwide process. Moreover, the Swiss system has proven time and again that it never takes action, particularly on important issues, without carefully and democratically examining it, so there is no reason to believe that this reality of stronger identity politics would result in an increasing control of the majority over the minorities.

The enormous diversity of Switzerland and the deepening divide between the two main linguistic-cultural groups (ibid.) means that the potential for future conflict remains high. At the same time, there seems to be a consensus in the country that "minority interests should not be pursued with violence but rather by peaceful political means." Moreover, a shared commitment to the same political values has emerged in Switzerland, "combining in a unique way the principles of shared rule and self rule, that is: the autonomy of canton and municipalities" (Fleiner 2002).

The establishment of the new Canton Jura has demonstrated the capacity of the Swiss political system not only to respond to an ethnically based challenge, an issue that has existed within the Swiss body politic for over a century and that has escalated significantly after World War II, but also to respond appropriately, effectively, and democratically to that challenge. Not only was the right of self-determination granted to the people of the Jura but also a new and constitutionally complicated procedure was adopted so that every district, and in some cases even individual municipalities, could determine – by a majority vote – the future of their governmental institutions. The final borderline between the old canton (Berne) and the new one was determined through this process, and it reflected a successful method in introducing change. The peaceful secession of the Jura, accepted by most if not all people directly impacted by it, was proof of the success of the process as a whole. Above all, it was an agreed-upon process, not a unilateral, forced, or hegemonic one.

The Jura separation case, as Swiss politics in general, demonstrates the possibilities open to a multiethnic polity to overcome the tendency to establish a tyranny of the majority the way it is done in hegemonic states, even those presumed to be fully democratic. Moreover, the case demonstrates the ability to further enhance genuine democracy where democracy already exists. In this sense, Switzerland joins Canada, Spain, and the United Kingdom as an example of the impact of relatively small changes on the enhancement of the quality of democracy in countries that could have conceivably evolved in a different direction. In all four countries there is a clear-cut majority of one ethnic, cultural, and linguistic group, and in some of them (e.g., Spain or Canada) there is a history of uneasy relationships between the majority and minorities.

All four cases dealt with in this chapter are, ultimately, not as much about whether you have democracy or not but about the quality of the democratic regime you have. In the post–Cold War era, which is when election became a commonly used measure to judge whether a country is democratic or not, we need a more sensitive and accurate instrument to assess the quality of a democracy. One of the situations where democracy is seriously lacking, but where it might look as if it prevails, is that in which you have a combination of three conditions: (1) a deeply divided society (usually on an ethnic basis); (2) a highly centralized state where all power is held at the political center (Jacobinism); (3) an electoral system based on the "one person, one vote" principle that is not balanced by any consociational arrangements (power sharing at the center), federal or semifederal structures that take ethnicity into account, autonomy arrangements, and the like. In such a centralized state the minority is perpetually losing, and it lives permanently at the mercy of the majority, even though it looks as if democracy might be fulfilled through periodic, open, general elections. The four cases analyzed here are about the efforts to overcome this democratic illusion or, alternatively, to improve on a problematical democratic situation.

Interestingly enough, neither the Anglo-Saxon democratic model (often known as Westminster democracy) nor the European-Continental territorial democracy emerging after the French Revolution (and often known as Jacobinism) has a convincing answer to the conditions of the permanent minority in such a centralized, "winner takes all" state. Although both types of system might enact special legislation to protect minorities (as individuals or as groups) against outright discrimination, and they might even promote a policy of multiculturalism "celebrating" these minorities' uniqueness and cultural values, neither is likely to grant minorities qua minorities real political power because to do so would be to negate their very essence.

The Swiss model, and to a lesser extent the other three cases dealt with in this chapter, could be looked upon as an alternative democratic design to the Westminster and the Jacobin models, those that the current volume views as "hegemonic" or at least potentially hegemonic, particularly in ethnically divided societies. The Swiss model, in essence, challenges the often-hidden assumption of the Westminster and Jacobin models that democracy is about producing majorities through general, equal elections, so that these majorities can govern effectively or even reflect the overall political will of the "people." The Achilles heel of these models is that they focus entirely and, I would argue, in an unbalanced manner on a single democratic value, that of "majority rule," while ignoring other values.

In contrast with both Westminster and the Jacobins, the Swiss model emphasizes community in its narrower definition – not the national community but a local one. The Swiss tradition has been based for over seven hundred years on the idea that the small community has not only a right to exist but also the prerogative to govern itself as it sees fit, exercise extensive self-determination, maintain its own characteristics (e.g., in terms of language and religion), and so forth. Put differently, Swiss democracy is community based, rather than based on the presumed equality of all individuals and their right to form a majority (as the Westminster model does) or on the amorphous notion of the state as representing the people as a whole (as Jacobinism assumes).

Although the Swiss model might not have emerged in the first place on the basis of a careful analysis of the advantages of communal democracy versus its Westminsterian or Jacobinistic alternatives, its principles could be judged rather attractive in the contemporary world. In a growingly uniformist, globalizing, economically controlled world, a world in which identity is still important for people, the Swiss model is important; it might be essential for an ethnic minority.

Summary

The four rather different cases of gradual transformation presented here – the quasi-federalizing but ethnically based Spanish case, the multicultural Canadian policy combined with the equalization of the French language and the limited recognition of Quebec's uniqueness, the post-1997 devolution policy of Great Britain, and the Swiss readiness to create yet another canton (Jura) to satisfy ethnoterritorial demands – suggest that political systems can cope with ethnic conflict in a peaceful way through enlightened, creative, and far-sighted public policy. Moreover, in all four cases there has been close cooperation between some elements within the central government, heavily influenced by the dominant ethnic group, and some elements within the minority ethnic group seeking recognition. Most important, all processes discussed in this chapter were introduced using democratic means.

By and large, in these four and other cases (e.g., the case of the German minority in the Italian region of Alto Adige) the willingness of the central government to recognize the rights of the minority led to a significant decline in the motivation of the ethnoterritorial minority to engage in violent action; even the intensity of the minority's political struggle declined significantly in response to inclusionary policies. An analysis of these four cases demonstrates that although there is no one method or single technique for settling ethnically based conflict, there is a series of tools available to the contemporary and largely democratic polity to respond creatively to ethnonational pressures. Although the accommodationist route is never easy, people of goodwill and political ingenuity can find solutions for issues that are, by their very nature, complicated.

On the whole, the gradual approach analyzed in this chapter is preferable to the more radical approach dwelt on in the next chapter, although in some situations there is no way but to adopt a radical, metaconstitutional approach to solve deep ethnic conflicts.

The four cases represented in this chapter are taken from the developed and democratic world where gradual changes – steps that require by their very nature compromise – are easier to implement than large, metaconstitutional revolutions. In these four cases and others (e.g., Belgium's emergent federalism or Greenland's demands of autonomy toward Denmark), ethnoterritorial claims led to some type of negotiation and at least partial accommodation between the larger, sovereign polity and the smaller political unit(s) within it. Moreover, comparative research has shown that accommodation efforts "frequently reduced the saliency of ethnoterritorial politics" (Rudolph and Thompson 1985, 304).

It is clear that in many countries, especially developed and democratic ones, certain citizens see themselves as having a dual identity, and that they can live with this duality with no resort to violence. A person can be Flemish and Belgian, a Scot and a Brit, a Quebecois and a Canadian, a Catalan and a Spaniard. Although the duality of identity may lead to conflict and even bloodshed, the four cases analyzed in this chapter indicate that such duality does not have to inevitably lead to that result.

Political institutions and leaders may enhance the possibility of compromise by not pushing the issue of loyalty toward conflict and in seeking accommodation between conflicting groups and interests. In numerous instances, accommodation efforts "appear to have softened the saliency of ethnoterritorial politics" (ibid., 305). As demonstrated in this chapter, this could be done through the establishment of regional autonomy, the recognition of personal autonomy, the enhancement of devolution, cantonization and even subcantonization, federalization or semifederalization formulae, and enhanced recognition of the minority's identity.

5

Transforming Uni-national Hegemony

Megaconstitutional Engineering

> Even in the most severely divided society, ties of blood do not lead ineluctably to rivers of blood.
>
> Donald L. Horowitz 1985, 684

Daring to Dream: Redesigning the Political Order

In the previous chapter several modes and specific cases of gradual, mild, and incremental transformation of hegemonic systems were discussed. The cases were judged to be "mild" insofar as the transformation did not result in complete overhaul of the system, let alone its total dismemberment, but resulted in the emergence of new patterns of governmental behaviors or new political institutions. Thus post-Franco Spain saw a transformation from a centralized and ethnicized polity to a decentralized and semifederal one, explicitly recognizing the diverse ethnic character of the Spanish state but without demolishing its essential fabric. Similarly, in the case of Canada over the last four decades there has been an increasing willingness to recognize the unique character of Canada's French-speaking minority yet maintain the polity's fundamental structure. In the case of the United Kingdom, devolution was adopted as a method for Recognizing the traditional ethnic or national mosaic of the British Isles, attempting to change the system, albeit marginally, to head off possible deterioration of relations between the prominent group, the English, and the Scots, Welch, and Irish. Finally, the case of Switzerland in general, and that of the establishment of the Canton Jura in particular, is an example of the ability of the system to adjust to new or intensified pressures by further dividing itself. All of these cases and others (e.g., Italy's autonomy to the German-speaking minority in Alto Adige) are good examples of the ability of a contemporary political system with traditional hegemonic structures to initiate a transformation and reemerge in a new and presumably more inclusive form.

In this chapter, our attention turns to a more fundamental systemic change in a hegemonic polity, a megaconstitutional transformation that redefines the political system in a basic, deep, long-lasting manner. At least four distinct modes of such transformation are defined in this chapter along with concrete historical examples. First, there is the peaceful division of an existing national territory into its ethnic or national components, as was done in the case of Czechoslovakia (considered by many Slovaks to have been dominated by the Czechs) and in very few other historical cases (e.g., Sweden and Norway in the early twentieth century). Second, contentious and often violent partition of an existing hegemonic polity is discussed by focusing on the rise and fall of the Republic of Cyprus. Other interesting cases of partition include the split of East Pakistan (Bangladesh) from the Pakistani state in the 1970s and the case of the former Yugoslavia in the 1990s. Smooha and Hanf (1992, 28) usefully distinguish between "partition after violence" and "preemptive violence." Third, the consociationalization of a hegemonic system (as was attempted in the 1998 Good Friday agreement in Northern Ireland) is presented as a solution to excessive, long-term hegemony. Finally, the establishment of a majoritarian government, and possibly even a liberal democracy (which does not necessarily follow majoritarianism), in a previously hegemonic state is discussed by focusing on the transformation of South Africa. This is a particularly interesting case insofar as its transformation could have gone in a consociational or majoritarian direction, and with liberal or illiberal democracy (Zakaria 1997) resulting.

Although some cases might be difficult to classify in terms of being transformed "moderately" or "substantially" (i.e., megaconstitutionally), the key is whether the new system resembles the old one or whether it exhibits truly new structural and behavioral patterns. No one would question the fact that the post-1993 Czech Republic and Slovakia are truly different than the previous Czechoslovakia, Cyprus divided is different than the old Republic of Cyprus, South Africa changed its complexion entirely once apartheid passed from this scene, and the Good Friday Agreement envisioned a different Northern Ireland than the one known to us from the pre-1998 era. It is evident the United Kingdom changed only minimally with the initiation of devolution, Switzerland with the Canton Jura is basically the same country as before (but with an additional canton), and Canada changed somewhat in the 1970s with the acceptance of French as coequal to English and the initiation of the policy of multiculturalism, but the change was not dramatic. The case of Spain in the post-Franco years could be included, admittedly, in either the gradual category or in the metaconstitutional category. It is included in this study among the gradual cases because the country has not adopted a full-fledged federal structure (replacing its centralized form), although the adoption of democracy has surely changed all aspects of political behavior in the land.

The nine questions presented at the beginning of Chapter 4 in regard to the process of gradual or mild transformation ought to be asked also in regard to the process of megaconstitutional transformation: did it come about as a result of violent or nonviolent process? Not surprisingly, three out of four cases of megaconstitutional transformation (Cyprus, Northern Ireland, and South Africa) involved a massive amount of violence and/or threat of violence; only the case of the split between the Czechs and the Slovak came about peacefully. A second question to be asked is in regard to the role of external factors rather than internal ones (including intercommunal violence) in leading toward transformation. It seems that, in contrast to cases of mild transformation, in all cases of metaconstitutional change external pressures are significant; in some cases they are crucial (e.g., Cyprus and South Africa), and in other cases (e.g., Czechoslovakia or Northern Ireland) the role of outside actors is more marginal.

The substance of the megaconstitutional transformations is shown in the following text in some detail in each of the four cases. Several key questions are raised in regard to the substance. First, to what extent has the transformation of the system changed the conditions in regard to citizens' access to the public sphere? It seems that in some cases, such as South Africa, the change in regard to access has been most dramatic, and in other cases (e.g., Czechoslovakia or Northern Ireland) it might have been significantly smaller. A second substantive question is the extent to which the megaconstitutional transformation led to the evolvement of an overarching, common identity within the political system (e.g., South Africa in the postapartheid era) or possibly a reduction in the intensity of such identity (Cyprus in the post-1963 era comes to mind). Most important is the question of the overall direction taken by the transformation. Has it been in the direction of the enhancement of democracy, inclusion, and systemic openness (South Africa in the postapartheid era is a good example, as is Northern Ireland's attempt in 1998 to establish a consociational system) or in the direction of further ethnicization and more exclusionary policies (see Chapter 6). Finally, there is the question of what substantive internal change has occurred: the establishment of majoritarian rule (South Africa) or consociationalism.

Radical Modes of Transformation: Alternative Variants

Peaceful Separation: The Case of Czechoslovakia

As a result of the end of the Cold War, several multiethnic Communist-ruled federations (the USSR, Yugoslavia, and Czechoslovakia) were dismantled. Those authoritarian federations imploded under the weight of their own ethnic diversity and nondemocratic practices, as well as by the impact of international pressures, including expectations that democracy will be established in the new states. The dismantling of a multiethnic state as a result of and a solution to interethnic animosity is an interesting phenomenon from the perspective of hegemonic rule and its replacement with democratic practices.

It is important to note that the Czechoslovak case was quite different than the cases of both the Soviet Union and Yugoslavia. First, the country was substantially smaller, both geographically and demographically. Second, only two nations – the Czechs and the Slovaks – were involved in the dissolution of the federal structure, simplifying considerably the political game, especially at the

end. Third, the multinational structure was dismantled with no bloodshed but
through an agreement, albeit a very narrow agreement reached between the
leading elites of the two constituent nations. Fourth, unlike Yugoslavia, there
was no violence and mass genocidal murder in the history and collective memory of the Czechs and the Slovaks: the record of the past was mixed. In this
section, an analysis of the Czechoslovak dissolution from an ethnic perspective
will be offered, emphasizing the division of the state as a possible solution to a
long-term interethnic animosity.

Although the dissolution of Czechoslovakia could be explained by focusing
on numerous factors (Hilde 1999, 648–9; Kraus and Stanger 2000, 7–8; Zajac
2000, 261), that split would not have come about without an infrastructural
ethnic divide within the Czechoslovak body politic. The division of the state
along ethnic lines is highly important; it is incumbent on the analyst to inquire
into the fact that the dismemberment of the multinational polity came about
in an unusually quick and peaceful manner despite the fact that the majority
among Czechs and Slovaks seemed to have opposed it.

Several prominent ethnic factors played a role in the history of Czechoslovakia and its eventual dissolution. From its first days following World War I
and until its dissolution in 1992, Czechoslovakia suffered from lack of a unified, overarching national identity. Most Czechs and Slovaks saw themselves
as members of the Czech or Slovak nations, respectively, and not as members
of the Czechoslovak nation. The hope of the Republic's Founding Fathers of
creating a single nation, neither Czech nor Slovak but Czechoslovak, was never
achieved, particularly in regards to the Slovaks (Pithart and Spencer 1998, 191).
Interethnic suspicion, hostility, and resentment were constant in the successive
eras of that tortured polity: in the interwar era (1918–39), during World War II
(1939–45), following the liberation from Nazi rule (1945–8), under the first
period of Communist rule (1949–68) and following the Prague Spring (1968–
89), and eventually after the fall of the communists (1989–92).

Although it is difficult to prove that the dissolution of Czechoslovakia was
"inevitable," despite the prominence of the ethnic divide, the inability or unwill-
ingness of the Czechs and the Slovaks to forge or invent a Czechoslovak identity
made the eventual split more likely than not. A polity suffering from what Linz
and Stepan call (1996a, 123) a "stateness problem" – a situation where a significant proportion of the population does not accept the state boundaries as
a legitimate political unit to which they owe obedience – might be doomed in
the long run to disintegration. Leff has shown that Czechoslovakia "clearly
suffered from a stateness problem from its inception" (2000, 29).

The stateness problem gave birth to alternative views of and expectations
from the Czechoslovak polity, dividing the Czech and Slovak elites in almost
every stage of the evolving Czechoslovak experiment. Although those elites
did not necessarily control the majority of their people, at critical historical
junctures they influenced decisively the outcome of the political game. One
such juncture was following the 1992 elections conducted in both parts of the
republic on June 5–6, 1992. Those elections brought to power Vaclav Klaus in

Prague and Vladimir Mečiar in Bratislava. Many observers thought that Klaus and his associates were primarily interested in quick economic development and wanted to get rid of Slovakia as it was clearly the least developed province of the Czechoslovak state, while Mečiar and people around him looked for ways to strengthen the Slovak identity through independence (Rutland 1993–4). Although Klaus preferred a functioning federation to partition, he clearly preferred partition to a federation in which the minority could block the majority. Mečiar agreed in principle to a common state with the Czechs but insisted on sovereignty for and international recognition of Slovakia, an unacceptable demand to his Czech counterpart.

Rychlik believes that the results of the June 1992 elections to the Federal Assembly were "the key to the fate of Czechoslovakia" particularly in regard to Slovakia. He also views Havel's request that Klaus form the government as "most unfortunate," becase there was a tradition that when the president is a Czech the prime minister should be a Slovak (Rychlik 2000, 58–9). Be that as it may, the Klaus-Mečiar negotiations led them both to conclude that the only agreed upon solution is one that spells the end of Czechoslovakia, that is, a division of the country. Once the decision to split was made, the Czech side insisted on a complete as well as quick division, leaving the impression that this was Klaus's goal from the very beginning.

Although some of the institutions of the Czechoslovak polity softened the impact of the interethnic hostility, they did not eliminate it altogether. During the First Republic (1919–38), potential and real outside pressures, combined with the presence of large German and Hungarian minorities within the state, were powerful enough to justify the need for a centralized, unitary state in the mind of most Czechs and even many Slovaks. Significant autonomy to Slovakia was perceived as a prelude to unbearable pressure to grant such autonomy to the Germans and the Hungarians. The result was a Czechoslovakia in which the Slovaks "found ready expression in electoral politics and assured parliamentary representation," but in which they did not have "a decisive voice in governance" (Leff 2000, 31). The national problem was sustained and remained unresolved. The politicians believed that they could solve the Slovak question through social engineering; they were much too optimistic. Thus it was hoped that educational advances in Slovakia would produce a generation of Slovaks more inclined to accept a common Czechoslovak identity (Leff 1988; Leff 2000, 34). The result was exactly the opposite.

The national problem continued under the Communists, although it was covered up better. After 1948 the Communists continued and even intensified the policy of heavy economic investment in Slovakia as a means for equalizing the conditions between it and the Czech lands and to solve the national problem once and for all (Wolchik 1991). The Slovaks were treated asymmetrically in the political sphere also, allowing them to establish a separate Slovak Communist Party as well as a Slovak National Council (without equivalent institutions in the Czech lands). All-important decisions continued to be made at the center (Prague) despite these concessions. There is no evidence that the modernization policy of the Communists or the structural revisions introduced by them were more effective than the policies carried out by the First Republic democrats.

Following the repression of the liberal forces within the country by the Soviet Union and its allies, Czechoslovakia became a federal state in October 1968, replacing the unitary state it was before. The Czech Socialist Republic and the Slovak Socialist Republic (the two national components of the reformed polity) had their own parliaments and governments. Moreover, the Federal Assembly had two chambers, minority veto was instituted, and a special majority require- ment was established in regard to the election of a president. It seems as if these provisions guaranteed all the demands of the Slovak minority.

In reality, however, the new federal framework had minimal significance on Czech-Slovak relations. Vaclav Havel called the new, post-1968 polity "federal- ized totalitarianism" (rather than "authentic federalism"), a centralized system imported from the Soviet Union. The federal government remained in full con- trol of the country as a whole. Just as in the cases of the USSR and Yugoslavia, the division of the "federal" country into ethnically based provinces, strength- ened rather than controlled or even managed ethnicity. The so-called normal- ization period did not produce more interethnic empathy: the Czechs viewed themselves as subsiding Slovak development (now more than ever before) and viewed the Slovaks as lacking gratitude; many Slovaks saw the entire Czechoslo- vak history, including the post-1968 era, as an exercise in Czech control.

Interestingly enough, even though the dominant political figure between the years 1969–89 was a Slovak, Gustav Husak, the Slovaks were just as dissatisfied with the new federation as were the Czechs. They wanted a system in which the most important decisions regarding their lives could be made in Bratislava, not in Prague. Yet in the centralized state, albeit in theory a federation, decisions were made in the capital.

The national question came back to the fore once the authoritarian Com- munist state was gone. The underlining ethnic infrastructure came to dominate the entire political game despite the fact that many had hoped that authen- tic federalism would be established and would finally give the Czechs and the Slovaks an opportunity of solving their conflict. Yet the state disintegrated within three years. An overarching identity has not emerged: on the contrary, the Czechoslovak society became increasingly segmented (Leff 1988, 287). By late 1989, every Slovak demanded the enhancement of Slovakia's autonomy, and some of them demanded vigorously outright independence.

The federal structure of the state did not help in alleviating hostility. Specifi- cally, the minority veto, guaranteed in the federal constitution, made the Czechs determined not to surrender the country's future to Slovak veto. In a more gen- eral way, it is possible to argue that ethnically based federalism could become an invitation to the dissolution of any multinational state. Under the best of circumstances this dissolution might be peaceful, as it was in the case of Czechoslovakia.

Although many hoped that the combination of democratization, federalism, and the promise of integration within Europe would guarantee the common future of the Czechs and Slovaks within the Czechoslovak polity, in reality this was not the net result of that combination. The Slovaks were reluctant to adopt the economic revisions required by the European Union as conditions for joining it, and the Czechs believed that the Slovaks' reluctance and poor economic performance would prevent the state from quickly joining "Europe." Moreover, the incentives for internal cooperation that existed within the Czechoslovak framework faded away. Within an open, democratic system there were increasing pressures on politicians to adopt populist – that is, nationalist – positions. As happened in other contexts (e.g., Yugoslavia), moderate politicians were outbid and denounced as antipatriotic. In Bratislava "Czechoslovakism" was perceived as a negation of Slovak identity and even Vladimir Mečiar was charged with "Czecoslovak leanings" (Leff 2000, 41).

Although the Czechoslovak case was deeply influenced by the economic disparities between the Czech lands and Slovakia, without the infrastructural ethnic divides the economic disparities would not be as detrimental to the eventual breakup of the polity as they have become. The economic disparities fed the animosity of the Slovaks toward the better-off Czechs and made the Czechs look with disdain at the Slovaks as underdeveloped people. From the very beginning of the Czechoslovak republic, economic disparities existed between the two provinces. During the Communist era, however, the Slovaks received a disproportionate share of the investment to equalize their conditions to those of the Czechs. This initiative largely eliminated the long-standing gaps between the two parts of the Republic (Wolchik 1991, 186–95). Yet at the critical juncture of June 1992 Czech unemployment was less than 3 percent, while it was over 11 percent in Slovakia (Pithart and Spencer 1998, 191). The Czechs were afraid that the Slovaks would drag them down (Draper 1993; Young 1994).

The economic program, although somewhat successful or perceived as such (at least in the short run), did not eliminate the interethnic hostility. Moreover, once the Communist regime expired, the less-developed Slovakia suffered disproportionately from high unemployment (over threefold that of the Czech unemployment rate). The Slovak economy depended heavily on markets for the products of Slovakia's heavy industry, mainly weapons, and when demand for these products declined the gaps between the Czech lands and Slovakia became even more prominent than before.

Mutual recrimination between Czechs and Slovaks increased after 1989. The Czechs saw themselves as subsidizing Slovakia's inefficient economy while the Slovaks complained about Czech control and unfair advantage. The ethnic beast was fed by real or perceived economic disparities. Several economists thought that perception more than economic reality came to influence the situation. Although, in real economic terms, by 1989 the Slovaks had caught up with the Czechs, the old envies were sustained. "Politics and perceptions largely trumped economic realities," state Kraus and Stanger (2000, 17). The Czechs saw Slovaks as trying to gain "Slovak independence with Czech insurance," not as people negotiating in good faith to sustain the common state. The strength of the ethnic factor, in and of itself and relative to the economic factor, was clearly demonstrated during the last few months of Czechoslovakia.

The ethnic factor within post-Communist Czechoslovakia was strengthened in the post–Cold War era, as the ideological division between East and West declined. In the new Europe, the Slovaks, or many among them, saw themselves as a sovereign nation that deserved full international recognition while still preserving its union, although a loose union, with the Czechs. The Czechs rejected that vision.

One of the dominant factors that made the Czechoslovak split possible was the disappearance, for the first time in over seventy years, of any serious external threat to the republic. When the Czechoslovak union emerged after World War I, the logic for it was self-evident: the two small and related nations in central Europe, the Czechs and the Slovaks, needed unity in the face of their powerful neighbors of the past, present, or future, particularly Hungary, Austria, and Germany. With the rise to power of the Nazis in Germany this reality became all too clear, and it was further reinforced by the results of World War II and the emergence of the USSR as a superpower. Yet in 1989, for the first time since 1918, there was no apparent danger from any external quarters for the security or independence of either the Czechs or the Slovaks. One of the main rationales for unity was gone and an internal ethnic conflict became possible or at least not out of the question.

What became known as the Velvet Divorce – the peaceful dissolution of Czechoslovakia following its famous Velvet Revolution – was produced by a series of impersonal factors such as the different historical experiences of the two nations involved, the intensity of Slovak nationalism, the long-term Czech-Slovak animosity, and Czech desire to quickly join "Europe" as an economically viable and strong entity. But, at the same time, it was also produced by the very personal ambitions of political figures on both sides of the divide. The ethnic factor – individuals and groups viewing themselves as Czechs or Slovaks but not as Czechoslovaks – seems to have played a crucial role both as an impersonal given and as a personal motivator of individual leaders.

The early 1990s battle over the name of the newly democratic state, known as the hyphen war, was an indication of the deep lack of empathy between Czechs and Slovaks. In that battle, both sides exhibited ample disregard for the national sensitivities of the other group. The Czechs were unable or unwilling to respond to Slovak desires for recognition. Thus Havel's proposal (1990) to call the state the Czechoslovak Republic (replacing the Czechoslovak Socialist Republic) ignored the disdain of most Slovaks to the name "Czechoslovak," which they viewed as merely covering up the fact that the state has always been ruled by the Czechs. The Slovaks, on their part, did not take into account Czech sensitivity in regard to post-Munich Czechoslovakia when they insisted that the state ought to be called the Federation of Czecho-Slovakia (indicating that the polity consisted of two separate states). The final "compromise" – calling the country the Czech and Slovak Federative Republic – satisfied very few. An indication of this was that thereafter the unofficial name,

Czechoslovakia, would be written in Czech as one word but written in Slovak with a hyphen.

Although the dissolution of Czechoslovakia could be looked upon as a tragedy, and most Czechs and Slovaks accepted it with a measure of considerable sadness, it could also be perceived as a reasonable, civilized, nonviolent solution to what has become an endless if nonviolent ethnic conflict. Between the Czech goal of maintaining a functioning, even if federal, state and the Slovak desire for real independence, there was no solution but partition. In implementing a negotiated partition through legal settlement rather than through war (as in the case of Cyprus) – although a partition lacking in full popular legitimization – Czechoslovakia looks a great deal better than, for example, Yugoslavia.

From the perspective of the current study, it is important to note that the many consociational (or what some might view as semiconsociational) institutions of Czechoslovakia did not prevent the dissolution of the republic. They might have helped in guaranteeing a relativly soft landing when disintegration occurred, that is, peaceful and nonviolent partition. In a series of writings, Arend Lijphart identified nine typical consociational conditions (see, in particular, Lijphart 1984 and 1996). Kopecky has shown (2000, 81) that, in terms of consociationalism, only three of Lijphart's conditions existed, and that they could have helped in terms of maintaining the Czechoslovak system: (1) the Slovak minority was overrepresented on the federal level; (2) the Czechs and the Slovaks were geographically concentrated so that a territorial federation was possible; and (3) the negotiation about keeping the states involved only two groups. The rest of Lijphart's consociational requirements did not exist: (1) the Czechs and the Slovaks lacked a tradition of elite accommodation, (2) overarching loyalty to the Czechoslovak entity rather than the particularistic Czech and Slovak nationalism did not develop, (3) large socioeconomic differences among the two nations prevailed, (4) the larger group (the Czechs) pushed toward majoritarian rule, (5) there was never a demographic balance between the two nations (with a solid two-third Czech majority prevailing throughout the history of the state), (6) by the late 1980s all external threats to the state disappeared, and (7) despite the small size of the population "the post-communist elite was not particularly characterized by long-standing mutual exchange" (Kopecky 2000, 80).

Although the "consociational balance" could not have prevented the dissolution of the state, Kopecky believes that the three positive factors "combined to play a positive role in the peaceful character of the Czechoslovak separation" (ibid., 81). There is no question that the division of Czechoslovakia can be looked upon as "a sad story of egotism, short-sightedness, and misunderstanding," although it can also be looked upon, more positively, as a relatively painless and bloodless form of separation (Pithart and Spencer 1998, 185).

Forced Partition: The Case of the Republic of Cyprus

When Cyprus received its independence from Great Britain in 1960, it adopted a governmental design that was fundamentally unitary but with several consociational built-in features designed to protect the Turkish minority from the arbitrary, hegemonic control of the Greek majority. In some regards the Republic of Cyprus resembled Czechoslovakia, although the history of these two countries was quite different. First, like Czechoslovakia, the island had only two major communities, with several other significantly smaller minorities. Second, there was a clear demographic dominance for one of the communities (the Greeks with over 75 percent of the population). Third, uneasy relations between the national communities existed. There were, however, also significant differences between the Czechoslovak and the Cypriot cases. Most important, at least two foreign countries, Greece and Turkey, had a strong interest in the future of "their" communities on the island, a feature that would prove crucial in the eventual partition of the small island into two polities. Moreover, those two countries, along with the United Kingdom as the colonial power since the late nineteenth century, were deeply involved in negotiating Cypriot independence, and the solution they reached was not necessarily popular with the local communities. At least one author called the new state "a reluctant republic" (Xydis 1973). It is no wonder that although Czechoslovakia managed to survive between 1918–89 (albeit with the bloody interregnum of 1939–45), the Cypriot state disintegrated for all intents and purposes within three years of its proclamation, among the fastest polities to ever dissolve. Moreover, while the breakup of Czechoslovakia was peaceful, the Cypriot disintegration was accompanied by substantial violence, a large number of deaths, refugees on both sides, and eventually a large-scale Turkish military invasion leading to a de facto partition of the island.

Even a brief historical inquiry brings out the negative features that led eventually to the failure of the Cypriot experiment in power sharing. Nationalist Greek Cypriots under Colonel George Grivas started a violent campaign against the British rulers of Cyprus in the mid-1950s. Their platform, however, was not merely the liberation of the island from colonial rule but also its unification with Greece, the motherland of most of its inhabitants. The Greek campaign for *Enosis* (unification) was counterbalanced by the demand of the Turkish minority for partition. In 1960 an agreement among the British, the Greeks, and the Turks was reached. The Republic of Cyprus was established, based on a complicated constitution that adopted several governmental mechanisms designed to divide political power between the two communities. Archbishop Makarios, the head of the Cypriot Greek Orthodox church, assumed the presidency, and the Turkish Cypriot Dr. Kutchuk became vice president. The Turkish minority (about 18 percent of the island's population) received three out of ten seats in the government, 30 percent of the jobs in the Republic's bureaucracy, 40 percent of the positions in the military, and separate municipal services in Cyprus's five largest towns. Most important, the House of Representatives was divided between fifty-six Greek Cypriots and twenty-four Turkish Cypriots.

In general, the 1960 constitution could be regarded as an ambitious attempt at establishing a republic in which both communities would share power and in which the majority of Greek Cypriots (77 percent) would not be able to gain hegemonic, unrestrained control over the much smaller Turkish minority. Many Greek Cypriots opposed the deal and demanded a revision to the constitution, eliminating the veto rights and many other ethnic clauses benefiting the Turks. Tensions between the two communities came to a head by December 1963 when violence erupted in Nicosia. By that time the Turks withdrew from the government and the Republic began its slide toward disintegration. The next few years saw the creation of a sizeable refugee problem (with about 265,000 displaced persons) in both communities, with the Turks establishing enclaves and eventually a "government" in the northern part of the island, while the Greeks dominated the south and appropriated the institutions of the Republic.

Despite efforts to resolve the escalating conflict – mostly by going back to the 1960 constitution or a version thereof – no agreed-upon formula was adopted. Moreover, the situation worsened considerably when right-wing nationalist elements on the island (headed by ex-EOKA fighter Nicos Sampson) and in Greece (ruled by a military junta) engineered an anti-Makarios coup. The plan was to implement Enosis, a solution that would leave the Turkish minority at the mercy of a nondemocratic Greek government.

This hegemonic gambit backfired, damaging (maybe permanently) the chances of achieving a compromise, a power-sharing deal between the two warring communities. Although the Sampson regime collapsed before it had a chance to firmly establish itself, Turkey reacted to Greece's intervention by invading Northern Cyprus. By August 1974 the Turkish army controlled about 37 percent of the island, and by 1983 the Turkish Republic of Northern Cyprus (TRNC) was formally established.

Despite considerable efforts to solve the Cypriot problem, to date no agreement has been reached. In effect, four distinct solutions could be identified:

1. A return to the unitary but semiconsociational state that existed between 1960–3 (or a variation of that governmental design); a solution preferred by the Greek community but strongly opposed by the Turks.
2. A partition of the island into two states along the existing lines, in which the Greeks would control 63 percent of the island while the Turks would control 37 percent; a solution preferred by most people in the Turkish community but rejected by the Greeks.
3. Establishing a Cypriot federal state: there is already an agreement on the principle of establishing a federation, but no concrete framework has been adopted despite numerous attempts to formulate such a framework.
4. Establishing a confederation between two independent polities, Greek and Turkish.

The first solution, a return to a common unitary state (with semiconsociational features), is unlikely in view of the mutual hostility between the island's two communities. This hostility has probably deepened through the years and it cannot be easily (if at all) overcome. The lack of an overarching, common identity between the two communities is a major reason for not going back to the status quo ante, the situation of 1960–3.

The second solution, a permanent partition of Cyprus into two states, might be perpetuated as a de facto solution if no negotiated settlement is reached; chances of formulating it as a mutually accepted solution are slim at best. Such a solution is unlikely to be agreed to by the Greek community, which has always viewed Cyprus in its entirety as Hellenic. The Greeks' desire to reestablish their hegemonic rule on the island is, ironically, a major impediment for the reemergence of Cyprus as a unified polity and a cardinal reason for the Turks' preference for a permanent partition.

A federation or confederation, the third or fourth solutions, is where a solution to the Cypriot dilemma might eventually be found. Although these are not the preferred solutions for either of the parties, a federal solution with a strong central government is the second best solution for most Greek Cypriots because it will reunify the island and might promote long-lasting stability (Theophanous 2000, 218). A loose confederal solution might be the best for the Turks if they cannot achieve permanent partition and a wide recognition of their state, and if they are effectively pressured to settle on a framework other than a two-state solution. Some analysts have even suggested a federation with confederal elements (ibid.), and such a solution might be more acceptable to two asymmetric and antagonistic communities than a concept of a federal overarching cultural political union (Duchacek 1987; Duchacek, Latouche, and Stevenson 1988).

Following a history of communal conflict (particularly in the preindependence 1950s era), the establishment of a unitary Cypriot state in 1960 was woefully unrealistic. The framers of the Cypriot constitution were aware of the difficult Greek-Turkish relations. Therefore they introduced consociational elements into the governmental design, a mode of limiting the dominance of the Greek community. The Greeks were given the presidency, but the Turks were guaranteed the vice presidency; each was granted a veto power over foreign affairs, defense, and security, thus in effect negating the supposition of a majoritarian democracy. The Turkish Cypriots were granted 30 percent of the positions in all levels of government (despite their mere 18 percent of the population); legislation regarding some important issues required separate majorities of Greek and Turkish representatives (Bahcheli 2000, 204).

Although many analysts offered a critique of that system (Joseph 1999, 24–30; Kyriakides 1968, 166–70), there was no other way of establishing a unified country but by granting the minority power beyond its demographic size and erecting a power-sharing system. The problem with the Cypriot consociational or semiconsociational system was that the interethnic divide between the two communities was extremely deep, there was no history of cooperation among elites, and no sense of a larger Cypriot community ever developed.

The 1960 constitution was quite satisfying from a Turkish perspective, both that of the Cypriot Turks and that of the Turkish government. The relatively small minority of Cypriot Turks was given an effective veto power over the actions of the island's government, and Turkey saw itself as entitled to intervene, even by the force of arms, to defend "its" people on the island.

The Greek Cypriots, however, were quite dissatisfied. Given their clear numerical advantage on the island, they wanted to see a majoritarian rule established. Their leader, President Makarios, in 1963 proposed the substitution of communal rights established in the constitution with individual rights for the Turks (Necatigil 1998, 21–2), thereby erasing the power-sharing clauses of the 1960 constitutional settlement. The violence that erupted shortly thereafter doomed the power-sharing deal altogether, leading eventually to the division of the island and to Turkish occupation of its northern part.

In pushing for hegemony based on their numerical advantage, the Greek Cypriots miscalculated. Rather than accepting the limitations imposed on the majority in 1960, they pushed for an unrestrained majority rule, a system that often does not work in deeply divided societies. First, Archbishop Makarios demanded constitutional revisions that would have changed fundamentally the essence of the agreed-upon constitutional order in favor of the Greek Cypriots. Second, the Greek government supported a coup against the duly-elected Makarios (July 15, 1974) to bring about Enosis. The fact that the anti-Makarios coup was planned outside Cyprus (Ehrlich 1974) internationalized the conflict and gave Turkey the reason or the excuse to intervene militarily. The maneuvers among the Greeks, on and off the island, brought about the eventual Turkish intervention and the occupation of about one-third of the island, thus creating a de facto two-state "solution" or partition (*taksim* for the Turks).

If anything, the divide between Greeks and Turks has deepened over the last forty years. The hands of the Cypriot Turks were strengthened by the presence of tens of thousands of Turkish soldiers in the northern part of the island. In 1983 the Turkish Republic of Northern Cyprus was officially declared, formally confirming the long-term and possibly permanent division of the island.

The strengthening of the Turkish hand led to a more moderate, accommodating Greek position. Thus the Greeks have accepted the federal principle although, at the same time, they have continued to oppose a separate Turkish state anywhere in Cyprus. The Cypriot Turkish position had become harder. Their preference for a two-state solution or, at a minimum, a confederation has crystallized. Moreover, the Turkish government and the leadership of the Cypriot Turks have encouraged a large number of Turks to immigrate to northern Cyprus, increasing the number of Turks on the island to about 24 percent. Many of those new arrivals received the properties of Greek Cypriots who became refugees as a result of the formation of the Turkish Republic of Northern Cyprus.

The de facto division of Cyprus, Turkish interests in maintaining a strategic presence in the northern part of the island, and the diametrically divergent attitudes of the two Cypriot communities makes the genuine and complete reunification of the island rather unlikely. The Greeks will never accept partition, and the Turks reject the re-creation of the unitary Cypriot state. A federal solution is possible, in principle, but the Turks are anxious that this could lead to the reestablishment of Greek hegemony in which they will be a controlled minority.

Rauf Denktash, the long-time leader of the Cypriot Turks (until April 2005), has clearly preferred independence; however, it seems that he or his successors may settle for a loose confederation in which the Turkish community will be, for all intents and purposes, independent. Yet the vast majority of Greek Cypriots are as opposed to confederation as they are to partition. Formal partition or confederation will divide the island geographically, ethnically, and politically in a permanent and formal manner, a solution to which the Greeks are adamantly opposed.

Even more than Czechs and Slovaks, it seems that Greek and Turkish Cypriots simply do not trust each other, making stable and peaceful political cohabitation unlikely. The distance between Turks and Greeks in terms of religion and culture is substantially greater than the distance between Czechs and Slovaks, and if the latter could not maintain a united polity can we expect the former to do so? Although a federal solution is, in theory, possible and even desirable, in reality it is not very likely to succeed in Cyprus. Federalism requires a significant measure of mutual trust.

For those reasons, dividing the island between the two warring communities might not be an unreasonable solution. The Cyprus conflict is, at heart, an identity-based conflict (Fisher 2001, 307), rather than an interest-based or resource-based conflict (Rothman 1997). It is extremely difficult to resolve that type of conflict on the basis of shared political institutions of any kind.

The international community has invested significant efforts in trying to resolve the Cypriot conflict. The Secretary-General of the United Nations, Kofi Annan, presented a plan on April 24, 2004, that carries his name for restoring the demolished state under the new name of the "United Cyprus Republic." The "Annan Plan," reflective of the Swiss confederal model, the Bosnia-Herzegovina arrangement, and even the 1960 Cypriot constitution, proposed a loose confederation of two constituent states, a Greek Cypriot and Turkish Cypriot. It provided for a minimal federal apparatus.

In many ways the Annan Plan seems to favor the Turkish minority. It called for a collective Presidential Council made of six voting members and three non-voting members, both groups divided between the majority and the minority on a 2:1 basis (i.e., the minority will have two voting members and one nonvoting member in a council of nine individuals). The Presidential Council would elect a president and a vice president, one from each community, but these two will rotate their functions every twenty months. A bicameral legislature will include an evenly split senate (upper house) with forty-eight members and a Chamber of Deputies (lower house) with forty-eight members. In counting the votes for the chamber, the ballots of Turkish Cypriots will count twice as much as those of Greek Cypriots. A supreme court will be established, with equal representation from each community but with three additional foreign judges.

The purpose of the Annan Plan was clear – try to reunify Cyprus by convincing the Turkish Cypriots to come back into the fold by guaranteeing them de facto independence – it did not achieve its goal. In the Turkish Northern Sector the plan was endorsed by almost 65 percent of the votes (with 87 percent of the eligible voters exercising their vote). In the Greek Southern Sector, however, almost 76 percent voted against the plan offered by the Secretary-General (with 88 percent voting).

Despite its failure, the Annan Plan could be looked upon as a reasonable solution to the difficult Cyprus issue. The assumption of the plan was that of communal equality (regardless of numerical strength), the right of both groups to govern themselves with a minimal level of outside interference (including that of the state). If implemented, the Annan Plan would have prevented majority hegemony by creating a weak central authority and granting veto power to each community. If one remembers that the 1960 constitution was trying to do the same, and that the constitution collapsed under the pressure of Greek hegemonic push, the Annan Plan seems to make sense. It was trying to create an even stronger and more balanced situation than the defunct 1960 constitution. The logic of the Annan Plan was already inherent not only in that previous constitutional framework but also in the Makarios-Denktash 1977 agreement in which the two leaders agreed on a bicommunal, bizonal federation.

So why was the Annan Plan rejected by the vast majority of the Greek Cypriots? First, the Annan Plan ratified, in effect, the division of the island, an ideological defeat that the Greeks were not ready to accept. Second, the plan could easily be looked upon as unbalanced and overly pro-Turkish, especially because the Turks from the very beginning have been a relatively small minority in Cyprus, and the Annan Plan was even more favorable to them than the 1960 constitution. And third, the majority felt that allowing Turkish settlers to stay on the island and obtain citizenship was not merely against their interests (as changing the demographic picture in Cyprus) but also fundamentally unjust. Nevertheless, it is interesting to note that while the President of the Republic of Cyprus, Tassos Papadopoulos, and the AKEL (Progressive Party of Working People), Cyprus's largest party, came out against the Annan Plan, Greece's Prime Minister Karamanlis was "neutral" (although in reality probably opposed the plan) while the leader of the Greek opposition, Papandreou, spoke in favor of the proposal.

On the Turkish side there was more support than opposition, a reasonable position given that the plan was compatible with the long-term interests of both Turkey and the Turkish minority in Cyprus. An implementation of the plan would have meant an end to the political and economic isolation and exclusion of the Turkish Republic of Northern Cyprus; moreover, it would have eased Turkey's relations with the European Union. No wonder that the Turkish government endorsed the proposal. Rauf Denktash, the veteran leader of the Turkish Cypriots, expressed his opposition, while his prime minister, Mehmet Ali Talat, endorsed the plan. In April 2005, a year after the vote, Talat was elected as the new president of the Turkish Republic of Northern Cyprus.

A comparison of the Czechoslovak and the Cypriot partitions in terms of the questions asked in the first section of this chapter is rather revealing. First, the Cypriot partition was accompanied by violence, and the Czechoslovak partition was nonviolent. The latter was based on an explicit agreement between the governments involved, and the former was, in effect, a forced partition. The Czechoslovak partition was a no-fault divorce and, therefore, left relatively few marks of bitterness, recrimination, and hostility on the people involved. The Cypriot partition came about as a result of the complete deterioration of the relations between the island's communities and the Turkish invasion of 1974, leaving the warring communities in a noncompromising disposition.

In terms of the rest of the questions introduced, it is clear that the change occurring in the Czechoslovak case was significantly different than the one occurring in the Cypriot one. The transformation of Czechoslovakia came about mostly as a result of internal factors, although the fact that the country ceased being a potential target of international aggression (as in the 1930s) or a player of any significance in the European balance of power (as during the Cold War) made the Velvet Divorce possible. The desire of the Czech economic elite to join the European Union, and their sense that Slovakia may prevent them from doing so, played a significant role in the Czech decision to agree to the partition. Nevertheless, on balance, the breakup of the Czechoslovak federation came about as a result of deep internal divisions between the two national components of the formerly Communist state. The disappearance of the authoritarian regime made the split possible. From the perspective of the Slovaks, and especially nationalist elements assembled around Vladimir Mečiar, this was an opportune moment to challenge or even break Czech hegemony.

In the case of Cyprus, it could be argued, internal and external factors played an almost equal role in the dissolution of the ill-fated new republic. The hostile relations between the two ethnic groups on the island, Greek Cypriots and Turkish Cypriots, were a close reflection of the negative relations between their two respective motherlands, Greece and Turkey. The motherlands played an active, even aggressive, role in leading to the eventual disintegration of the fledgling republic. The Greeks on the island and the homeland were trying to replace the consociational republic with a hegemonic, majoritarian regime.

Despite the fact that the results in the Czechoslovak and Cypriot cases might look similar – a partition of an existing state into two separate national components – the short- and long-term consequences of the transformation occurring in Czechoslovakia and Cyprus were dramatically different. The peaceful change in Czechoslovakia enabled the two new states, the Czech Republic and Slovakia, to develop fairly good relationships since 1993. The bitterness and violence involved in the breakdown of Cyprus led to negative relations between the Greek and the Turkish polities on the island. Although there are no prospects for the Czechs and the Slovaks to reestablish their defunct federation, the Greeks and Turks might eventually find a way of reinventing their dismembered republic, surely in a different form than the one produced in 1960.

In the Czechoslovak and the Cypriot cases we have been witnessing a metaconstitutional transformation of polities that were close to being hegemonic (Czechoslovakia) or moving potentially toward hegemony (Cyprus). In both cases this condition was eliminated or averted by a violent (Cyprus) or peaceful (Czechoslovakia) transformation based on resigned acceptance

(Czechoslovakia) or coercion (Cyprus). In both cases the absence of a sense of overarching or common identity prevented the polity from functioning properly in the first place, and an overarching identity has not developed since the breakup.

Consociationalism: The Case of Northern Ireland

The changes attempted in Northern Ireland over the last several years, like those implemented in Canada and Spain, are another example of conscious efforts to transform a political system through large-scale constitutional reform. Moreover, these changes constitute a bold attempt to change well-developed ideological positions and even deeper held identities based on separation, antagonism, and conflict between two communities. The overall goal of these changes has been that of moving from long-existing exclusivity constructions that have existed in Northern Ireland for generations to a new governmental design based on inclusion and intercommunal power sharing. Long-held exclusivist positions, often associated with Ulster Loyalist or Unionist segments of the Northern Irish society and with personalities such as that of the Reverend Ian Paisley (Cash 1998), have been marginalized for a while by compromise proposals, although reversals in the fate of these efforts at reconciliation have returned these personalities and the positions that they represent to center stage.

The most important constitutional effort to change the nature of political life in Northern Ireland came with the April 1998 Good Friday (or Belfast) Agreement, a negotiated settlement that repeated the main features of the 1973 Sunningdale Agreement. The two alternative designations of that agreement are indicative of the deep divide that ought to be overcome before a new reality could be created in Northern Ireland on a long-term or permanent basis. That divide is surely recognized by the framers of the 1998 agreement as an extremely bold, comprehensive, and imaginative way of solving this long-term dispute. Nevertheless, this serious effort might eventually prove to be insufficient.

Shane O'Neill (in Gagnon and Tully 2001, 223) goes as far as to describe the remarkable 1998 agreement as "the twentieth century's greatest achievement in the quest for legitimate government on the island of Ireland." It is important to note that this "quest," despite its endorsement of such fundamental revisions in the status quo, was approved by 71 percent of the voters in Northern Ireland, a somewhat smaller majority than the one endorsing the Spanish constitution of 1978 but still an impressive majority. As many as 94 percent of the voters of the Republic of Ireland endorsed the agreement.

Any constitutional change of large proportions has to be assessed against the past that it tries to erase, an exercise attempted in regard to Northern Ireland by John McGarry (2002). The 1998 Irish agreement must be regarded as another attempt, this time consociational in nature, to convince the Northern Irish nationalists, mostly Catholics, that they can have an equitable share in the Northern Irish polity. It does so by asking Northern Ireland's unionists, mostly Protestants, to give up the privileges that they have enjoyed traditionally. Therefore, opposition to the agreement has been particularly strong among the privileged unionists (or loyalists), a pattern that has appeared among other hegemonic groups (e.g., Greeks in Cyprus, Serbs in Yugoslavia, Afrikaners in South Africa).

Although the Spanish strategy toward the transformation of hegemonic relations has been semifederal, the constitutional strategy chosen by the framers of the Northern Irish deal was consociational. The small size of the territory in question and the more even demographic distribution of the population suggest that consociationalism might work in Northern Ireland. Reynolds maintains that this is "the most obvious present-day example of fully-blown consociationalism, that is, an institutionally based power-sharing agreement within government, brokered between well defined segments of society that may be joined by citizenship but divided by religion, ethnicity or language" (1999–2000, 613). The consociational accord, while recognizing the position of Northern Ireland within the United Kingdom, upholds minority rights and cultural demands, as well as gives the minority substantial political power; thus it is consociational through and through.

The revolutionary nature of the agreement has to be understood, and greatly appreciated, particularly within the broader structure of the governmental tradition of the United Kingdom. As such, the Good Friday Agreement could be looked upon as a form of devolution, and radical devolution at that. An area that is part of the United Kingdom is the subject of a treaty between the United Kingdom and the Republic of Ireland. Moreover, the future of that area is to be determined by the people of Ireland, not merely those living in the north. The power of the British government at Westminster is limited in regard to Northern Ireland, introducing a federal element into a traditionally unitary governmental design. Northern Ireland can even leave the United Kingdom in the future (Nairn 2001; Stewart and Shirlow 1999), insofar as the agreement recognizes the legitimacy of whatever choice is made by a majority of the people of Northern Ireland with regard to its status. The options open to the people are explicitly referred to as the continuation of the union with Great Britain or the establishment of a sovereign united Ireland (meaning, in effect, the cessation of Northern Ireland from the United Kingdom).

From the perspective of this study, it is essential to emphasize that the 1998 agreement reflects a true transformation toward an inclusive political system. It does so in several respects:

1. It establishes several democratic institutions that are truly consociational, that is, based on power sharing between the different communities in devolved areas and not reflecting merely the desires of majorities composed of individuals. Thus the 108-member Northern Ireland Assembly envisioned in the 1998 agreement is to be elected by proportional representation, a hallmark of consociationalism, and the allocation of committee chairs, ministers, and committee membership is also in proportion to party strength. The executive branch is headed jointly by a first minister and a deputy first minister, elected together by the assembly, thus

creating in effect a dual premiership (somewhat like the ill-fated Cypriot deal of 1960). The proportionality principle is also applied to governmental departments.

2. Different rules guarantee the equality of the two communities in the North; these include a set of minority veto rights that protect the nationalists from unionist dominance (or vice versa). Key decisions, including the budget, require cross-community support in the assembly (O'Leary 1999, 70). These decisions are made either by "parallel consent" (i.e., majorities within the "unionist" and "nationalist" camps in the Northern Ireland Assembly [NIA]) or a weighted majority of 60 percent of members present and voting, including at least 40 percent of each of the unionist and nationalist camps. Among the key decisions are the election of the chair of the assembly, the first minister and his deputy, budgetary allocations, and so forth. The competing aspirations of the two communities are thus clearly recognized, sharply distinguishing the 1998 agreement from Northern Ireland's traditional hegemonic past.

3. To assure the stability of the agreement, it is based not merely on the relations between Northern Ireland's two rival communities, groups with a long history of conflict, but also on links between Northern Ireland and the Republic of Ireland to its south, between Northern Ireland and the United Kingdom (of which it remains a part), as well as between the United Kingdom and the Republic of Ireland.

4. The agreement demands equal opportunity in all social and economic activity regardless of any societal divides (including ethnicity), and it establishes a new Human Rights Commission. Thus consociationalism is supplemented by the fundamental principles of liberal democracy.

From a broader perspective, it is important to realize that the 1998 agreement does not try to resolve the long-lasting conflict, its framers having realized that this is simply not possible, at least not in the short term. Rather, the agreement tries to offer an effective and peaceful way of managing the conflict politically. The main conceptual breakthrough inherent in the 1998 deal is the recognition that in Northern Ireland there is not one but two political communities, and that both ought to be fully engaged in the decision-making process to create stability and bring an end to violence. In some ways this seminal agreement is not merely consociational but binational (O'Leary 1999, 73, 76). This character of the agreement could be seen in the fact that it offers a voting system that is entirely different than the one existing in the rest of the United Kingdom, where simple majority has been thoroughly institutionalized for generations. The simple majority rule is replaced in the 1998 agreement by a requirement for the consent of both communities.

Other provisions point in the same direction. Thus, for example, nationalist ministers in the government of Northern Ireland do not have to swear an oath of allegiance to the Crown or the Union; they can take merely a "Pledge of Office." I argue that their integrity as Irish is being maintained, even though they serve within a branch of the British government (Northern Ireland continues to be part of the United Kingdom).

One of the most far-reaching provisions of the 1998 agreement is the fact that the United Kingdom acknowledges that Northern Ireland has the right to join the Republic of Ireland on a basis of referendum conducted in Northern Ireland. In a way, this is the equivalent of the Supreme Court of Canada's ruling on recognizing the validity of a cessation referendum in Quebec. Although it is difficult to predict where this provision could lead in the future, Northern Ireland's autonomy clearly is enhanced by that provision.

The 1998 agreement includes many additional important elements, including a call for the decommissioning of weapons and the establishment of a representative and impartial police force. This is important in view of the fact that the Protestant-dominated police have served as a major control mechanism in the hands of the majority.

Above everything else, this agreement is historical because it includes explicit and mutual recognition between unionists and nationalists, legitimizing these communities as political actors in the determination of the future of Northern Ireland.

Unfortunately, despite the impressive constitutional façade erected to create a new constitutional reality in Northern Ireland, the implementation of the 1998 agreement has not been carried out smoothly. Issues such as the decommissioning of arms (disarming the paramilitary groups) have not progressed satisfactorily, and, as a result, political instability has prevailed. The worst of it had been that the United Kingdom, the sovereign in Northern Ireland, felt that it had to take power back and suspend the devolutionary Northern Ireland deal.

The Northern Ireland Assembly, the most important institutional component of the Good Friday Agreement, has been out of business since October 2002 when it was dissolved by Tony Blair, the British prime minister. Although Gerry Adams and David Trimble came close to an agreement in October 2003, trying to revive the implementation of the original agreement, the latter backed out at the last minute, and the effort to return to the orderly implementation of the 1998 agreement faltered. Trimble felt that the Irish Republican Army (IRA) failed to deliver a convincing statement permanently renouncing armed struggle along with a visible decommissioning of its weapons.

The future of the 1998 agreement seems uncertain. The attitude that Bew called "Paisleyism" (2003), continued confrontation with and lack of tolerance toward the other side, has been on the rise. At the same time, the 1998 agreement has not been scrapped, and a deal between the two communities, represented now by the Protestant Democratic Unionist Party (DUP) and the Catholic Sinn Fein, has been rumored to be "just round the corner" for quite some time (ibid.). This hope may not be fulfilled soon in view of the fact that in both communities radicals have become the majority. However, even radicals might realize that only a political deal can settle this dispute, not the force of arms.

Some people have observed that the old tribalism of the past has reemerged, along with disillusion with the 1998 agreement and a feeling that "the other side get everything, we get nothing." But even Paisley's Loyalists want devolution, and they are "smart enough to know that without Sinn Fein there will be no devolution" (McKittrick 2003). So despite the electoral victory of the hard liners on both sides of the religious-political, the logic of the situation may lead to the resurrection of the 1998 agreement.

Some analysts have gone as far as pronouncing the Good Friday Agreement "brain-dead," maintaining that it was deeply flawed from the beginning. "Power-sharing based on proportional representation in divided communities is inherently unstable.... It drives leaders constantly to look over their shoulders to their hinterland, and voters rushing at every crisis to the extremist parties," asserted one commentator as the Trimble-Adams deal collapsed (Jenkins 2003).

The problem with such rushed analysis, written invariably under the impact of negative political developments, is that it often ignores the alternatives to power sharing. The fact is that Protestant majoritarianism has led to Loyalist hegemony, accompanied by systematic discrimination of Catholics as well as massive violence. The 1998 agreement has to be understood as an attempt to change this reality by institutionalizing equality and reducing violence.

Between the early 1920s and the early 1970s, the devolved government in Northern Ireland, a self-governing region within the United Kingdom, ruled the six counties exclusively, maintaining all power in the hand of the Protestant unionists. The 1998 agreement might be looked upon as an attempt to rid the region from that entrenched control system after a process that lasted almost thirty years. The goal of the process is to move from one-side hegemony to two-side power sharing. The cornerstone of the proposed deal is "the requirement of cross-community support for all key decisions" to ensure that "neither community can dominate the other" (Ahern 2003, 28).

It is important to note that despite the difficulties in implementing the 1998 agreement, leading to the suspension of the devolved administration of Northern Ireland by the British government, the Good Friday Agreement has not been repudiated by either of the parties in Northern Ireland. It is clear that the governments of both the Republic of Ireland and the United Kingdom are fully committed to the agreement, and it seems that the parties in the conflict-ridden province do not have any choice but to stick with the 1998 deal, as imperfect as it may be.

John McGarry has successfully shown that the consociational model is best suited for the conditions now prevailing in Northern Ireland, particularly when compared with alternatives tried in Northern Ireland before. He noted that "virtually all unionist politicians are now formally committed to some form of power sharing" (2002, 456). If and when the political institutions of Northern Ireland as envisioned in the 1998 agreement are restored, the peace process of the last few years could be back on track. The establishment, or reestablishment, of a consociational rule in Northern Ireland will complement well the closer, friendlier relations between the Republic of Ireland and the United Kingdom (Cullen 2005).

Majoritarian Transformation: The Case of South Africa

The case of South Africa is particularly interesting from the overall theoretical perspective of this volume. First, although in the case of Czechoslovakia or Cyprus, for example, one may question whether full-fledged hegemony ever existed in the pretransformation era (and I would argue that it did, at least in the minds of many minority members, Slovaks and Turkish Cypriots alike), there can be no question as to the breadth and depth of hegemony under South Africa's apartheid regime. Second, the South African situation was rather unusual in the sense that it was a particularly rare form of hegemonism – minority hegemony (most hegemonic cases have been of a majority dominance variety). Third, the South African situation generated unusual interest on the part of the international community, thus allowing us to assess the impact of that community on political transformation, at least in extreme cases. Fourth, in the case of South Africa, maybe more than in any other case, several models of resolution – and particularly consociationalism versus majoritarianism – were discussed and debated by political actors, ethnicity scholars, and South Africa experts. Donald Horowitz identified as many as twelve different perspectives on the country's future (1991, 1991b, 3–7). This fascinating constitutional debate has continued after the elimination of apartheid (Maphai 1999) and is extremely instructive for the purposes of this book. Finally, South Africa was considered by most observers as one of the countries least likely to become democratic (Giliomee 1995, 83). For these reasons and others, the South African case is ideal for examining the transition process, particularly its political-engineering aspects.

In evaluating the case of South Africa, this section will describe the multi-dimensional hegemony that was apartheid. A brief description of the factors leading to apartheid's demise will be given. A discussion of the process through which the hegemonic regime was terminated will be presented, dwelling on the alternative governmental designs debated by the participants. Finally, an assessment of where the country is now, and where it might be going in the foreseeable future, will be given. One of the most important questions to be asked is whether the changes introduced over the last fifteen years or so are sustainable.

Of all the hegemonic systems in existence, none was more hegemonic in terms of its multidimensionality, the depth of the control exercised, and the very fact that it was carried out by a minority than South Africa. Although the white minority was under 20 percent of the population, it controlled the disenfranchised black majority by legal, economic, military, and political means. This control was based on Afrikaner nationalism, itself rooted in Calvinism, German Romanticism, and a theology of choseness (Moodie 1975; Sparks 1990).

The conflict in South Africa has deep historical roots. Of special relevance for the eventual development of apartheid and its demise after more than four decades (and for contemporary politics) were the uneasy relationships between the first European settlers, Afrikaners, and two other groups, the British colonialists and the indigenous African population. Similar to Canada,

South Africa's history was influenced by the competition between European colonial powers.

The first Europeans to arrive in what was to become "South Africa" were the Dutch. In 1652 the Dutch founded the Cape Colony through the Dutch East India Company (Lester 1998, ch. 1). The settlers' regime was harsh and included slavery for the black natives (Hauss 2001, 81). British colonial interests arrived during the Napoleonic wars in the early nineteenth century, seizing the Cape from the Dutch. Both the Afrikaners (Dutch) and the British established control over the black African population in their ever-expanding territories, although the British were more liberal and abolished slavery. The Afrikaner-British competition was severe (especially after diamonds and gold were found in the country), resulting in periodic violence. Especially important in this regard was the bloody Anglo-Boer War of 1899–1902.

Following the signing of a peace treaty (1902), the Union of South Africa came into being following lengthy British-Dutch negotiations (May 1910). The Union was a self-governing dominion within the British Empire (later the Commonwealth). From the beginning it institutionalized white privilege. Thus a bicameral parliament was elected by the white population and only a handful of Africans and Coloureds. The Union eventually became the Republic of South Africa (1961) when South Africa withdrew from the British Commonwealth.

The most important event, from the perspective of the establishment of hegemonic order in South Africa, was the unexpected victory of the Afrikaner-based National Party under D. F. Malan in the 1948 elections. The new government formalized and extended the long-existing policies of racial segregation establishing the policy of apartheid (separateness). This highly comprehensive legal system divided the races in all respects, imposed racial designation on all persons, required Africans to carry "passes," limited the rights of Africans to live in certain areas, and removed millions of them arbitrarily in what amounted to ethnic cleansing (Christopher 1995, 9), and segregated public facilities on a racial basis. The premiership of H. F. Verwoerd (1958–66) witnessed the further expansion of apartheid. It became an elaborate ideology of Afrikaner nationalism (Giliomee and Schlemmer 1989, ch. 3) that endorsed the idea of "separate development" for the different races under which whites were greatly privileged politically, economically and socially while blacks were massively discriminated against and condemned to severe inequalities. This led to the establishment of eight poor, underdeveloped black "homelands" (Christopher 1995, 5). To top it all, "the regime meticulously removed all but White voters from the electorate" (Horowitz 1991a, 11). According to some estimates, apartheid resulted in the killing of over forty thousand people (Hauss 2001, 83).

The policy of Verwoerd and his successors invigorated the opponents of the regime such as the African National congress, the world's oldest "liberation movement" (Friedman 2004, 237; see also Kotze 2000, 80), leading to turmoil in the black townships, a series of wildcat strikes, and worldwide condemnation of (and eventually sanctions against) the regime. Although the government of

P. W. Botha initiated what they called "reforms" (1977–84), apartheid remained intact (Kotze 1998). The political conflict increasingly grew more violent.

Under enormous internal and external pressure, however, the South African regime began to change, indicating that even the most entrenched hegemonic order is not immune to at least gradual and limited transformation. First, in 1983, Coloureds and Indians were given limited political representation, a half-measure that was designed to divide the opposition to apartheid but made the negation of political rights of the black majority even more glaring. Second, National Party officials began a series of secret meetings with imprisoned African National Congress (ANC) leaders (e.g., the unpublicized meetings between Justice Minister Coetsee with Nelson Mandela beginning in July 1984); those contacts led eventually to a Botha-Mandela meeting on July 5, 1989. The resignation of Botha a month later gave a negotiated political solution yet another boost. Botha's more flexible successor, F. W. de Klerk, delivered a truly historic speech on February 2, 1990 in which he legalized scores of anti-apartheid organizations, released from prison eight political prisoners (including Mandela), and declared that he intended to negotiate a new, democratic constitution. The door for a postapartheid South Africa was thus opened, although the way toward that goal was still long and arduous.

What led the apartheid regime, one of the most ideologically inflexible and hegemonic polities of the modern era, toward negotiations? In answering this question we might be able to identify the factors needed to undermine, in general, an entrenched hegemonic regime. Although it is difficult to offer the exact weighing of the factors leading to the South African transformation, several elements could be identified as central (not necessarily in order of importance):

1. The internal resistance to the regime became increasingly violent. Some estimates of the number of deaths between 1984–97 put the figure at twenty-three thousand (Kotze, 2000, 86). This internal resistance, escalating since the Soweto uprising of 1976, was supported by outside forces such as the USSR and its allies (the South African Communist Party was an ANC ally). Other external forces supportive of the ANC included the African states (through the Organization of African States [OAS] or especially South Africa's neighboring countries housing guerrilla forces) and other Third World countries. The South African intervention in Angola's civil war proved not only costly in blood and treasure but also eventually unsuccessful (Guelke 1999, 15). Negotiations in which both the United States and the USSR served as honest brokers led to the resolution of the conflict, raising the question of whether similar negotiations could resolve the South African conflict in the same way (Giliomee 1995).

2. The South African economy was in decline as a direct result of the apartheid policy. Banks denied the country badly needed loans. Some companies left the country or refused to follow its discriminatory policies. Trade restrictions were imposed. The sanctions eroded "support for hard-line apartheid policies" (Hauss 2001, 101). To many white South

Africans the future, dominated by economic stagnation, looked bleak. The handwriting was on the wall: increases in the gross domestic product declined from 5.7 percent in the 1960s, to 3.4 percent in the 1970s, and then to 1.5 percent in the 1980s (Giliomee 1995).

3. The apartheid regime generated, by the 1960s and 1970s, a series of international sanctions (Crawford and Klotz 1999; Klotz 1995). Some of these sanctions were introduced by the United Nations (e.g., the 1977 Security Council arms embargo, the 1984 General Assembly definition of *apartheid* as *crime against humanity*) and the European Union. Other actions were taken by individual states although the policies of key countries, particularly the United Kingdom and United States, were often inconsistent. The general direction was that of tightening the screws on the South African regime. Particularly painful was the United States' Comprehensive Anti-Apartheid Act of October 1986, passed despite President Reagan's veto.

4. The South African regime began to lose its legitimacy after the Sharpeville massacre (March 21, 1960) and gradually became a pariah within the international community. On the one hand, the Dutch Reformed Church (the main Afrikaner church) was expelled from the World Alliance of Reformed Churches, and South Africa was expelled from international athletic competitions and increasingly from scientific and academic circles. On the other hand, antiapartheid activists, such as Nelson Mandela and Desmond Tutu, gained worldwide popularity, and antiapartheid films such as *Cry Freedom* became popular all over the world and their heroes (e.g., Steve Biko) became household names. Apartheid became synonymous with unacceptable governmental practices. Most whites, who wanted desperately to be accepted in the Western world, began to understand that the price for readmission into the family of nations would be the deestablishment of hegemonic apartheid.

5. The overall situation amounted to what Hauss called "the hurting stalemate" – the realization that neither side could "win a definitive and decisive victory" (2001, 101). It was clear that only a political solution, that is, a negotiated settlement, could lead to significant improvement. Moreover, at least some key members of the elite realized that the conflict between the government and its opponents "did not necessarily have to be zero-sum" (Kotze 2000, 82).

6. The leadership on both sides was ready (or maybe even forced) to take chances and act decisively in critical moments. Among the opposition leaders, Nelson Mandela, Desmond Tutu, and Joe Slovo pushed for multiracial democracy and insisted that revenge had no place in the new South Africa. Among the ruling whites, and especially the Afrikaners, there was a growing realization that a change was needed, a realization strengthened by the loss of support for the ruling National Party to both left-wing and right-wing parties in the general election of September 1989. The greatest change of all, and possibly the most relevant for the

eventual political transformation, occurred in the thinking of the new prime minister, F. W. de Klerk.

7. Important divides within the white community in South Africa had major impact on the decision to abandon apartheid. By the late 1980s the cabinet was divided between hard-line "securocrats" who still believed in military solutions, and those who believed in negotiations. In 1986 the Dutch Reformed Church declared that apartheid was incompatible with Christian ethics. It was a serious blow to the Afrikaner community as well as to the South African regime, that is, an assault on the hegemonic infrastructure. Moreover, South African academics criticized the regime severely.

8. Changes in the international environment played a significant and probably crucial role in de Klerk's decision to move beyond apartheid. The Soviet Union experienced serious instability during the last months of 1989, making it "easier for President de Klerk to embark on his major initiative" (Guelke 1999, 39). The Soviets apparently told the ANC, which it had supported for years, that the South Africans would have to reach a political accommodation. De Klerk and his associates believed that without Soviet support the ANC would be easier to contain, especially because the Americans promised to pressure both the majority and the minority in South Africa to negotiate in good faith (Giliomee 1995). The end of the Angolan war (1988) and the independence of Namibia meant that the ANC would be deprived of bases within reach of South Africa. The ANC knew full well that it could not defeat the South African regime just as the regime knew that it could not regain its position unless it negotiated.

By the late 1980s the South African regime was at an impasse, its future unclear but unpromising. The hegemonic policies, carried out vigorously for at least four decades by the National Party, were simply not working. Many among the ruling elite, let alone among those out of it, felt that far-reaching transformation was warranted. "Negotiations with black leaders within an apartheid framework had come to a dead end" (Giliomee 1995, 85). This sense led even Prime Minister Botha, the rigid conservative leader of the ruling National Party, to invite the imprisoned Nelson Mandela for a meeting in his office outside Cape Town (July 5, 1989).

Nevertheless, there was a growing sense among members of the white elite that "a change in approach was unlikely under the existing leadership" (Guelke 2005, 155). This feeling, and Botha's ill health, led to the president's resignation and to the selection of F. W. de Klerk as his successor.

Despite his reputation as a hard liner, de Klerk proved to be significantly more flexible than all of his predecessors. He was twenty years younger than Botha, much better educated, and, most importantly, more in touch with the outside world. He was convinced that continued coercion was not the solution and that a new, bold strategy was needed (Giliomee 1995); he also sensed that time was not on the side of the ruling white minority.

The February 2, 1990 speech by de Klerk opened the door to the dismantling of the carefully built hegemonic structure, although there is no indication
that the "messenger" understood this to be the real meaning of the "message"
(not unlike Gorbachev's reforms in the Soviet Union). It has been argued that
de Klerk miscalculated: had he foreseen the outcome, he would have chosen a
different course of action (Guelke 2005, 164; Sparks 1994, 12). What is clear
is that de Klerk envisioned some kind of power-sharing deal based on federal
models, an arrangement that would protect "his" group from others' domination. The ANC wanted a majoritarian, egalitarian, and centralized regime.
Despite the different visions of the political opponents, de Klerk's decision to
release the leaders of the opposition and legalize their organizations, as well
as his commitment to negotiate a new constitution with them, amounted not
merely to public recognition that the existing regime was at the end of its way
but also that a very different governmental design – yet unknown – was about
to be born. The February 2 speech spelled the beginning of the end for racial
hegemony in South Africa while, at the same time, leaving the precise shape of
the alternative rather unclear.

Constitutional negotiations began, dealing with alternative designs for the
new political order and, particularly, the forms of the transitory and permanent
constitutions. The National Party, still governing the republic, and the Mandela-
led ANC intended to move jointly toward a resolution of the deep-seated conflict (Sisk 1995) although it could be argued that while the National Party
wanted minimal transformation, the ANC envisioned what this study calls a
metaconstitutional transformation. The parties recognized their mutual dependence, the need for cooperation and compromise, and the fact that a peaceful
resolution could be produced only in stages. In a series of interim agreements,
the ANC suspended the armed struggle, the government agreed to release all
political prisoners, and the parties committed themselves to political reform
through negotiations. On September 14, 1991, representatives of twenty-seven
political parties and interest groups signed a National Peace Accord. A year
later Mandela and de Klerk committed their parties to establishing a five-year
interim Government of National Unity. Following the election for a new parliament – the first multiracial parliament in the tragic history of the land – the
new body would draft a permanent constitution.

The compromising mood in moving from hegemonic to democratic structure
was evident in this stage already, despite (or possibly because of) the enormous
difficulties. Thus it was agreed that the elected president (eventually Mandela)
would have two vice presidents (one of them was de Klerk). It was also agreed
that any party that won at least 5 percent of the parliamentary seats in the
elections would be represented in the cabinet. Thus the ANC, clearly the largest
political force in South Africa, accepted the idea of power sharing with its bitter
opponents, the National Party, but only for a transition period. The agreement
to postpone the enactment of a permanent constitution by at least five years (i.e.,
to postpone the establishment of majority rule) represented a major concession
by the ANC. It reflected a sense of realism on the part of Mandela and his

associates and an effort (which eventually paid off) to assure the white minority that they could benefit from working together with the black majority.

On the whole, the five-year Government of National Unity had several important achievements. It saw the weakening of radicals, particularly right-wing white extremists among the Afrikaners, as well as the co-optation of regional, ethnic leaders (e.g., Inkata's leader Buthelezi) into the new government. It gave South Africa the necessary breathing time to negotiate a permanent (although changeable) constitution. It restored the country's badly damaged reputation as a respectable member of the international community.

The 142-page Interim Constitution of South Africa was ratified by late 1993 and went into effect in April 1994. The lengthy, complicated document committed the country to a multiparty democracy where all adults had a right to vote and where individual rights without discrimination were guaranteed, a major deviation from the old hegemonic, discriminatory, racist state. It established a bicameral parliament comprised of a four-hundred-member National Assembly and a ninety-member Senate (consisting of ten members representing each of nine provinces). The most important function of the Interim Constitution was to reassure the white minority that it could work with the black majority, and it was achieved by guaranteeing minority representation in the Mandela-led cabinet, institutionalizing property rights, and introducing a measure of decentralization (although not full-fledged federalism).

As expected, the ANC easily won the first democratic elections in South Africa, receiving 62 percent of the vote. The new president, Mandela, managed the difficult transition successfully by including his old opponents, the Afrikaner-led National Party, in the government (albeit without giving up on important issues such as permanent minority privileges), keeping the white civil servants, adopting market-oriented economic policies despite the ANC socialist commitments and its affiliation with the South African Communist Party, and appointing a Truth and Reconciliation Commission for dealing with the country's painful past. What could be called the "Mandela Approach" could be thought of as the only workable strategy for successful transition from a hegemonic to an inclusive regime.

In adopting a conciliatory approach Mandela was able to convince most whites that they could survive in a democratically ruled South Africa in which blacks would forever be the majority.

This attitude was crucial for successfully negotiating the all-important final constitution, a monumental task given the country's deep divisions. These negotiations, based on principles adopted in 1993, were conducted by twenty-six parliamentary and extraparliamentary groups in a forum entitled the Convention for a Democratic South Africa (CODESA). The final constitution was adopted in 1996 and went into effect in February 1997.

The new and final South African constitution continued to reflect the spirit of compromise between the parties, although with one important caveat – the determination of Mandela and his colleagues to establish a majoritarian rule in the country, negating the minority demand for a special and protected status. Implementing the principles adopted by the parties in 1993 (Gloppen 1997, 277–83), a series of important provisions were included in the 1996 constitution:

1. A bicameral parliament was established, although the ANC initially favored a unicameral body to fully reflect the principle of majority rule. The lower house, South Africa's National Assembly, has four hundred members, two hundred elected from a national list and the other two hundred elected proportionally from the provincial lists. The upper house, called the National Council of Provinces, consists of ninety members, ten from each province. The National Party proposed a second chamber in which all political parties with a certain percentage of support would have equal representation (Kotze 2000, 82), thus limiting the majority rule. This proposal was not accepted. Yet the proportionality selection process, bicameralism, and establishment of a central organ to represent the provinces are all reflective of consociational principles.

2. Although South Africa did not establish a full-fledged federal system, nine provinces were recognized. The formation of the provinces was, again, a compromise between the ANC goal of creating "one South Africa" and the autonomous and even separatist goals of some of the whites, especially among the Afrikaners (who failed to establish what they called a "volkstaat") and possibly even among some of the blacks (e.g., the Zulu). Most important, the powers of the provinces as determined by the 1996 constitution are not designed to encourage ethnic politics and "the 'final' constitution paints the picture of a relatively centralized state" by granting the provincial legislatures limited powers in comparison to the national legislature (Gloppen 1997, 223).

3. Most important, from the perspective of this study, the adopted alternative to ethnohegemony was not a consociational deal protecting the minority through complicated power-sharing mechanisms but a system enshrining individual rights for all South Africans, that is, majoritarian liberal democracy. Moreover, some provisions designed to give the minority special protection that were included in the 1993 interim constitution (e.g., giving the National Party the vice presidency) were pointedly dropped from the 1996 constitution, emphasizing its commitment to majority rule. Collective rights were not included in the 1996 constitution, either on a territorial or nonterritorial basis.

Despite the country's huge problems – especially social fragmentation and wrenching poverty among the blacks – the 1999 elections were conducted peacefully. Thabo Mbeki and his ANC won, although they fell just short of the two-third majority that could have given them a free hand in amending the constitution on their own.

In the April 2004 election the ANC further enhanced its majority but President Mbeki hastened to state that the ruling party would not use its overwhelming majority in parliament to change the constitution.

There are several important lessons from the South African case – lessons with wide implications for other hegemonic situations. The first lesson is that there is a danger not merely for democracy but also to stability in a situation where the interests of a particular ethnonational group (as defined by its elite) form the very infrastructure of the political regime and when that regime infrastructure is implemented comprehensively and with no restraint by state institutions.

In the case of South Africa, and in principle in the case of all hegemonic Ethnic Constitutional Orders, the following situation prevails:

Ethnonational Interests = Regime Infrastructure = State Institutions

In a liberal democracy the state takes, at least in principle, a neutral position; its most important role is to facilitate the participation of all citizens in the political process on an equal basis. In an Ethnic Constitutional Order the role of the state is to perpetuate the domination of one ethnonational group. The case of South Africa, due to the unique and flagrant violation of democratic principles, reflects this theoretical linkage more than any other contemporary case, and it is particularly more obvious than cases in which the ethno-national interests are represented by the majority, because the majority can "hide" behind formal democracy.

The second lesson of the South African case is that hegemonic behavior, at least when it is protracted and pervasive as it was in the case of South Africa, might close off the possibilities for power sharing even if power sharing is theoretically sensible and normatively desirable. In the case of South Africa, power sharing lost its appeal and even feasibility because "ethnicity has become for blacks an euphemism for apartheid and hence lacked any legitimacy" (Smooha and Hanf 1992). In a comparative vein it could be argued that hegemony in general closes off alternatives to cooperation and compromise, as proven, for example, in the cases of Cyprus, Sri Lanka, or Yugoslavia, as well as in the case of South Africa.

The third lesson of total hegemony is that, if and when it is finally overwhelmed, a determined effort to repair the fabric of society is needed to avoid large-scale violence. When Mandela took over as South Africa's leader, and even before, he understood the need to create a climate of reconciliation between the races, erasing the notion that it is in the interest of whites to oppress blacks (or vice versa) by using the power of the state. As president, Mandela was trying to create an overarching South African identity, despite (and because of) the deep racial divides. He vigorously supported South African sporting teams, including rugby (Amabokoboko) associated with the Afrikaners and soccer (Bafanabafana), thus generating an all–South African pride. He also visited Verwoerd's widow in Orania, the "homeland" of the right-wing Afrikaners, discussed issues with veteran apartheid supporters and Dutch Reformed Church officials (which endorsed apartheid beyond the mid-1980), and initiated other substantive and symbolic acts across ethnic barriers to promote a climate of tolerance (Kotze 2000, 85–6). Mandela clearly understood the organic link between the demolition of South African hegemony and the ideology of apartheid and the task of building a new, democratic, and above all inclusive South Africa.

One of the lessons that we should *not* draw from the South Africa case is that consociational solutions are, in and of themselves, either wrong in principle (i.e., unjust or undemocratic) or politically unattractive. What the South African case does show is that consociational concessions for minorities that have enjoyed hegemonic positions are going to be resisted by the majority because they will be, understandably, perceived as the perpetuation of the minority's hegemony. In a more general way it might be possible to argue that, ironically, consociational concessions are easier to make to weak minorities (e.g., the Turks in Cyprus) than to strong minorities (e.g. the whites in South Africa).

The results of the South African transformation are not all positive. Poverty prevails, crime is rampant, corruption is widespread, and economic development is slow. Yet the current situation has to be assessed against the pre-1990 apartheid regime and, more speculatively, against what might have happened had apartheid been allowed to survive. There can be no question that the transition, carried out under the most difficult of circumstances, created a racially inclusive democracy. The tight merger that went under the name of apartheid – white (especially Afrikaner) interests, the regime infrastructure (including its ideology and even theology), and all the state's institutions – was dismantled and replaced by a new governmental form that, while very imperfect, holds promise for all South African citizens.

Critics of the settlement reached by the ANC and the white elite argued that while "reconciliation" was pursued, economic apartheid remained untouched. Martin Murray, for example, argued that "the bargain that the white oligarchy has struck is to trade exclusive political power for continued economic advantage" (1994, 4). The question that such criticism raises is what could have been a more promising policy on the part of the ANC and other opponents of apartheid? Could the ANC in the 1990s have argued for massive nationalization of private property? Wouldn't such a policy result in determined resistance by the white minority as well as by the American government, thus condemning the volatile polity to chaos and the transition process to failure? These questions, for which there are no final answers, indicate once again that in the final analysis politics is the art of the possible, not the unilateral achievement of desirable goals. On the plus side, the transition in South Africa led to the establishment of a majoritarian, liberal democracy and a relatively "benign political outcome" (Guelke 2005, 1), infinitely better than the apartheid system that it succeeded.

6

The Reverse Trend

Sustaining or Strengthening Ethnic Hegemony

Effo tainu? [Where did we go wrong?]

Dan Pagis, "Applied Hebrew"

As argued in the thesis statement, some hegemonic states have felt it necessary to change under the pressure of new developments and political pressures of various types. Chapter 4 discusses four cases of gradual and altogether limited changes in deeply divided societies, most of them still under way and not necessarily finalized (e.g., Spain). Chapter 5 deals with more dramatic and profound, metaconstitutional transformation. Yet as argued in the thesis statement, the transformation of entrenched hegemonic systems is by no means preordained, inevitable, or even more likely than not. Hegemonic systems are inherently resistant to pressures designed to change them.

Having covered several cases in which hegemonic polities are transformed into more democratic and inclusive systems in Chapters 4 and 5, analysis of systems that try to sustain or even strengthen their hegemony will be offered in this chapter. The analysis will focus, first, on two political systems (Israel and Turkey) in which hegemonic polities change some of their institutions and practices in a democratic, exclusive direction but do so without changing the essence of their regime. The principle leading these systems is the maintenance of the status quo in essence, while introducing some "cosmetic" changes in a democratic, inclusive direction. In the second part of this chapter, analysis of several systems moving in the direction of relatively mild ethnicization will be offered, and in the third part the analysis of radical ethnicization will be addressed. Thus the entire gamut of theoretical possibilities will be covered.

Mild Democratization: Israel and Turkey

The cases of Israel and Turkey could be looked upon as two situations where mild (or cosmetic) transformation seems to have occurred over the last few years. Although these hegemonic states did not really change their overall constitutional order, which continues to be dominated by one ethnonational group, they have introduced modest changes and have done so in the overall direction of more equality and inclusion. Although the cases of Israel and Turkey are different in many respects, there is some similarity between them in the response to challenges to the system and, particularly important from the perspective of this section, in the way these systems have tried to introduce changes while maintaining the essence of their polities.

The Turkish case is interesting and complex. Modern Turkey was created in the early twentieth century in the wake of the collapse of the Ottoman Empire, a multiethnic polity that contained, in addition to ethnic Turks, Albanians, Bosnians, Circassians, Georgians, Kurds, and other distinct groups (Mutlu 1995). The new republic was "engineered" from above in a hegemonic fashion by determined, cohesive political and military elite. It was "modeled upon the nation-states of Western Europe, particularly France... Ataturk and his associates aimed to create a modern nation-state, an integrated, unitary polity of the French type" (Cornell, 2001, 33–4). Cognizant of Anatolia's cosmopolitan and multiethnic character, the members of the new elite called the new state the "Republic of Turkey" rather than the "Turkish Republic," which would have been a clear misnomer. "The founding elites were attempting to substitute Turkish identity for Ottoman identity" (Ergil 2000b, 52). Ottoman identity was a supra-identity (like Britishness), an identity that allowed other identities to coexist and be recognized; the Ottomans were truly neutral when it came to ethnicity. To many, Turkish identity was ethnic, even though the republic has denied it.

Although the republic seemed to have been fairly successful and quite stable for a while, it is now going through what some analysts have termed a "crisis of national identity" (Ergil 2000a; Waxman 2004). This crisis is characterized by the emergence of a multiplicity of interpretations regarding the essence of the state and society in Turkey and what these ought to be. Most important, the Islamic (Keyman 1995; Waxman 2000), Kurdish (Cornell 2001; Ergil 2000a; Kirisci and Winrow 1997; Mutlu 1995, 1996), and liberal challenges (Argun 1999) to the essence of Turkey are examples of those new voices.

In the case of Turkey, as in that of other counties, national identity was imposed from above by determined elite with minimal popular involvement. It was a case where the state invented the nation. The state's conception of "nation-building" has called for "standardizing the citizenry to make them Turkish in language and nationality, secular in orientation, and obedient to the state," leading to the "denial of diversity" and to the "repression of any other expression of group identity" (Ergil 2000b, 123). Ataturk's invention has developed into an extreme case of a Jacobin regime in a society that was and to a large extent remains deeply divided.

Although challenges to the hegemonic state and its identity were evident immediately upon the establishment of the Republic of Turkey, causing, for example, the large Kurdish uprising (or Sheik Said Rebellion) in 1925 (Kirisci and Winrow 1997, 97–8), these challenges came to the fore of the political scene mostly in the 1980s, an era that witnessed the revival of Kurdish, Alevi, Islamic, and other identities in Turkey (Van Bruinessen 1996; Waxman 2000). Identities that had been ignored, repressed, or marginalized for generations in the name of a shared nationhood based on Turkish nationalism (Salomone 1989, 238) began to be publicly expressed and noticed. The most important challenge to the traditional Turkish conception of the Republic was the ethnic one. While the ideology introduced by Ataturk and his colleagues was that there were no separate ethnic groups within the Turkish nation, although there are fifty-one such groups (Waxman 2004), elements within the largest ethnic group, the Kurds, became more and more assertive and even massively violent. The traditional position of the state, asserting that ethnic minorities did not exist and that all citizens of the republic were simply "Turks," proved unrealistic. This position on behalf of the republic was translated into a powerful prohibition on expressing any ethnic positions (Mutlu 1995), leading to harassment, prosecution, and even imprisonment of those who insisted on emphasizing their Kurdish identity.

Although the Republic of Turkey was home for millions of Kurds, the Kemalist ideology was fundamentally opposed to the recognition of any separate identity on the part of Kurds or other ethnic minorities. While other non-Turkish Muslims living in Turkey (e.g., Albanians, Bosnians, Circassians, Georgians) accepted Turkishness and were assimilated, the Kurds, due to the remoteness of their ancestral homeland and their tribal social structure, remained relatively unaffected by the policy of assimilation (Ergil 2000b, 125). Many of them did not become part of the larger Turkish nation (Saatci 2002, 113). Moreover, although many other minorities were immigrants, the Kurds were an indigenous group (Cornell 2001, 35). Through the years the Kurdish population grew dramatically, and it is now about thirteen million people or even more (Icduygu, Romano, Sirkeci 1999, 1001; Mutlu 1996; *Economist*, June 12, 2004).

While the republic allowed Kurds, as individuals, to rise to any prominent position within the state, and several Turkish presidents and prime ministers were Kurds, those Kurds could rise to prominence only as "Turks." The state did not have a problem with Kurds as individuals, as long as these Kurds did not insist on their Kurdishness. Simply put, "the Republican Turkish state denied that the Kurds existed" (Yegen 1999, 555). The "Turkish state discourse enunciated the exclusion of Kurdish identity" (Yegen 1996). Although the position of the state was highly consistent and even principled, and it did not discriminate against individuals on the basis of ethnicity, by ignoring any kind of group identity this position was not sustainable either internally or (particularly) internationally. The Kurdish guerrilla campaign against the Turkish military, beginning in the 1980s, and the political activism by the Kurds in Southeastern Turkey and abroad (e.g., among Kurds in Germany) kept the "Kurdish Question" on the agenda.

Although it is not easy to determine with considerable precision the reasons for the recent emergence of challenges to the hegemonic Turkish state and to its interpretation of national identity, several explanations come to mind. First, the ongoing violent conflict in Turkey (especially after the initiation of the Kuridistan Workers' Party [PKK] campaign in 1984), costing the lives of at least thirty thousand people, made the denial of the existing problem seem unrealistic and detached from any factual basis. Second, as argued in the thesis statement (introduction), in a globalized world the Turkish position of not only denying the existence of a "problem" but also rejecting the need for a solution that would be acceptable to the minority (or some within it) became untenable. In a globalizing world, an increasing number of Turks had begun to feel that their system, characterized by a strong interventionist role of the military in political affairs and the total denial of Kurdish identity, simply did not conform to the worldwide (and especially European) democratic political culture and rights discourse. Third, and more poignantly, with the growing interest of Turkey in joining the European Union, increasing pressure was put on the state to liberalize its laws, institutions, and practices in regard to the Kurdish minority and otherwise. Finally, the Kurds' conditions, which Icduygu et al. (1999, 991) called "an environment of insecurity," and that had material and nonmaterial aspects, had created long-term instability within Turkey.

The traditional rules, regulations, and laws of the Republic of Turkey against all things Kurdish were extensive. The Turkish government emphasized linguistic homogeneity as a way of assimilating non-Turks. Not only were Kurds referred to as "mountain Turks," but also limitations were put on speaking and particularly teaching Kurdish, publishing in Kurdish was illegal, broadcasting was banned, and so forth. Notably, the use of the Kurdish language was strictly prohibited in all state institutions, including the schools and the courts. Yet in the 1990s these prohibitions, including linguistic suppression, began to fall to the side. Denying the Kurdish factor became more and more difficult. In April 1991, Ozal's government lifted the ban on the use of the Kurdish language (Gunter 1997, 62). Its successor, the Demirel government, lifted the ban on giving children Kurdish names; it also allowed the publication of a Kurdish newspaper (ibid., 67). Yet while these limited measures were adopted, the overall repressive policy toward the Kurdish minority remained intact, especially in the face of the intense campaign against the PKK.

In February 2000 the PKK declared a unilateral ceasefire, following the capture and conviction of its leader, Abdullah Ocalan. This development enabled the republic to adopt a more liberal approach to the Kurdish issue, responding to both the improved security situation and to the intense pressure by the European Union. In 2002 parliament passed legislation eliminating the ban on books, publications, and television programs in Kurdish. Although Kurds remained unrecognized as a minority, recognition that would have undermined the Kemalist ideology of the republic altogether, this was the beginning of a trend toward recognizing the cultural rights of the sizeable Kurdish minority. It seems that Turkey had begun to accept, willy-nilly and belatedly, its own heterogeneity.

This development was quite revolutionary, given that the Kemalist ideology was, in theory, "civic." The theory was that everyone who was a Turkish citizen, regardless of his or her ethnic background, was to be equal and that the state was to be not merely neutral toward ethnicity but even refuse to recognize its existence. Yet many citizens, particularly Kurds, have rejected this construct, believing that it deprived them of their ethnic identity or that it supported, in effect, Turkish nationalist interests. Some citizens of the republic wanted to go beyond the existing national identity: they supported an ethnically based Turkish national identity that sought to promote aggressively the interests of the Turkish people wherever they may be (e.g., in Cyprus or in several of the former Soviets republics). A third position in regard to identity came from the Islamists, people who believed that the Kemalist project of Westernization and secularization was wrong from its inception. The Islamists rose to power in the 1990s, triggering in 1997 an intervention by the military that forced the Welfare Party from office. Yet this radical action did not end the challenge to the Kemalist project from Islamic quarters.

In general, it seems that in the struggle between the hegemonic state, determined to impose its Kemalist unitary notions on a traditional and diverse society, and the forces that demand more inclusive ethnic or religious recognition, there is a trend toward more recognition of diversity, more openness toward that which is not secular and "Turkish." This trend was strengthened when Turgut Ozal, who served as premier and president in the 1980s and 1990s (and whose own grandmother was a Kurd), broke the long-term taboo on using the term *Kurd* by referring to the inhabitants of eastern Anatolia as Kurds.

At the same time, the changes that have been enacted in the direction of liberalization and inclusion are relatively minor and have not been always implemented consistently. Thus, in July 2003, Parliament amended the Census Law to allow parents to give Kurdish names to their children. Yet numerous reports indicate that the law has not been implemented systematically by local authorities in different parts of the country. Obstacles were also evident in implementing laws from 2002 designed to allow broadcasts in Kurdish; such broadcasts remain limited (Kinzer 2006). On June 9, 2004, the first-ever broadcast in the most widely spoken Kurdish dialect, Kurmandji, occurred. The teaching of Kurdish and other languages in private courses has also been on the agenda. In view of the state's long-held ideological position, the stakes in regard to the Kurdish issue are high: Ergil believes that "the inclusion of the issue of Kurdish identity on the political agenda would mean changing the Turkish definition of the nation" (2000b, 130).

Although Turkey is not about to become a binational Turkish-Kurdish state or even a multicultural society in the vein of Canada, it is evident that under enormous internal and especially international pressures its regime is seeking ways to liberalize. At the same time, although the state lost its monopoly over the right to decide exclusively on all issues of national identity, it is still by far the most powerful actor in the political field, and it still views itself as a unitary actor. But just as the state-run Turkish Radio and Television Corporation today is not the only voice available publicly, so is the situation in other areas: there are alternative voices.

Liberal changes in Turkey have been greatly impacted by the balance of power between state and society. Traditionally the Turkish civil society was weak, totally dependent on the state and deferential toward it. The typical attitude of the citizenry was to accept quietly the actions of the state. Today, however, it is quite common to criticize the state and its ideology and to publicly question its institutions. This tendency reflects the liberalization of the Turkish society. If the state accepts this new reality and responds to international pressures and expectations, it might accelerate its democratization and eventually fully recognize the cultural rights of minorities, particularly the Kurds. Some observers believe that there is now "a window of opportunity...to press forward with reforms on human rights and democratization" (Cornell 2001, 44). The Turkish government seems to have come to the realization that many of its oppressive policies are simply counterproductive and must be changed (Van Bruinessen 1996, 7). Cultural and linguistic grievances are now dealt with in a much more liberal manner. In addition, the Turkish government has been involved in large-scale investment in Eastern Anatolia (Radu 2001, 58), having recognized the link between economic conditions and ethnic consciousness.

The complexity of liberalizing the Republic of Turkey and the duality of advancement and retreat at one and the same time is evident in the case of instruction in the Kurdish language. In all public schools in the country the language of instruction has always been exclusively Turkish. Yet, under pressure from the European Union in 2004 the Turkish government authorized the opening of eight private schools dedicated to the teaching of Kurdish. Within the context of modern Turkish history this was a substantial step because until 1991 it was illegal to speak Kurdish, let alone teach it.

The issue of the private schools has become a hot potato. Turkish nationalists opposed the move, viewing it as emboldening Kurdish separatism. Many Kurds saw it as an insufficient, halfhearted step. They argued that Kurdish must be taught in public schools as part of the regular curriculum and pointed out that most Kurds were too poor to afford private schools. Moreover, as in other areas, the implementation of policies lagged behind the law. Thus it was pointed out that although it took the government two to three months to approve most private schools, it took it up to eighteen months to grant permits for the opening of Kurdish-language schools. In early August 2005 the directors of the eight schools announced that they intend to close them down.

In the final analysis, the Kurdish issue and its disposition might decide the future of Turkey, and particularly the quality of its democracy. The chances of Turkey being admitted into the European Union will increase immeasurably if it can resolve the Kurdish issue (Somer 2004). It seems that Turkey's political elite has concluded that the best way of resolving the Kurdish issue is through a combination of moving toward a more liberal-democratic regime (with emphasis on fundamental rights such as free expression), some recognition of the "Kurdishness" of millions of Turkey's citizens, and economic development for the southeastern regions of Anatolia.

In the Israeli case, as in that of Turkey, there is evidence of a trend toward the establishment of a more liberal and more inclusive political system in terms of majority-minority relations. At the same time, the essence of the hegemonic polity in which the majority dominates has not changed substantially and is unlikely to do so in the foreseeable future. There are, of course, important differences between the two systems. The most important among them from the perspective of this volume are (1) Israel was established from the beginning as a democracy (albeit not a liberal democracy: Peleg 2000), and Turkey was not; (2) Israel immediately established an Arab-language school system, and in Turkey Kurdish was in effect an illegal language until 1991; and (3) Israel was established as an ethnocentric polity, a "Jewish Republic," and Turkey was established as state-centric, meaningfully called the Republic of Turkey.

Although the differences between Turkey and Israel are many and obvious, the similarities between them as majority hegemonies are remarkable. First, both the Republic of Turkey and the State of Israel were invented polities, the product of elaborate ideologies promoted by willful Founding Fathers and ruling elites. Second, both polities emphasized what might be called "Statism." Ben-Gurion's "mamlachtiut" (Dowty 2000; Medding 1990; Peleg 1998a; Yanai 1989) and Ataturk's "Turkish" nationhood were remarkably similar in claiming a supreme status for the state. Third, both Ataturk's Turkey and Ben-Gurion's Israel had a major ethnic "problem" that has persisted and in some ways worsened through the years: a large minority that did not have a place in the state conception and within the national identity. Fourth, neither Israel nor Turkey has been able to resolve their respective religious dilemma within their respective majorities, although both sought "statist" solutions: Israel attempted to solve the issue of religion by not only recognizing the Orthodox religious establishment but also formally granting it power over the religious and personal matters of all Jews (including secular ones), and Turkey tried to resolve its religious problem by declaring itself secular. Both diametrically different approaches failed in neutralizing the impact of religion as a political force. In the case of Israel, this failure has a direct impact on the state's ability to deal with its ethnic problem.

In analyzing the Israeli political system, as in analyzing that of Turkey, it is important to look, however briefly, at the fundamental ideology that led to the establishment of Israel (Zionism), the foundational decisions made in 1948 and later (in the formative years of the State of Israel), the developments since then, the challenges that the Israeli polity is facing now, and its response to them.

Israel is a product of Zionism, an ideological movement that emerged among European Jews at the latter part of the nineteenth century (Hertzberg 1997). Although it is forever associated with the name of Theodor Herzl's *The Jewish State* (1988, orig. 1896), several versions of Zionism developed between the early 1880s, when committed Zionists began arriving in Palestine, and 1948, when Israel was established as a sovereign state. There were important differences between Zionists of different stripes over issues of strategy and tactics; however, they all aimed at establishing a Jewish state, where Jews would be a clear majority. Most of them also emphasized the Jewish character of the state to be – in language (Hebrew), culture, location (Eretz Israel), and so forth. So when Israel came into being, after a long and bloody struggle with the Arabs of Palestine and beyond, it was quite easy for the ruling party, Mapai, and its domineering leader, David Ben-Gurion, to establish what was in effect an ethnically based Jewish republic (Peleg 1998a, 235).

Even a cursory review reveals that all alternatives to ethnic hegemonism were rejected and that, furthermore, none was even seriously considered. Although Ben-Gurion talked about establishing a socialist Israel, Mapai deserted any serious commitment to comprehensive egalitarianism long before 1948 (Sternhell 1995). Equally, even though Ben-Gurion wanted a Jewish state, he rejected the idea of a religiously Jewish state based on the Halacha. Finally, and most relevant from the perspective of this study and that of Israel's dilemmas at present, Ben-Gurion and most of his associates did not want to establish a liberal democracy, based on full civil equality in law and in practice, and enshrined in a written constitution and a comprehensive bill of rights. Israel's Founding Fathers preferred organic to civic nationalism (ibid., 19–22) as an overall design for nation building; their clear preference for an ethnocentric order rather than a liberal democracy was reflected both in the overall character of the regime and in key decisions that determined the trajectory of the constitutional order for generations.

Israel's decision not to enact a constitution is an early example of the strong illiberal inclinations of the Founding Fathers and Ben-Gurion in particular (Shapiro 1996a, 1996b). A short time after the 1949 election for a Constituent Assembly, a body elected specifically to adopt a constitution, Ben-Gurion suddenly announced that there was no need for a constitution. Evidence suggests that the venerable leader acted so as to enable himself and his associates maximum leeway. He wanted to govern with no constitutional restrictions to take whatever action he deemed necessary to establish the state as an ethnocentric entity. Most specifically, the absence of a constitution, a bill of rights, or an equality clause in Israel's constitutional framework enabled the government to maintain military rule in areas inhabited by Arabs and to initiate large-scale expropriation of Arab lands (Jiryis 1969; Lustick 1980b).

The absence of a binding constitution enshrining equality enabled the government to ignore the commitment made in the country's declaration of independence to "maintain complete social and political equality" among the citizens. This created a particularly dangerous situation from the perspective of erecting a truly liberal democracy because the declaration, laws that followed its adoption, and practically all the state's institutions were fully committed to establishing a Jewish state; the absence of any legal barrier to the control of the majority was ominous to the minority and to the quality of the country's democracy in general.

The history of the State of Israel since 1948 indicates that while the state has developed many democratic institutions (e.g., a regularly elected parliament, a relatively transparent executive, an independent judiciary, and a free press) as well as democratic practices (e.g., ability to access the High Court of Justice, demonstrate peacefully, and publicly express opinion), in many ways Israel remains an illiberal democracy with inherent flaws. The single most problem-atical aspect of the Israeli regime has been and remains the treatment of members of the Arab minority, and the minority as such, by the state. Thus not only were Israeli Arabs under military government control between 1948–66 but also since the establishment of the state they have lost control over most of their land, ending up with the control of merely 3.5 percent of state land despite their 18 percent share of the population. Until now, Arabs could not purchase land in large parts of Israel that had been acquired by organizations such as the Jewish Agency or the Jewish National Fund.

As in Turkey, there is in Israel widespread, but no unanimous, recognition that the equalization of conditions of all citizens (i.e., a move in the direction of liberal democracy) might be needed. Yet this recognition rarely results in real change "on the ground" and is equally opposed to by powerful forces. Thus after the riots of October 2000 resulted in the death of thirteen Arabs, the government issued a formal commitment to invest heavily in the Arab sector. To date, however, no dramatic change has occurred.

One of the most important governmental institutions that has attempted to liberalize the Israeli society and make it more inclusive has been the High Court of Justice. The court's rulings have met with some success, although the court avoided dealing with fundamental problems relating to the "essence" of the state and in some cases its decisions were ignored. Thus in March 2000, the High Court of Justice ruled in the case of Katzir, a communal settlement in northern Israel that denied land to an Arab family, stating that Katzir, the Jewish agency that controlled Katzir's land, and the State of Israel that transferred the land to the Jewish agency could not "allocate State land . . . on the basis of discrimination between Jews and non-Jews" (*Bagatz 6698/95 Qaadan vs. ILA, Katzir and Others*). Although the court established the principle of equality, its decision was narrowly construed. It left to the discretion of the respondents – the Jewish agency, Katzir, and ultimately the State of Israel – whether or not to implement the decision, stated that the court decision does not apply to past practices (where discrimination was rampant), and it offered several escape routes that could facilitate future discrimination. In other words, the historic 2000 decision did not amount to reversal of the policy of "judaizing" the country by transferring the control of land from Arabs to Jews (Yiftachel and Kedar 2000).

In terms of services given by the state to the Arab minority, as opposed to those given to the Jewish majority, a similar pattern exists: there is a long history of discrimination, and there are some minor improvements (Peleg 2004b, 423). Discrimination could be shown, in addition to the important area of land control and regional development, especially in terms of housing, civil service hiring, governmental allocations to municipalities, and education (as shown in a series of reports by the Arab-Jewish organization Sikkuy, the Arab legal advocacy organization Adalah, and in numerous other places). The authors of one report, *After the Rift*, concluded that the Arab education system is "a tool for ideological control in the hands of the State" (Rabinowitz et al. 2000, 40).

The analytical framework included in this volume suggests that Israel, like Turkey, is an archetype of a majority-hegemonic system. Since its establishment it has maintained strong distinction between Jews and non-Jews, particularly Arabs. The Israeli regime does not meet the strict definition of Western liberal democracy either in the sense of equal treatment to all individuals or in the sense of state neutrality toward all social groups. At the same time, the state has granted all citizens, including members of the minority, a substantial package of liberties and freedoms traditionally associated with liberal democracy. In terms of group rights, the Israeli state has been thoroughly identified with Jewish nationality and religion – although there are deep disagreements within the Israeli Jewish public as to the desired essence of the state, often characterized as Kulturkampf (Peleg 1998c).

In regard to the Arab minority in Israel three generalizations could be formulated: (1) the policy of the state toward the minority has been discriminatory; (2) some of the discriminatory policies have been moderated over the last decade or so; and (3) there has not been a decisive move toward the elimination of all discriminatory practices, a move that will demand the erasure of the ethnonational character of the state.

Among examples for moderating the discriminatory policies there are several judicial rulings by the High Court of Justice (e.g., the Qaadan/Katzir decision mentioned before, a ruling in favor of using Arabic road signage in mixed towns and thus recognizing the status of Arabic as one of Israel's official languages), the advancement of Arabs as civil servants (e.g., the recent nomination of an Arab judge to Israel's High Court of Justice), government's commitment to equalize financial allocations to Arab local municipalities, a 2003 decision to allow two Arab nationalist parties to run in the general elections, and so forth.

Although these are significant steps toward greater liberalization, they do not amount to a fundamental or long-term transformation of the character of the State of Israel as a "Jewish Republic." The country will continue to witness a tug-of-war between the dual commitment of most Israelis to both Jewishness and democracy, however these "essentially contested concepts" are precisely defined by the warring camps (Gallie 1962; Peleg 2002–3). The conservative, nationalist forces within the Israeli body politics will insist on maintaining the ethnonationalist infrastructure that was established in 1948 and possibly even strengthen it. The more liberal forces within the polity will push toward more inclusive, accommodationist policies: the nomination of Arabs to positions of responsibility in all parts of the Israeli bureaucracy, the establishment of aggressive antidiscriminatory policies and even institutions, the enactment of a comprehensive equality clause and possibly a full-fledged constitution with a bill of rights, the adoption of a symbolic language that might generate a sense of belonging among non-Jews, and so forth.

Israel today is facing not only a complicated peace process with the Palestinians outside and inside its borders but also a sharp division within its dominant ethnonational group. This division has been conceptualized alternatively as that between "Jewishness" and "Israeliness" (Aronoff and Atlas 1998), a

Kulturkampf (Peleg 1998c), a clash between different "ethnic" and "territorial" imperatives (Barzilai and Peleg 1994), and so forth. In regard to the dynamic process of transforming the Israeli polity from a hegemonic and ethnically exclusive system to an inclusive liberal democracy, it is useful to analyze contemporary Israel in terms of the country's ethnonationalist agenda versus its liberal-democratic agenda.

Israeli ethnonationalists would like to see the State of Israel pursuing what they view as a "Jewish" agenda, an agenda based on the presumed interest of Israel's Jewish majority. Among the items on the ethnonationalist agenda there is the continuation of Israel's control over the Occupied Territories or significant parts of these areas, maintaining the preferential position of Jews within Israel emphasizing the Jewishness of the state rather than its Israeliness in all respects (including the state's symbols), and so forth. The liberal-democratic agenda among Israeli Jews is rather different. It includes a two-state solution (with the assumption and hope that it would ease Arab-Jewish relations in Israel proper), steps toward the equalization of the conditions of the Arab minority in Israel (at least as individuals if not as a group), the liberalization of the Israeli society in regard to discriminated groups such as homosexuals or women, and even symbolic steps toward the inclusion of non-Jews as equals (e.g., by adding inclusive verses to the Israeli national anthem, recognizing the exodus of Arabs from Israel in 1948, marking destroyed Palestinian villages). In general, members of the first group adopt ethnic nationalism by viewing Israel's mission as implementing a Jewish agenda that includes the interests of non-Israeli Jews, wherever they may live. Liberal democrats, however, tend to be more sympathetic toward civic nationalism, even if their position is not purely a-national: they view the State of Israel as the state of all of its citizens, even if most of them still see it as a "Jewish state" in terms of its overall character or even in terms of its immigration policies. It is, however, important to realize that this theoretical distinction between two types of Israeli-Jewish nationalists is, in reality, more a matter of degree than of kind. In the final analysis even liberal-democratic Zionists are committed to a national agenda, even if it is defended by them as a form of "liberal nationalism" (Tamir 1993).

Although most press reports on Israel focus on the evolving situation in the Occupied Territories (West bank and Gaza Strip), the battle royal in Israel is about the essence of the state today and in the future rather than about the final status of the relationships between Israelis and West Bankers. Many liberal Israelis would like to see Israel transformed into "a truly democratic state in which all of its citizens are equal under the law . . . a state that belongs not only to its Jewish majority but to its Arab minority, whose members are still treated as second-class citizens" (Hadar 1999, 77). Such a transformation would be momentous. To date the steps in that direction have been relatively modest.

As could be expected, in both Israel and Turkey one can easily find powerful forces opposed to any fundamental changes in the well-established majority-hegemonic system. The language used by those who oppose fundamental changes in Israel is often ideological. Some have argued for the seemingly contradictory "liberal nationalism" (Tamir 1993). Others have used more blatant nationalistic, collectivistic arguments (Hazony 2000; Steinberg 2000) or even religious ones. Analysts have noticed the essence of the struggle as being between particularistic and universalistic forces (Peleg 1998a, 2003a; Yadgar 2002).

It seems that in view of the countervailing pressures within the Israeli society – further recognition of the rights of the minority and the equalization of rights of its members versus maintaining the existing order and even strengthening it – in the foreseeable future changes will be fairly limited. Yet the general direction in Israel, as in Turkey, will be toward greater inclusion. In view of counterpressures, occasional reversal in this overall trend could be expected.

In Turkey the engine of change has been outside pressure, the pressure in Israel has been almost exclusively internal. Liberal forces have been led by academics and, mostly, by the High Court of Justice. Yet even the court's support for a liberal agenda on the nationalist front has not been unanimous or unqualified. Thus in May 2006, the High Court of Justice upheld by the narrowest of margins (6:5) the Citizenship and Entry law that bans the right of Palestinians in Israel who marry a non-Israeli, often a West Banker, to bring their spouse into Israel proper. In making the ruling, the High Court of Justice asserted that the security of the State, or even demographic considerations, is superior to individual rights. The decision highlighted the difficulty in liberalizing the Israeli polity insofar as the rights of the minority are concerned.

Mild Ethnicization: Estonia and Latvia

Over the last few years a number of countries have gone through what might be looked upon as a process of purposeful ethnicization. Rather than moving in the direction of more inclusion, the dominant national or ethnic majority in these countries has adopted policies designed to marginalize their minorities. At the same time, in practically all of these countries there is an ongoing struggle between a push toward hegemony of the dominant group versus pressures to maintain the openness of the system to all its members.

The cases of the Baltic republics of Estonia and Latvia in the post-Soviet era demonstrate clearly the dilemmas faced by the political system in deeply divided societies and the options open for such systems. Although the Estonians and the Latvians have lived on their lands for hundreds of years, they never enjoyed independence until the end of World War I. Yet this independence was short lived and by 1940 these newly established republics were conquered and annexed by the Soviet Union.

During the time of Soviet control, which the Estonians and the Latvians bitterly resented and resisted, a large number of non-Baltic Soviet citizens, ethnically Russian for the most part, moved into these two republics, changing the demographic balance in a pro-Russian direction. At the beginning of World War II the Russian population of Estonia accounted for a mere 8.2 percent of the total population and somewhat less than 10 percent in Latvia (Johns 2002, 108). By the time independence was reestablished, 30 percent of Estonia's inhabitants were Russians (Kirch, Kirch, and Tuisk 1993, 174), and 34 percent of all Latvia's inhabitants were Russians (Zvidrin 1992, 364). By and large, the Russian population did not assimilate (Johns 2002, 109). The vast majority of the ethnic Russians in Estonia settled in cities such as Tallinn and Sillamae (Ott et al. 1996, 39), and in Latvia the Russians constituted the majority in four out of the seven largest cities, including Riga (Zvidrin 1992, 365). Thus history and demographics made an ethnic confrontation between the "restored" Baltic States and their Russian populations almost inevitable.

Some scholars concluded, in the early post-Soviet era, that "Estonia and Latvia must face the fact that the injustices inflicted on them have turned them into bi-national states" and that "there is no way of turning back the clock" (Tamir 1993, 159). Yet those old-new states were determined to change their situation, rejected binationalism, and, in the language of this study, resolved to ethnicize their polities.

In dealing with the Russian minorities in their midst, the Latvians and the Estonians had a dilemma. On the one hand, they wanted to restore their dominance within their national states, viewing the Russian minorities as dangerous for their future and as historically unjust. On the other hand, they had to accept these minorities as a fact of life that cannot be erased through harsh and violent action, particularly in the face of the presence of the huge Russian state to their east and the enormous pressure of the European Union for dealing with the minorities fairly. In between these countervailing pressures, Estonia and Latvia seem to have adopted what might be called a policy of mild ethnicization. Moreover, the outside pressures and even some internal forces seem to have produced a more inclusive policy in recent years than the one established in the immediate postindependence era.

In the case of Estonia, the early post-Soviet period looked auspicious from the perspective of interethnic relations. The overall policy of the new regime was that of Estonization, with the aim being the restoration of the situation between the world wars and reversal of the Russification policy of the Soviet Union. In regard to citizenship, the single most important element of ethnicization, the Estonian parliament decided in 1992 not to grant citizenship to nonethnic Estonians. The law recognized the citizenship of pre-1940 citizens of Estonia (when about 92 percent were ethnic Estonians) as well as their descendants. Other inhabitants of the country, mostly ethnic Russians that immigrated after 1940 and their descendants, were not recognized as citizens and thus became stateless "aliens" (O'Connor 2003). The minority was, thus, divided and thereby easier to dominate. The constitution adopted later that year in a referendum (where many of the Russians could not vote) obliged the state to preserve the Estonian nation, culture, and language.

The issue of citizenship for ethnic Russians has become highly controversial because the law turned long-time Estonian residents with Soviet citizenship into "aliens" if they happened to be non-Estonian by ethnicity. To become citizens of the Republic of Estonia such aliens now needed to reside on a permanent basis in Estonia for at least five years, earn a steady income, and pledge their loyalty to the state and its character (which is, according to the constitution, "Estonian"). A special civics exam, in Estonian, was added later to the naturalization requirements, making it even more difficult than before to become a citizen. Under the new circumstances, many Russians emigrated. Of those who remained, over 40 percent remained stateless (Yiftachel and Ghanem, 2004a). This segment of the population tended to hold jobs with lower status.

A similar situation evolved in Latvia. Stringent citizenship laws required extensive language examination, a ten-year residency, and evidence of knowing the Latvian constitution (Johns 2002). The state made concrete efforts to establish linguistic control and marginalize the Russian language. It banned Russian on street signs and as the tongue of governmental transactions. It also required that only 25 percent of all televised programs may be in a language other than Latvian (O'Connor 2003).

The ethnic commitment of Estonia has been reflected in policies regarding many areas. Thus civil service was restricted to Estonian citizens (Article 30), forcing all Russians out. The political arena was taken over exclusively by Estonians. During the first ten years of independence not even one non-Estonian was appointed as a minister until in 2002 an Estonian of Tatar origin joined the government (Pettai and Hallik 2002, 517, 527). Moreover, the language policy became a tool for ethnic domination. The overall goal of the policy has been to make Estonian the dominant language and to relegate Russian to merely another foreign language. Estonian is the only language recognized now in most public spheres, such as street signage, education, and government offices and activities (including parliament and local councils). Proficiency in Estonian became not only a requirement for citizenship but also in many situations a precondition for professional employment. The minority language, Russian, is recognized only in areas where the Russians are the majority.

While the special status of the majority was thus enshrined in the constitutional order, minority rights were not recognized. There is no official church in Estonia, and the constitution states specifically that "there is no state church" (Article 40). The state recognizes the Protestant holidays but not the Orthodox Russian ones; Estonia's Orthodox Church is not recognized by the state. Russians tend to be underrepresented in parliament, and they are always in opposition.

Despite this strong ethnic tilt after the restoration of independence and the determination of the Estonian leadership to openly adopt a model of ethnic control (Lustick 1979, 1980a; Pettai and Hallik 2002), over the last several years there have been significant changes. Most of these have tended to blunt the edge of aggressive ethnicization. Thus, for example, the naturalization of Russians has now become easier through language acquisition, military service, or contribution to the Estonian society (Berg 2002; Pettai and Hallik 2002). Although ethnicization has been the overall policy, it seems to have been moderated over the last several years. Moreover, Estonian ethnicization has never been accompanied by violence, and it has become increasingly influenced by the expectations and pressures of outside forces, including the European Union and the international human-rights community.

Some scholars have argued that the control model and unilateral Estonian measures have worked well for post-Soviet Estonia (Pettai and Hallik 2002). However, one could argue that consociational mechanisms and intercommunal negotiations could have made the transition from Soviet rule to Estonian independence smoother and the quality of Estonian democracy higher.

Over the last few years, Estonia initiated what is often referred to as the "integration program," despite opposition from nationalist circles. The overall goal of the program is to create a stable status for Estonian minorities, especially the Russians, and to progress beyond the mono-ethnic state building of the early 1990s. By mid-1993, initiatives had been taken by the Estonian government to improve ethnic relations, including the enactment of the Law on Cultural Autonomy (Blum 2001, 107). This program was approved by the Estonian government on February 10, 1998 and by the parliament four months later (Pettai and Hallik 2002, 521). The purpose of the program was to move toward closer relationships between the majority and the minority, a goal reflected also in an interim "Action Plan" adopted by the Estonian government in 1999.

These documents reveal that the Estonian approach is to focus on the individual and not on the collective rights of groups, namely that the Russian minority will not be granted such rights. These documents speak of the common societal core, but it is clear that this core is to be based on the Estonian language and culture. The Action Plan talks explicitly on "Estonian cultural predominance": "Whereas society may become multicultural, the state is and shall remain Estonia-centered" (Pettai and Hallik 2002, 523).

The integration policy was further "liberalized" in a March 2000 version, entitled "State Program: Integration in Estonian Society 2000–2007." The newer document speaks about "cultural pluralism," and it recognizes Estonia's cultural diversity. The document emphasizes "the opportunities for the preservation of cultural and ethnic distinctiveness" by different minorities. Assimilation of minority culture into Estonian culture was eliminated as a goal for integration and even the predominance of Estonian culture disappeared, as well as the Estonian dominance of the state.

Yet it is still unclear as to what these changes mean beyond the desire of the Estonian government to respond to outside pressures. Pettai and Hallik conclude that "the Estonian language continued to be the key to integration." There is no question that Estonia is and intends to remain an ethnic state, not a neutral civic state. At the same time, even scholars sympathetic to the ethnic ideal are talking recently about "a process of re-equilibration," while recognizing that despite "liberalization through the creation of an integration program and even the proclamation of a policy of 'multiculturalism,' this bedrock ethnic view remained" (Pettai and Hallik, 2002 524–5).

An examination of the policies stemming from the integration program reveals that the teaching of Estonian to non-Estonians has been the "centerpiece" of the program, thus helping increase the dominance of the Estonian language in the country. Support for minority projects has been limited and even declining, and some have seen it as merely "symbolic or passive commitment to minority rights" (Blum 2001, 108). Data about the rate of naturalization among Russians in Estonia indicate that more Russians are becoming citizens. At the same time, the number of Russians leaving Estonia declined. These figures indicate that integration might be working.

The developments and trends in Latvia have been generally similar to those in Estonia. The immediate post-Soviet era saw the non-Latvians losing their citizenship, public and government jobs becoming the exclusive province of ethnic Latvians, and other such elements of radical ethnicization. Russian and European pressures have clearly moderated some policies. Thus facing that external pressure in 1995, the Latvian parliament amended the constitution to allow naturalization of noncitizens, and in May 2002 the parliament dropped a provision that required candidates for political office to speak a high level of Latvian. Reports indicated that there seems to be "less and less hostility" between the groups in recent years (*New York Times*, August 4, 2002).

It seems that in the case of Estonia, the state "was able to reconcile its so-called 'ethnic democracy' with the EU Copenhagen criteria requiring the 'respect for and protection of minorities'" (Smith 2003, 1). In the immediate postindependence era Estonia and Latvia adopted and implemented what might be called an aggressive ethnicization policy, however they have moved in the late 1990s toward a more moderate policy based on some recognition of minority rights, multiculturalism, and possibly even some form of autonomy.

The Estonian and Latvian cases have implications for this study in general. These cases demonstrate that it might be possible to identify a middle ground between the hegemonic impulse to ethnicize the state to the highest degree possible and the need to recognize the rights of existing minorities. Although the desire of the Estonian and Latvian majorities to restore their dominance within their newly established states could easily be justified, particularly by taking into account the circumstances under which they have been annexed by the USSR, the need for some measure of protection for the Russian minority is self-evident. In this balance of countervailing forces, the Baltic States seem now to have moved toward a "EU-sponsored multiculturalist paradigm" (Smith 2003, 31) and improved majority-minority relations.

Radical Ethnicization: Sri Lanka and Rwanda

In the first two sections of his chapter we examined cases in which hegemonic systems moved in a relatively mild manner toward the creation of more inclusive polities (the cases of Turkey and Israel) or toward somewhat more ethnicized and exclusive polities (the cases of Estonia and Latvia). In Chapters 4 and 5 we have already dealt extensively with political systems that have moved away from hegemonism, either gradually or metaconstitutionally. In this section, attention is being turned toward cases in which already hegemonic systems adopt even more radical forms of hegemonism. Despite their similarities, the cases presented here are different in character. In the case of Sri Lanka we witness a liberal democracy that has moved first toward mild hegemonism and then toward radical hegemonism, implemented through majoritarianism. In the case of Serbia (or the Former Yugoslavia), particularly under Slobodan Milosevic, we witness a country with a tradition of recognizing the rights of its minorities move toward the negation of those rights and ending up with ethnic cleansing on a significant scale. In the case of Rwanda of 1994, we had a binational or biethnic country adopting a policy of full-fledged genocide; it is a case of radical hegemonism. Although these three cases might look quite different, Sri Lanka, Serbia, and Rwanda share in common the determination of the majority to eliminate the minority politically or even physically.

The case of Sri Lanka is one in which a country starting with at least some of the liberal-democratic tradition of its colonial master (by adopting, in effect, Britain's Westminster system) quickly became, as a result of governmental policies and complex political processes (DeVotta 2005), a full-fledged ethnohegemonic state facing a bloody civil war. In Sri Lanka, the original design of "civic nationalism" was deserted in favor of "ethnic nationalism" when the dominant group appropriated the state, initially conceived as neutral, and all its institutions for its purposes. As in the case of other hegemonic polities, nation and state became one in the case of Sri Lanka, and both were totally identified with merely a segment of the population, leaving the marginalized minority vulnerable and resentful. Through the years, the Sri Lankan state had become "increasingly ethnocentric and culturally exclusive." Efforts by the ethnic minorities to redress the situation by civil protest led to further repression (Isaac 1996, 179).

The Sri Lankan conflict, like all majority-minority disputes in the contemporary world, has deep historical roots. Some analysts focus on the South Indian invasions of about a thousand years ago as the source of the conflict. When the Portuguese arrived on the island in the early sixteenth century (1505), they found separate Tamil kingdoms in the north and in the east and Sinhalese kingdoms in the south (Singer 1992). When the Dutch ruled the island (1656–1796), they divided the territory into three parts: in the midwest and southeast the chief vernacular was Sinhalese, and in the north and east it was Tamil (Hoole 1998, 255). This history means, for the purposes of our discussion, that the two main contending groups in contemporary Sri Lanka have had a presence on the island for many hundreds of years and that both could legitimately perceive the island, or parts thereof, as their ancestral homeland.

The British took over the island in 1796. During the nineteenth century one could witness the development of ethnic consciousness in Ceylon. From 1871 onward the British census reports designate the "nationality of inhabitants," partly on the basis of language, but even then some analysts found that there was on the island a "spirit of pluralism" (ibid., 256). Yet during the twentieth century, increasing nationalism produced tensions between different groups.

The fact that the Tamils held positions in the upper civil service and the professions far in excess of their proportion in the population (Singer 1992, 712) did not help those tensions.

Ceylon received its independence from Britain in 1948. Its population had a majority of Buddhist Sinhalese and a minority of Hindu Tamils. Violence between the two groups led eventually to a civil war, but in 2002 a ceasefire between the government and the Tamil guerrillas was signed through Norwegian mediation.

If one looks at the dynamics that led to the deterioration of the ethnic relations, it is evident that it resulted from the increasing determination of the majority to rule the island on its own and create a form of *majoritarian populism* (Hoole 1998, 258). After independence the majority took a series of actions designed to guarantee its unilateral control. First, citizenship rights were denied to about 50 percent of the Indian Tamils ("Estate Tamils"), nearly one million people, who were settled by the British in the highlands of the south and south-central Ceylon in the nineteenth century. This move was taken to create a more favorable demographic balance from the perspective of the Sinhalese, already a clear majority in the country.

Second, the majority moved to establish the linguistic hegemony of its tongue and acted to marginalize the language of the minority. When Ceylon became independent, there had been a consensus that Tamil and Sinhalese should jointly replace English as official languages (ibid.). Yet after the momentous 1956 election Sinhala was made the sole national language. Although Tamil was later reinstalled as the official language in the Tamil-inhabited areas, this early struggle poisoned the relationships between the two groups. The language policy had symbolic significance but also produced negative results by restricting the educational and employment opportunities for the Tamils. The policy included the replacement of English by Sinhala at the universities.

Third, the majority established Buddhism as the state religion, thus deserting the notion of developing a modern, secular, liberal democracy. Ancient, religiously inspired programs, such as building a "just society" were revived. The Buddhist clergy (Sangha) led this process, reviving old mythologies according to which the Sinhalese people, as the chosen people, were the custodians of Buddhism. In a diverse country this meant the exclusion of non-Buddhists.

Fourth, the government acted to settle the Sinhalese in traditional Tamil-dominated areas in the northern and eastern provinces. This demographic colonizing policy was naturally perceived by the Tamils as threatening the character of their ancestral home. This was especially the case following every violent outburst after 1958 because large numbers of Tamils fled to these areas.

Fifth, discriminatory policies were implemented in regard to admission into universities, and employment opportunities for Tamils were cut significantly.

Sixth, important symbolic changes were introduced, including the change of the name of the state from Ceylon to Sri Lanka, emphasizing the new identity of the state. These symbolic changes were designed to restore the past glory of the country and its Buddhist civilization, in other words, to erase its pluralist character. Pro-Tamil analysts believe that the fundamental reason behind these changes and the nationalist ideology is the Sinhalese self-perception of being a beleaguered minority (despite being the clear majority), people whose duty is to preserve the island for Buddhism (ibid., 259).

As could be expected, this determined campaign to change the character of the polity from a liberal, somewhat binational and multicultural endeavor to a uniethnic hegemonic entity quickly led to riots and eventually to a civil war of major proportions. In the 1950s many Tamils realized that they could not rely on the state to protect them from the majority, a feeling that was further strengthened after the assassination, at the hand of a Buddhist monk, of Prime Minister Bandaranaike (September 1959). The state became, in effect, a machinery to "outmaneuver the minorities" (ibid.), as it has been in other hegemonic polities.

What makes the Sri Lanka case so interesting from the perspective of this volume is that the country started with a balanced document known as the Soulbury Constitution (1948). Although some of the Tamils argued in the late 1940s for the so-called fifty-fifty formula whereby they would share power on equal basis with the Sinhalese, Lord Soulbury and his commission recommended the establishment of a Westminster-type polity, a secular state with adherence to liberal and democratic principles. The original constitution included a clause (Section 29.2) that protected minorities from legislative discrimination (Clarance 2002, 43). This clause, and the power of the courts to review legislation, was dropped after the 1970 election, signifying deterioration in majority-minority relations. It seems that the hegemonic, intolerant ethnonationalist majority resisted any limitation on its power. That attitude eventually pushed the minority toward separatist counternationalism and increasing violence.

Solutions for the conflict have been offered throughout the years and finally, in 2002, a precarious ceasefire was announced. To date, the Sinhalese majority has refused to agree to a federalist solution or extensive autonomy for the Tamil minority, governmental designs that could have reversed the hegemonic step taken by this majority. Some analysts have suggested that Sri Lanka has emerged, at least on paper, as a type of "ethnic democracy" (Smooha 1997), where all citizens have individual rights but only the majority has group rights. Yet it is difficult to see how the system is democratic.

A large number of solutions have been discussed throughout the years. In terms of demographic distribution, the island could sustain a loose federation rather well, with the Tamil areas in the north and northeast enjoying federal rights within the larger Sri Lankan state. With a clear-cut demographic advantage – there are about fifteen million Sinhalese and merely three million Tamils – there is no real reason for the majority to fear the minority. The reality "on the ground" is such that the army cannot, in any event, take over the Tamil-controlled area nor can the Tamil rebel defeat the state.

Despite (or maybe because of) promising negotiations over the last few years between the Sri Lankan government and the Tamil rebels, President

Kumaratunga dismissed parliament in November 2003. Her intent was to abort a deal for a federal Sri Lanka that the Wickremesinghe government was discussing with the rebels. The April 2004 elections brought in a more nationalist government. The president was afraid that Sri Lanka would disintegrate.

In opposing a federal Sri Lanka, the president was strongly supported by Sinhalese ultranationalists and religionists, especially Sinhalese-Buddhist clergy, a coalition maintaining that "the peace process would undermine Sri Lanka's status as an exclusive state-protected and state-promoted Buddhist state" (Ganguly 2004, 911). In the language of this volume, you had, once again, a powerful pressure from a group within the majority that wanted to maintain the hegemony of that majority. In general, no solution will be possible without the leading forces within the Sinhalese-Buddhist community agreeing to either share or divide power with the country's minorities, particularly the Tamils. Only a change in that position could lead to a peaceful Sri Lanka.

In terms of long-term solutions to the Sri Lankan conflict, there are in principle three solutions. The extremist Sinhalese want a completely unitary state under their exclusive control. The extremist Tamils want a totally independent Tamil Eelam. Neither of these solutions can bring the violence to an end. In between these two extremes there are large numbers of options that divide power between the central government – where the weight of the Sinhalese majority would be heavily felt – and other governmental agencies below it, agencies that will give the Tamil minority a measure of protection and power.

For Sri Lanka to move away from ethnic hegemonism – promoted relentlessly by the majority for over fifty years – a solution must be found somewhere in between extensive autonomy and genuine federalism. Tamil region or regions, contiguous or not, must get significant political power. The solution lies in the details of such an arrangement: how precisely to divide power between the central and the regional governments, what region(s) to include in the Tamil autonomous or federal "enclave," the status of the Tamil language in Sri Lanka (including its courts, universities, and government agencies), the role of proportional representation or other formulae for dividing the state's resources, and so forth.

To achieve such a momentous, complicated deal, Sri Lankan politicians, from the minority but particularly from the majority, must cease resorting to "ethnic outbidding as a means to attain power," something they have done since the 1950s. Such political tactics caused the marginalization of the minority Tamils, led to their mobilization, and eventually to the violent conflict of the last quarter century (DeVotta 2005, 141).

The case of the Rwandan genocide of 1994 is among the most radical cases of a systematic effort by the dominant group to strengthen its control over the polity by physically eliminating the minority. The most important fact to note (from the perspective of this study) is that in the Rwandan case, as in that of Serbia and Sri Lanka, the violent actions of the majority have been planned and executed by the country's government, and that state institutions (e.g., the army, security forces) were used as instruments of achieving ethnohegemony.

Genocides, ethnic cleansings, and even lesser acts of violence are often not spontaneous acts by social groups but planned from above by governments.

There are complex reasons for the eventual Rwandan genocide: however, there can be no question that the goal was to liquidate as many Tutsi as possible and any moderate Hutu seen as opposed to the government (Newbury 1995, 12) and that forces associated directly with the Rwandan government saw the genocide as a way of clinging to power.

The Rwandan case, as the Sri Lankan and Serbian ones (and in many ways most majority-minority relations), evolved and reached its tragic climax due to the manner in which groups defined their interests, imagined their identities (Anderson 1993), and articulated their policies toward each other. Their visions determined their actions and the consequences of these actions. In other words, ultimately *constructed identities* were at the basis of the Rwandan tragedy. Many analysts spoke about the Rwandan society as clearly divided into three distinct groups – Hutu (85 percent), Tutsi (14 percent), and Twa (1 percent). In reality these have not been distinct racial groups and not "really ethnic groups in the conventional sense" (Newbury 1995, 12). Moreover, their definitions as groups have changed over time and were influenced particularly by the role of the state (Newbury 1988). Hintjens and others believe that "the notion of two exclusive and incompatible Hutu and Tutsi identities was constructed gradually" (1999, 251), namely that it reflects what Hobsbawm and Ranger call the "invention of tradition." In this sense, the 1994 genocide could be looked upon as a tragic self-fulfilling prophecy, reflecting the racial or ethnic definition that groups chose to adopt.

The people of Rwanda share many traits. For example, they all speak a single language, Kinyarwanda. When the Europeans arrived, the country was governed by a Tutsi-dominated monarchy. As in other places (e.g., Sri Lanka), colonial rule intensified and formalized the differentiation between "ethnic" groups, promoting a system of rigid ethnic classification unknown before. The Tutsi were the initial favorites of the European colonists and, in general, they were better off than the Hutus, enjoying superiority in all walks of life. The 1959 "social revolution" was perceived by many Hutu as a struggle against the Tutsi; tens of thousands of Tutsi became refugees as a result of that upheaval. By the time Rwanda gained independence (1962), ten thousand Tutsi were killed (Hintjens 1999, 248). The events of 1959–62 were as anticolonial (gaining independence from Belgium) as they were anti-Tutsi. The ideology of the revolution was that Rwanda belongs to the Hutu, the original inhabitants of the land who had been subjugated by the Tutsi and then by the Europeans (Uvin 1997, 98). Thus relationships between the country's two main groups were already highly negative from the beginning of Rwandan independence.

The two groups in Rwanda have adopted different historical narratives, linking those to the legitimacy of their cause. The Hutus, in particular, had a strong sense of victimhood: they perceived their history as a continuous saga of exploitation by the Tutsi. When the Hutu took over, their political elite developed a policy of systematic discrimination against the Tutsi, limiting their vertical mobility and access to power (ibid., 100). State institutions thus became a key for ethnic discrimination as they are in all hegemonic states. In a critical moment in 1994, they would be "activated" by a skillful leadership in the service of genocide.

In 1973 Juvenal Habyarimana took power through a coup. His regime was harsh, although it went after all opponents, Hutu as well as Tutsi. But after the attack of the Rwandese Patriotic Front (RPF) on October 1, 1990, the ethnic instrument became more prominent in the regime's arsenal and in 1994, argues Newbury (1995, 13), ethnic conflict was purposefully used by the regime for its own benefit. In terms of this book's argument, the Rwandan case is a quintessential example of the link between hegemonic state and inhumane, undemocratic, and oppressive action. The history of Hutu-Tutsi relations facilitated the use of this instrument.

Extreme elements within the government, and especially the military, used the RPF incursions of October 1990 to promote the expansion of the security forces, a move that would later prove significant in implementing the 1994 genocide swiftly. The army grew from five thousand to thirty thousand men. Because all Tutsi in Rwanda were accused as supporters of the RPF, this move was a frightening omen for the future.

The human-rights situation in Rwanda deteriorated after 1990. About two thousand Tutsi were killed between 1990–3 in what looks, in retrospect, to be a preparation for the 1994 genocide. An international commission of inquiry that visited Rwanda in January 1993 found that these attacks, which were not limited to Tutsi, were directed from the security services in the office of the president (ibid., 14).

To a large extent, the Rwandan genocide ought to be understood as a result of the interaction between several important factors: (1) the determination of the country's leadership to manipulate ethnic rivalries to extend its power by using the fears and suspicions that had deep historical resonance within the Rwandan society; (2) the deteriorating economic crisis in the country in the late 1980s and early 1990s; and (3) the lack of resolve, effectiveness, and even understanding of the complexity of the situation by the international community and scholars specializing in ethnic relations (Smooha and Hanf 1992, 29).

In terms of the first factor, the *political context* of the events, it is important to note that at the beginning of the 1990s there was enormous political pressure on the Rwandan regime and great internal discontent. The evidence is enormous that in view of this crisis situation, events were manipulated by the top echelons of the Rwandan government. The regime has a history of fostering ethnic politics to divert attention from economic problems and intra-Hutu divisions (Physicians for Human Rights, 1994), and in the early 1990s it began to push this agenda even more aggressively than before. There was a dramatic increase in the size of the army and in arms purchases: Rwanda became militarized as never before. Human Rights Watch and others noted the rapid para-militarization of the Rwandan society, including the appearance of militias and death squads. More important in terms of what was to come, a group of senior military and civilian officials called *akazu* (a "small house") emerged around President Habyarimana in the pregenocide period; it dominated the most strategic positions within the government, established a "state within a state," and was determined to keep its privileged position at all cost (Hintjens 1999, 259–61). The 1994 genocide "represented a last-ditch attempt by an increasingly autocratic and unpopular regime to cling on to state power" (ibid., 247). In the terms used in this book, it is important to emphasize the link between the dominant ethnic group and the hegemonic state that it came to control. In the words of Peter Uvin, the structural violence of the state was mobilized in all spheres (1997). Genocide, in this sense, could be looked upon as the last-ditch effort by ethnohegemonists to defend that which cannot be defended by other means. Benedict Anderson already observed that racism justifies domestic repression and domination more than foreign war (Anderson 1983). Rwanda is a case in point.

In terms of the *economic situation*, it started deteriorating when coffee prices fell in 1986–7. President Habyarimana began accusing "parasitic traders and misguided intellectuals" who allegedly exploited the "little man" and undermined social cohesion (Van de Meeren 1996, 257). It was clear to the president's listeners that he marked the Tutsi in general as responsible for the country's misfortunes. The economic crisis of the early 1990s meant the deterioration of health services, a rise in maternal and infant mortality, food shortages, and a sharp decline in agricultural production. Hintjens believes that instead of dealing with these problems, extremist politicians "set their faces toward genocide as the only 'final solution' to their problems" (1999, 258).

The *international response* to the situation in Rwanda was not effective either, and in some cases it was entirely counterproductive. Under the Arusha Accords (August 1993), the Rwandan government had to democratize and become more pluralistic. Thus the accords included a requirement that the RPF be incorporated within the Rwandan Armed Forces and be allocated 40 percent of all officer posts, a demand that the *akazu* perceived as the last straw (Prunier 1995, 159–64). There was a powerful faction within the Rwandan army that feared for its own survival under the power-sharing agreement with the RPF (Hintjens 1999, 249). "The international community neglected the existence of important and powerful factions in society that were totally opposed to any form of powersharing," Peter Uvin reminds us (1997, 109). Some analysts believe that this enormous and possibly misguided outside pressure on the beleaguered regime hastened the steps toward genocide.

This combination of events created the critical mass that produced the 1994 genocide. Rumors of a forthcoming "apocalypse" became widespread and frequent, and the actual preparation for it by the regime and its associates rather obvious. Genocide became almost inevitable; however, the international community ignored the early warnings. The massacre began on April 7 following the assassination of the president, reflecting the ability of the regime to control the behavior of the citizens (Prunier 1995, 3). The orders to kill came from the top and were implemented by the army and the militias. Very few Rwandans refused to carry the orders that came from above, confirming the general inclination of most people to obey orders given to them by authority figures (Milgram 1974) and the specific reputation of the Rwandans for obedience. The genocide was state-sponsored throughout, activating racist notions that have evolved in the Rwandan society for generations.

7

Beyond Hegemony in Deeply Divided Societies

Transforming Hegemonic Systems

> Everything is foreseen but free will is given.
>
> Rabbi Akiba, Pirkei Avot 3:15

The Terminological Debate: The Nature of Ethnohegemony

This study demonstrated through both theoretical analysis and a series of empirical cases that several types of cooperative relationships might develop between an ethnically dominant group and a minority in deeply divided societies. Lijphart's concept of consociationalism and the vast literature on federalism and autonomy (and even the more limited one on cantonization) have focused on the possibilities of interethnic accommodation through power sharing or power division. The assumption of this literature, borne out by several examples used in the current study, is that ethnically differentiated groups are not necessarily destined to live in endless, bloody conflict.

Focusing on hegemonic states, however, this volume has covered not only cooperative options but also situations where one group dominates other group(s). To analyze such domination, Yiftachel has introduced the notion of ethnocracy in an important series of publications (1998, 2000b, 2001, 2006). Yiftachel's conceptualization is insightful. However, its foundational dichotomy between democracy and ethnocracy is overdrawn and, consequently, loses its potency as an analytical tool when applied to many (although by no means all) specific cases. Yiftachel argues, in effect, that regimes that promote an ethnic agenda are no longer democratic but are ethnocratic, a different and new regime type. The difficulty in accepting that logic is that numerous regimes, some included in this study (e.g., Estonia, Israel, and Turkey), although adopting on occasion democratically questionable methods, are by most standards democratic. Yiftachel's conceptualization thus *equates democratic defects with nondemocracy*, leading him to conceptually "invent" a new type of regime. By his standards, the forceful promotion of "Frenchness" by the Paris-based elite, used in numerous other European countries throughout the modern era, would turn France (and other countries) into a nondemocracy.

Smooha (1997, 2002) offers an alternative conceptualization to that of Yiftachel. He identifies hegemonic regimes of the type analyzed in this volume as Ethnic Democracies, a regime type where the state and all its institutions "belong" exclusively to the dominant ethnic group, while individual members of the subordinate group enjoy some "liberal" rights but no collective ("republican") rights (Peled 1992). Yiftachel insists that serious democratic deviations make an ethnonational regime nondemocratic; Smooha accepts such "ethnic" deviations by not insisting that their existence contradict the very essence of modern democracy: individual equality before the law and protection of minorities. To make things even harder, other analysts struggling with the tension between ethnic domination and genuine democracy use the notion of majoritarian populism (Hoole 1998) or simple majoritarianism (Peled and Navot 2005) to describe a political system in which the dominant ethnic group uses its numerical advantage to dictate political solutions with complete disregard to the rights or interests of the minority.

In an effort to better understand the relations between majorities and minorities in hegemonic situations, this volume has introduced the notion of *Ethnic Constitutional Order*. The term has several characteristics that make it useful for analyzing hegemonic regimes and their transformations. First, the term broadens the meaning of hegemony beyond a political arrangement designed to benefit one ethnic group and beyond a foundational legal structure or a constitutional document and tradition. It reflects a multidimensional reality that includes, in addition to all these, a cultural dimension (e.g., the prevalence of the dominant group's language, culture, and traditions) and, very importantly, a deep psychological dimension that amounts to the thorough internalization of control thinking, domination, and a sense of the majority's exclusivity.

Second, the notion of Ethnic Constitutional Order, as used in this study, is meant to convey more flexibility and even fluidity than either ethnocracy or ethnic democracy. Many if not most contemporary nation-states are inherently ethnocratic to one degree or another (Dowty 1999). Even model democracies have a preferred language and often built-in intolerance toward alternative tongues, official church (regardless of the level of religiosity of their citizens or lack thereof), national holidays based on ancient traditions that some of their citizens may or may not share, "ethnic" symbols and historic narratives forced from above, and so forth. Although many such polities might be said to have ethnic orders, calling them ethnocracies (i.e., identifying them as nondemocracies) might be an exaggeration. Similarly, to call a polity dedicated single-mindedly to the promotion of the dominant group's hegemonic control an ethnic democracy might be construed as ignoring the true nature of the regime in question. Ethnic Constitutional Order, it is hoped, avoids these conceptual pitfalls.

Third, an Ethnic Constitutional Order could be democratic or not; the concept is designed to facilitate a more nuanced analysis of the democratic quality of a polity. On the one hand, it could not be assumed that ethnonational practices necessarily negate the democratic credentials of a country (turning it into an ethnocracy). On the other hand, it could not be assumed that such practices are compatible with democracy or a new type of democracy (i.e., ethnic democracy). To make a judgment on the quality of the country's democracy in a situation of complex majority-minority relations, one needs to adopt the type of detailed analysis of democracy that is offered in Chapter 2 and then apply it contextually to specific case studies. The different levels of democracy identified in Chapter 2 are designed to facilitate, specifically, a distinction between fully democratic polities and flawed democracies, the type often produced by Ethnic Constitutional Orders.

Fourth, the conceptualization of Ethnic Constitutional Order as offered here is designed to convey the notion that such an order is, above all, highly dynamic. The focus of this study has been on the transformation of hegemonic regimes, the question of whether such regimes may become more inclusive and therefore more democratic, or more exclusive and therefore more hegemonic. Designating a regime as ethnocratic or ethnodemocratic leaves little room for an empirical examination of the regime.

The dynamic nature of most Ethnic Constitutional Orders in the contemporary world suggests that, as a regime type, an ECO is almost invariably a regime with fundamental weaknesses. This is the situation especially in deeply divided societies and particularly in the current political atmosphere of promotion of equality, human rights, and participatory democracy. An ECO in all of its forms often leads to long-term, ongoing bloodshed, including ethnic cleansing and even genocide, or to the dismemberment of the polity through separatism or partition. Serbia under Milosevic, South Africa's apartheid, Sri Lanka for the last several decades, Franco's Spain, and Northern Ireland are but some historical examples for the lack of long-term viability of hegemonic regimes. Moreover, even what Smooha calls ethnic democracy and what Peled and Navot (2005) characterize as majoritarianism – both reflected in the Israeli and Turkish regimes – might not be sustainable in the long run; they will need to adapt to survive. When a liberal democracy moves toward hegemony (e.g., Sri Lanka) or when a consociational system does the same (e.g., Cyprus), the probability of achieving nonviolent stability is even lower. The bottom line is that neither a full-fledged ECO nor an ethnic order that hides behind ethnic democracy is viable in the long run.

What is most critical from the perspective of the sustainability of Ethnic Constitutional Orders is to identify the factors that might produce a regime change in deeply divided societies, including the direction in which a hegemonic polity might move (e.g., toward a more accommodationist or more exclusivist form of government) and the intensity of that move. To analyze the issue of sustainability, it is crucial to realize that practically all Ethnic Constitutional Orders in the modern world are heavily supported by the state. In this type of political order, the state becomes a primary tool for the enhancement and perpetuation of ethnic dominance or even the total hegemony of the leading ethnic group or (very often) elements that claim to speak in its name. Although classical writers such as Karl Marx and Alexis de Tocqueville emphasized the role of the state as an instrument of control, and some modern writers emphasized it as well, further attention must be paid to the specific role of the "ethnicized state" in converting a multi-ethnic social reality into a uniethnic political order (Chadda 2004; Peleg 2004a). The role of the state might explain the stability of ethnic orders; it might also explain their instability and the possibilities for their eventual disintegration.

Ethnicized states are often inherently unstable, particularly in an international system that is increasingly dominated by values that are quite alien to them. Once such values succeed in penetrating the state's "hegemonic shield," they are likely to enhance the motivation of the subordinate group to challenge the hegemonic order and at the same time increase the reluctance of elements within the dominant group to sustain the hegemonic order. In such circumstances, the state may be forced to transform incrementally or radically, although a change, its direction, and its intensity are not predetermined.

This book presented the thesis that by virtue of their fundamental incongruence with the values of democracy, equality, and rights, all Constitutional Ethnic Orders are today, and likely to be in the foreseeable future, under significant pressure from within and without to transform. At the same time, the sustainability of such regimes will continue to be high and many of them will be unlikely to agree to reform themselves. In some situations the reverse trend may occur: liberal or consociational regimes might decide to move toward greater hegemony as happened in several situations.

Five factors are likely to determine the dynamics of regime change in deeply divided societies dominated by Ethnic Constitutional Orders:

1. The balance of power between the dominant ethnic group and the subordinate group(s) and the nature of that balance (multidimensional or not).
2. The intensity and effectiveness of international pressure on the regime to reform itself from an ECO to a more open and inclusive regime.
3. The determination of the dominant group to hold on to its exclusive power, including its ability and willingness to suffer the consequences of sustaining hegemony.
4. The compromising proclivity within the polity or the extent to which it tends to be accommodationist or exclusivist in its approach.
5. The capacity of the system to engineer political change in a gradual or profound (megaconstitutional) manner.

Thus it might be argued that if the dominant group is only marginally dominant, the international pressure directed at it to reform is massive, the determination or capacity of the dominant group to withstand pressure limited, the proclivity for systemic compromise evident, and the capacity for initiating constitutional change significant, the result is likely to be a systemic transformation, probably in a consociational or federal direction (e.g., as happened in Spain or in Northern Ireland, although with different levels of success). If the prominence of the dominant group is total and multidimensional, the international pressure tolerable, the dominant elite intensely committed to hold and even increase exclusive power, the polity has no compromising inclination, and the capacity to introduce orderly change limited, systemic transformation is unlikely in either a gradual or metaconstitutional manner. Moreover, the system might move in the direction of further ethnicization (e.g., as happened in Cyprus and Sri Lanka), especially if the ruling elite feels threatened.

In today's world most ethnicized systems are unlikely to move radically in one direction or the other, that is, change completely in the direction of equitable power sharing or be able to totally ethnicize their polities. Given contemporary pressure to democratize, on the one hand, and the desire to maintain their own ethnic character, on the other, most ethnicized systems today are likely to end up somewhere in the middle. Under such circumstances, they might adopt a mixture of intermediate steps designed to enhance their liberality and consociationalism but without changing their basic character. Liberal changes would be designed to enhance equality on an individual basis, and consociational changes would be designed to enhance group equality. Countries such as Israel and Turkey might be models for such less-than-profound change.

At the same time, ethnicized regimes that feel threatened might decide to move away from equality and further ethnicize their institutions. They could do so by adopting either antiliberal steps, clamping down on individual rights in an ethnically biased manner, or by adopting anticonsociational measures designed to take away group rights (as was done by Milosevic toward Kosovo in 1989). The range of options open to an ethnicized regime is broad, and it goes all the way from enhancing the symbolic preference to the dominant group to ethnic cleansing (e.g., Serbia under Milosevic) and even full-fledged genocide directed against the dominated group (e.g., 1994 Rwanda).

The balancing act between the accommodationist and exclusivist policy available to ethnic regimes is quite complicated, and the consequences of the choice they make is rather profound. It is crucial to explore first the factors that might lead a hegemonic system to move in one direction or another and then the consequences that might ensue from adopting different policies.

Explaining the Transformation of Ethnic Constitutional Orders

It is the function of the analyst to identify the factors that are most important for determining the state's ethnic policies in a deeply divided society. A satisfactory explanation of such a widespread phenomenon, in numerous societies, is not easy to produce. This is merely the first "cut." Such a preliminary effort ought to be relatively complete and reasonably parsimonious in explaining the phenomenon; it cannot be expected to be, at this stage of our investigation, predictive of any specific case.

In this section I will identify five major factors that might play a major role in determining the policies that dominate the behavior of both the dominant group and the subordinate group in deeply divided societies experiencing hegemonic regime.

The Balance of Power between the Groups

A major factor determining the relations between the dominant ethnic group and subordinate group in a highly ethnicized polity is the balance of power between these groups, both in terms of the overall power relations between these groups and the dimensionality pattern of their relations. Although the demographic balance is important, it is not the only one to look at.

If the dominant group is in full control of the polity (i.e., if the balance of power is clearly in its favor) it might not be inclined or feel compelled to accept changes in the ethnic character of the polity. This could be the position of the dominant group especially if its dominance is not merely demographic but multidimensional and if it is seemingly permanent. For example, if the dominant group enjoys a large demographic advantage that is accompanied by a higher level of economic achievement, control over all or most political and military assets, an advantage in educational excellence, and so forth, it is less likely to be inclined toward compromise with a significantly weaker ethnic group, especially if the weaker group is perceived as a potential political adversary. Israel is a good example. If one group enjoys demographic superiority but another group is a leading force in the country's economy, as is the situation in Malaysia, the hegemonic nature of the regime might be curtailed.

In dealing with the balance of power between a dominant and a subordinate group within an ethnicized polity it is important to examine first the demographic balance between them. Using the informational base quoted by various databases (e.g., Freedom House annual reports or the *CIA World Factbook*) or by various scholars (Dowty 2000, Table 7, 212) it might be beneficial to calculate the balance between the dominant demographic group and subordinate groups in terms of what might be called the Demographic Dominance Ratio (DDR), a measure of how dominant a particular group is within a divided society.

In an ethnically divided society, the DDR could be theoretically between 99 percent (total demographic dominance) and 51 percent (marginal demographic advantage), although in societies with more than two ethnic groups the dominant group may have less than a majority. In terms of theoretical development it might be particularly useful to analyze the demographic balance between various groups on an ordinal scale. For example, we might conceive of a three-category scale in which *demographic hegemony* is defined as a condition in which the dominant group has at least 85 percent of the population (e.g., Egypt, Finland, France, Germany, New Zealand, Romania, the United Kingdom, and marginally Slovakia); *demographic prominence* is established when the larger group is between 65–84 percent (e.g., Bulgaria, Canada, Cyprus, marginally Estonia and Switzerland, India, Israel, Lithuania, Spain, Sri Lanka, and Turkey); and *demographic advantage* is in the range of 51–64 percent for the majority group (e.g., Belgium, Latvia, and possibly Czechoslovakia between the wars and before its disintegration in 1993). This categorization may be useful in developing generalizations about the relationships between dominant and subordinate groups and the likelihood of systemic transformation. Thus it could be quickly surmised that demographic hegemony might be a "pacifier" in terms of intergroup relations; more severe conflicts occur in countries with demographic prominence (e.g., Cyprus, Israel, Sri Lanka, and Turkey) and demographic advantage (e.g., Belgium, Latvia). At the same time, it is clear that demography is never, in and of itself, a single determinant of majority-minority relations.

Interesting cases of demographic hegemony (over 85 percent for the largest group) exist in Finland (93.4 percent Finns; 5.9 percent Swedes), Romania (89.5 percent for the majority), Slovakia (85.7 percent Slovaks versus 10.6 percent Hungarians according to the *CIA World Factbook*), and Egypt (94 percent Moslems versus 6 percent Coptic Christians). In none of these countries is there a major challenge to the demographic supremacy of the dominant group, but in at least some of them (e.g., Romania, Slovakia, Egypt and even France today) the hegemonic group may view the minority with suspicion due to its different real or perceived character. It is clear that the relations between the dominant and subordinate groups are not merely statistical or objective; psychological and subjective factors are equally important. The relations are invariably "constructed."

In many countries the dominant ethnic group might not enjoy demographic hegemony, but it has clear demographic prominence (defined here as between 65–84 percent of the population belonging to the majority). These cases are often more controversial and conflictual than cases of demographic hegemony because the dominant group may be concerned about its position, and it might take aggressive action designed to strengthen that position. In Bulgaria the majority is close to 84 percent and the Turkish minority is less than 10 percent, in India the Hindu are about 81 percent, in Israel the Jews are about 80.1 percent of the population versus 19.9 percent who are non-Jews and mostly Arab (CIA figures), in Turkey the minority of Kurds is assessed at about 20 percent (there are no official numbers), in Spain the Castilian Spaniards are about 74 percent (versus three distinct and considerably smaller ethnic groups), in Sri Lanka the Sinhalese are also assessed at 74 percent, in Lithuania the majority is roughly 80.6 percent versus 8.6 percent Russians and 7 percent Poles (a multigroup division that may be beneficial to the majority), and in Estonia the majority is merely 65.3 percent (with about 28.1 percent Russians, 2.5 percent Ukrainians, and an additional 1.5 percent Belarussians). In all these cases there are extremely uneasy majority-minority relations. In the case of Cyprus, with 77 percent Greeks and 18 percent Turks, this unease led to the eventual breakdown of the system, and in the case of Sri Lanka persistent violence has occurred for over two decades (as it did in Northern Ireland for decades).

Severe interethnic conflict, however, is not inevitable, regardless of the demographic balance within the polity. Although in Switzerland the dominant demographic and economic group of German speakers is 65 percent (and the minorities are 18 percent French speaking and 10 percent Italian speaking), ethnicity has been built into the federal and cantonal structure for centuries and has become a hallmark of a compromising political culture, a consociational mechanism if you will. In New Zealand the majority of whites is roughly 81 percent, while the largest minority (the Maori are 9.7 percent) is very weak socioeconomically. Nevertheless, the system has implemented equitable, progressive policies. In Spain the majority, Castilian Spaniards, and the minorities (Catalans with a significant 17 percent, Galicians 7 percent, and the Basques with merely 2 percent) have been moving toward a semifederal system over the last quarter century. Even in Northern Ireland, a traditionally conflictual territory, serious steps toward conflict resolution have been adopted. In contrast, in Cyprus and Sri Lanka the traditional rival groups have not been able to settle their differences peacefully.

The case of the United Kingdom is of interest from a demographic perspective. The demographic balance is clearly in favor of the English (81.5 percent), as against the Scots (9.6 percent), the Irish (2.4 percent), and the Welsh (1.9 percent). While the English are close to what might be considered demographically hegemonic, and their culture is by all means prominent, the level of inclusiveness of minorities is high. Moreover, there is an overarching British identity that has blunted the interethnic tensions for hundreds of years.

In numerous situations the larger group might have a clear demographic advantage (say, between 51 percent and 64 percent) but no prominence, let alone hegemony. In some of these situations (e.g., in Latvia where the balance between the Latvians and the Russians is 57–29 percent but with four other significant groups) the majority tries to strengthen its shaky position by all means at its disposal. In other situations (e.g., Belgium where the Flemish-Walloon balance is 58–31 percent) the majority and minority might move toward compromise in the form of power sharing and strong federalism. In other situations (e.g., Czechoslovakia) the uneasy balance might lead to partition. In some situations the majority has been fairly successful in dealing with a minority through constitutional and democratic means that avoid heavy-handed hegemonic practices; such is the case of Canada where the ratio of majority-minority, defined linguistically, is 56–23 percent. In South Africa the situation is much more complex; while the majority has 55 percent of the population, there are at least three significant minorities with 20 percent, 16 percent, and 9 percent of the population. Maybe this situation explains the possibility of moving toward majoritarian, Westminster democracy.

In his analysis of countries with a dominant ethnic group but also respectable political rights and civil liberties, Dowty concludes that eleven have some form of power sharing and fifteen do not (2000, 210–11). Moreover, in the power-sharing countries the dominant group averaged 67 percent of the population, while in the nonpower-sharing states the average size of the dominant group was 79 percent. Dowty also found that only one country with a minority of less than 20 percent (Finland) adopted power sharing, while ten of fourteen countries with minorities larger than 20 percent used power sharing.

These conclusions are logical. The more demographically hegemonic a country is, the less it is inclined or compelled to dilute its unique character by using power-sharing techniques. But when the dominant majority has to deal with a significant minority, especially if this minority is clearly distinct and views itself as such, it is compelled to accommodate it through power sharing. Liberalization (in the form of individual rights) is simply insufficient. Traditional France could have maintained its "Frenchness" and liberality as long as it did not have a strong and distinct, minority; will it be able to maintain either with a large, distinct and militant minority? It looks not. An even more severe challenge is facing Israel with its Arab minority, Turkey with its Kurdish minority and Sri Lanka with its Tamil minority, because these minorities are larger and more distinct. Although it is impossible to determine the tipping point mathematically, it seems that once the minority reaches about 15–20 percent of the population, as in the case of the Russians in Estonia and Latvia, the Tamils in Sri Lanka, the Arabs in Israel, the French speakers in Belgium, Canada, and Switzerland, the Catalans in Spain, the Catholics in Northern Ireland, and so forth, it cannot be ignored without generating serious instability.

It is interesting and important to note that there is no universally accepted, positive standard for the rights of a minority and no agreed-upon size of a minority that triggers the granting of certain prescribed rights. At the same time, there is an accepted, although often implicit and formally unspelled negative standard within modern democratic thought, particularly in the West: individuals or groups should not be discriminated against on the basis of ethnicity. This is an important factor in determining outside pressure applied to ethnic states.

A group with demographic hegemony might feel that it is immune from negative consequences while making substantial concessions to a subordinate group. Such hegemonic groups (e.g., the Finns in Finland with 94 percent of the population versus the small Swedish minority of roughly 6 percent) might feel safe and therefore willing to recognize the minority's rights. The demographic balance also has a dynamic aspect: a decline in the demographic hegemony could lead a group to enhance the equality of the subordinate group in recognition of the new emerging reality, or it can stiffen its opposition to such transformation to avoid what could be, demographically, inevitable. The decline of Maronite power in pre-1975 Lebanon is a case in point. It led to the redefinition of ethnic relations in the country.

If a group is dominant or prominent, and its relationships with the subordinate group are already negative, one could expect it to be unwilling to give up power regardless of demographic trends. Moreover, such a group would tend to use the state apparatus heavily to maintain its power in the face of a real, perceived, or potential minority challenge. The behavior of the Serb majority toward the Albanian minority in Kosovo is a case in point. This has also been the reaction of the Jewish majority in Israel, the Turks in Turkey, and the Sinhalese of Sri Lanka, with 81 percent, 80 percent, and 74 percent of the population, respectively. Strong ethnic identities do not crumble in the face of emerging demographic realities; they fight against them, often by adopting hegemonic tactics.

If and when the minority is significant and growing (i.e., the stronger group has a demographic advantage, but it is limited and shrinking), the dominant group might not be able to hold on to exclusive power in the long run. In such a situation, the dominant group and its leaders must choose between two basic options. One, the dominant group might agree to transform the hegemonic order through liberalization by granting individually based equal rights (as was done in the American South during and following the 1960s), consocialization by sharing power with the minority on the basis of group membership (as it was done in post-Franco Spain and tried in Northern Ireland), or even reach an agreement to partition the country (as was done in Czechoslovakia in early 1993). Second, the dominant group might decide to fight to maintain and even increase its supremacy. If demographic hegemony is what the majority is determined to enhance, that policy could logically lead to expulsions, ethnic cleansing, or even full-fledged genocide, as happened in the Former Yugoslavia, Rwanda, and other places.

One demographic factor that has to be taken into account in the determination of the relationships between majority and minority, whatever the DDR between them might be, is the Demographic Concentration Factor (DCF). If a minority is concentrated in a particular region of the county – like the Basques and Catalans in Spain, the French-speaking in Canada, or Switzerland's cantons – it might be able to have greater influence on the majority than if it is spread all over the national territory (as the Roma are in many countries, African-Americans in the United States, and the indigenous populations in Latin American countries).

All in all, it is clear that the demographic balance within an ethnicized polity is of great importance. At the same time it ought to be recognized that it rarely determines the relationships between ethnic groups in and of itself.

International Pressure

The relationship between a dominant and a subordinate group in an ethnicized state is often affected by outside pressure, sometimes significantly so. This is probably a growing phenomenon. In a rapidly shrinking world, barriers are falling and no state may deal with "its" minorities as it wishes. Not only is information and analysis of "internal" majority-minority relations available to "outside" observers, and often it dominates world news, but also today there is newly acquired legitimacy for intervention in domestic situations particularly when distinct ethnic groups are involved in a conflict. At the same time, there are great differences in the inclination of outside forces to intervene in an ethnic situation: some conflicts are central to the concerns of the international community (e.g. South Africa under apartheid), and other situations generate little or no international interest.

On the whole, it might be useful to distinguish between three different types of outside intervention in a sensitive ethnic situation within a polity. First, in many situations a country might interfere in the ethnic condition of people who share with it the same "nationhood" or ethnicity. Thus Hungary has shown great interest in the conditions of Hungarian minorities in Romania and Slovakia, Russia has been sensitive to the treatment of Russian minorities in the "Near Abroad" (former Soviet Republics), and Turkey has shown interest in the conditions of Turkish Cypriots.

Second, regional organizations might show special interest in the treatment of minorities in adjacent countries, especially if these countries have aspirations of establishing special relations with these organizations or are even interested in joining them. Thus the European Union has developed an elaborate system designed to assure that nations with significant minorities treat them fairly. In fact, European Union pressure has become a powerful tool in the promotion of minority rights. A particularly important case is that of Turkey and its relationships with its Kurdish minority, as well as its support for a settlement of the Cypriot issue.

Third, the international community could be activated from time to time to defend the rights of a minority in an extreme situation of persecution. Rhodesia (now Zimbabwe) and South Africa have been on the agenda of the international community for decades, and so was Iraq under Saddam Hussein and Serbia under Milosevic. All four hegemonic states eventually changed as a result of some type of international intervention through either sanctions or direct military engagement.

The vulnerability of regimes to outside pressure applied on behalf of their minorities by international actors is greatly uneven. Powerful countries such as Russia and the People's Republic of China have been able to successfully resist outside interference, while smaller countries such as Romania, Slovakia, or Estonia have been significantly more vulnerable to external pressure. There are, in general, a few cases where outside interference is truly effective in actually transforming hegemonic policy into liberal or consociational policy.

The tools used to pressure ethnicized states to deal fairly with their minorities are diverse. The most severe of these tools is, of course, a direct military intervention carried out by the international community or significant parts thereof against a government accused of violating minority rights. In the case of Serbia such intervention caused the Belgrade government to reverse its policy on Bosnia and Kosovo, leading eventually to the collapse of the Milosevic regime. Although military intervention is an exceptionally powerful instrument, more often gentler instruments, such as economic sanctions, are used.

To some extent, outside pressure on ethnicized regimes to change their behavior is haphazard if not entirely arbitrary. Thus international law, tradition, or expectations are unclear as to what absolute or relative size of a minority is entitled to schooling in its own language. Other positive rights are also often unclear. Nevertheless, in general it could be argued that the more sizeable the minority, in relative and absolute terms, the higher the expectations of that minority, its supporters abroad, and the international community at large that it would be treated "fairly" and that its distinctive position be recognized by the majority and by the state.

In special situations, outside interference could be a central factor in determining majority-minority relations within a hegemonic polity. This is particularly the situation when outside powers have self-evident legitimacy in interfering in what otherwise might appear to be an internal matter. The case of Northern Ireland demonstrates this point rather well. Both the Republic of Ireland and the United Kingdom have seen Northern Ireland as an issue of special interest to them, a view shared by others, because, in the first instance, the territory is on the Irish island and, in the second instance, the territory has been part of the state for generations. The special status of the United Kingdom and the Irish Republic has allowed them to engineer the 1998 Good Friday Agreement and to be involved in efforts to negotiate an end to the "troubles" in Northern Ireland.

A second case where outside interest is recognized as legitimate is the involvement of Russia in issues relating to the Russian minorities in former Soviet republics such as Estonia and Lithuania but also in some of the Asian republics. The considerable power of Russia, its recent control over these territories, and sometimes the harshness of the treatment given to Russian minorities in former Soviet republics have generated at least some legitimacy for Russia's interference on behalf of these minorities. It is interesting to note, in comparison, that Hungarian intervention in Romania or Slovakia has been perceived as less legitimate, reflecting Hungary's weaker position in comparison to Russia and the great sensitivity to Hungarian domination in the past. The "Status Law" passed by the Hungarian parliament caused significant opposition not only in Romania and Slovakia but also in other countries.

All in all, some situations of ethnicized conflicts in hegemonic states (e.g., Cyprus, Turkey, Northern Ireland, or South Africa) have been dominated by outside interest and intervention, and others (e.g., Quebec or Spain) have not generated legitimate intervention.

The Determination of the Dominant Group

A third factor that has to be taken into account as a determinant of the relationship between a dominant and a subordinate group in a hegemonic state is the will of the dominant group to resist internal and external pressure to change the character of the polity. Determination, a subjective factor, is no less important than demography, an objective factor, although its sources might be quite different. As an intangible factor, determination is not easy to assess. While the determination to keep the ethnicized character of the state intact is particularly powerful in relatively new states (Spinner-Halev 2002) (e.g., Israel, Sri Lanka, the Republic Turkey), the capacity to resist pressure might be more substantial in old and well-established polities.

As for determination to hold on to a privileged position, it is important to remember that many of the most highly ethnicized states came into being as a result of a long conflict between their dominant groups and their subordinate groups. Consequently, the dominant groups within these polities sometimes cannot imagine sharing political power with their minorities on a completely equal basis. Thus the Baltic populations have seen themselves since the early 1940s as "captive nations," occupied by the Soviet Union. The Soviets settled numerous ethnic Russians in those states to solidify their control. The current Baltic governments often view the Russian minorities as illegitimate settlers. They are determined to maintain the control in the hands of the "local" population and force the Russians to assimilate, immigrate, or accept second-class status (Berg 2002; Lievan and McGarry 1993; Pettai and Hallik 2002).

In trying to maintain the ethnicized nature of their regimes, Romanian and Slovak nationalists have often revived historical memories and tended to emphasize that in the past they have been dominated by the Hungarians. The past has thus been used as justification for maintaining hegemony and carrying out discrimination at present.

The vast majority of Israeli Jews view their relations with the Arab minority in Israel through the prism of the long Jewish-Palestinian conflict since the early twentieth century. The United Nations partition resolution of November 29, 1947, divided Mandatory Palestine into an Arab and a Jewish state. When the State of Israel came into being, it immediately defined itself as a Jewish state and its character as a Jewish state has remained intact ever since. There can be no question that the majority of Israeli Jews would like this situation to continue in the foreseeable future.

The determination of the dominant group to hold on to its privileged position is not a given. It could be cultivated and developed. The political elite of the dominant group is often engaged in intense efforts to strengthen the national or ethnic identity of their people. This could be done through the development of linguistic and cultural institutions, the invention and cultivation of legends and narratives, and the establishment of educational institutions.

The determination is reflected in what could be referred to as "cost tolerance," the willingness of the dominant group to sustain penalties to maintain the ethnicized character of "its" state. A determined dominant group can be rather dangerous to the minority when it views it as a challenger to its dominant position as well as, eventually, to its survival and the character of "its" state. Minorities identified as "enemies" are likely to suffer discrimination, persecution, expulsion, transfer, and sometimes full-fledged genocides. During the twentieth century in particular, determined majorities resorted to harsh means against powerless minorities: the Jews of Germany and Austria, German minorities in Poland and Czechoslovakia, Albanians in the Former Yugoslavia, Armenians in Turkey, Turks in Cyprus, a variety of groups in Stalin's Soviet Union, Tamils in Sri Lanka, Kurds in Turkey and in Iraq, and Tutsi in Rwanda have become victims to hegemonic ideologies. These are but some examples of the power of determination to maintain a "pure" country.

Compromising Proclivity in an Ethnicized System

The balance of power between ethnic or national groups is important in determining the relationships between dominant and subordinate groups in a multiethnic setting, along with the determination of the dominant group to maintain its exclusive hold on power and the outside pressure applied to it to change. The overall policy of the political elite and the dominant group that it represents is also of great importance. The question is whether these political elite have significant inclination to share or divide power with other elites.

In general, it is crucial to make an analytical distinction between an accommodationist and exclusivist posture taken by the dominant group's ruling elites and their opposing elites in multiethnic settings. Some multinational or multiethnic states try to accommodate at least the most important groups within their borders through consociational, federal, and other means. Other multinational states strive by all means at their disposal to maintain and even enhance the dominance of one national group over all others. In both cases the state becomes a central instrument in negotiating a deal and defining the relationships between the various groups in society.

An accommodationist state is one that is both ready to recognize its own diversity and act upon this recognition by forming structures and adopting policies designed to integrate the diverse reality into its political life. In contrast, the exclusivist state is fundamentally ethnocentric – all important policies are designed to enhance the power of the dominant "ethnos." In some situations such ethnocentric orders might be identified as state centric (etat centric?), but this is often a mistake. Their purpose is most likely to enhance the power of the ethnic group, the state is merely a tool for that goal and not the goal per se (Peleg 1998a).

In principle, the accommodationist state is, or could be, etat centric (state centric). The assumption of such state-centered order is that all citizens of the state, regardless of their ethnic origin (and, for that matter, their religion, race, and class) are equal before the law and are entitled to equal protection by the state. In theory, at least, one way for accommodation is for the state to pay no attention whatsoever to ethnicity (Van der Berghe 1981a). Alternatively, the accommodationist state may adopt a position by which all or most ethnic collectivities are recognized on an equal basis.

The accommodationist approach is inherently and significantly more democratic than the exclusivist one because it is based on the principle of individual and group equality, if groups are recognized at all. As such it is less likely to lead to violent results. An exclusivist system is by definition nondemocratic and might be regarded as unjust. As such it is also likely to be unstable, a major issue in assessing the consequences of its actions. The establishment of an accommodationist system in a multiethnic setting could be looked upon as a method of conflict management designed to maximize stability. The denial of a legitimate political role for a minority, or possibly even the denial of the very existence of that minority, is a recipe for instability.

Hegemonic states are by definition exclusivist and many hegemonic states are exclusivist in a blatant manner. They deny the existence or at least the legitimacy of their subordinate groups. Thus Jacobin France has traditionally dismissed Breton identity (and that of many other remote provinces) as "folkloric," Romanian politicians have often denied the "Hungarianess" of most

Transylvanians, and Turks tended to deny the existence of a Kurdish ethnicity, referring to Kurds as "mountain Turks."

In contrast to that approach, accommodationist states tend to respond favorably to at least some of the concerns of its minorities. Such a response could be reflected in the form of public recognition of the minority or through the neutralization of the state as the exclusive arena of the majority. Accommodationist regimes are ready to recognize diversity and even to value it as a positive characteristic of the system, and exclusivist regimes view diversity as a serious threat to the true nature of the polity. Accommodationist polities are based on the assumption or at least the hope that unity could be achieved despite diversity.

Although exclusivity and accommodationism are analytically separate, often they live side-by-side within one polity. Thus in the United States, "liberalism," an accommodationist governmental form, has often lived together, side-by-side, with the more exclusivist form of republicanism and even a thoroughly hegemonic form of ethnocentrism (Huntington 2002; Smith 1988). Shafir and Peled have shown a similar pattern in contemporary Israel (2002).

There are several good examples of accommodationist polities acting in the interest of interethnic understanding in the recent past. The United Kingdom's 1997 devolution program was designed to grant greater recognition to the nations of the British Isles, Spain in the post-Franco era has gone through a remarkable program of democratization and the recognition of the peninsula's various ethnic (or national) components, the framers of the 1998 Good Friday Agreement attempted to bring about a genuine consociational order in a territory ruled hegemonically by one group for decades, and so forth. Several states have been decidedly exclusivist in their policies: Sri Lanka over the last several decades, Mečiar's Slovakia, and Milosevic's Serbia are but some examples.

If accommodation is so clearly superior to exclusivity, and power sharing advantageous when compared to hegemonism, why have so many states chosen to establish an ECO and then sustain it? The reason is, I believe, sociopsychological. When the nation and its ethnicized state become the focus of societal myths and rituals and the object of supreme loyalty and reverence on the part of individuals, it replaces old-fashion religion (Gentile 2006). Individuals and groups are then ready to do everything for the nation, identifying any change in the character of the ethnicized state as blasphemous and any idea for a change as heresy. It is thus not entirely surprising that the compromising proclivity of many ethnicized polities, particularly on the part of their majority groups and governing elites, is not especially high, even though rationale and humane solutions are possible. The cases dealt with in this volume bear this conclusion.

The System's Political Engineering Capability

The last factor determining the relationships between dominant and subordinate groups is the capability of an ethnicized political system to engage in creative political engineering that could foster better relationships and avert violence and other forms of instability within the polity. Several systems have been able to engineer significant political changes that seem to have resulted in positive results, although not invariably or automatically implementable results:

1. In 1998 Northern Ireland saw the adoption of a plan for power sharing between traditionally hostile groups. The Good Friday (or Belfast) Agreement of April 1998 is a model of creative consociationalism. The agreement has not been implemented in full, and it has seen a series of ups and downs, however, it is an example of a conscious effort to solve a problem and create stability (McGarry 2002; McGarry and O'Leary 2004a, & 2004b).

2. Post-Franco Spain is another example of large-scale political engineering within the context of hegemonism. Although part of that particular exercise, reflected in Spain's 1978 constitution, was an effort to democratize Spain, another aspect was an effort to deethnicize it. Both efforts have proven quite successful to date (Moreno 2001b), although it is still unclear whether Spain will evolve into a full-fledged federal state.

3. The United Kingdom's devolution program is also an example of an attempt at political engineering, albeit a more modest example than the ones attempted in the cases of Northern Ireland and Spain (Bogdanor, 1999a, 2001; Pilkington 2002).

Hardcore ethnic hegemonies often have great, inherent difficulties engineering a fundamental political change, although they might be more open to gradual changes. This is the case because fundamental reforms may undermine the very logic of these ethnic regimes and spell their political end. This, for example, happened in South Africa during the 1990s.

What are the factors that might explain the willingness of a country to initiate political reform on a large scale? I believe that there might be at least three such factors, factors that might act on their own or in a variety of combinations:

1. Internalized national memory of the horrors of civil war (as in the case of post-Franco Spain) and a conscious effort of preventing the repetition of such horrors.

2. A long tradition of incremental reforms in the interest of compromise (as in the case of the United Kingdom) to produce social and political peace.

3. Massive unending violence (as in the case of Northern Ireland) and widespread feeling within the polity that only political settlement can lead to peace and stability.

Even though ethnic majorities are extremely reluctant to give up their superior positions, as demonstrated in the cases of the Greek Cypriots, Israeli Jews, and Sri Lanka's Sinhalese, under certain political conditions they may be forced to do so or reach the conclusion that it is in their best interest to do so. Several cases, notably those of Northern Ireland and South Africa, demonstrate the impact of a long-term, seemingly unending conflict as a motivator for large-scale change. Other cases, such as that of Canada and Switzerland, demonstrate the impact of the incremental and more massive tradition of reform as enabling a country to initiate change; to some degree such a tradition is part and parcel of democracy.

The Consequences of Unyielding Ethnic Hegemony

While hegemony might "work" in numerous situations, especially when the demographic advantage of the dominant group is accompanied by economic, military, and political prominence, as well as when there is relative indifference of the outside world to the fate of the dominated group(s), hegemonic regimes are quite vulnerable to instability and to internal and external demands for change. In the short run, demographic dominance could result in a relatively stable ethnicized polity, but it is often unlikely to be a stable regime in the long run. The larger the minority within an ethnicized polity and the more hegemonic the regime is, the more devastating the potential negative results.

There are several negative consequences to hegemony, as fully explained in Chapter 2:

1. Even under the best of circumstances, hegemony results in a fundamentally flawed democracy that exists in contradiction to the contemporary world's political culture. Ethnic hegemony is therefore almost invariably a source of considerable tension. The very notion of ethnic hegemony is a deviation from the democratic principle of individual and group equality. Lord Acton recognized already in the nineteenth century that nationalism leads to oppression of minorities (1907).

2. Ethnic hegemony is not only damaging to its "natural" victims, members of the minority group, but often to members of the majority group as well. Democracy is indivisible, and if one destroys one aspect of it (which ethnic hegemony does in the case of majority-minority relations) one is likely to harm other parts of the regime as well. Thus the oppression of a minority within a hegemonic ethnic regime is likely to lead to the militarization of that society to defend the status quo against inevitable challenges, the emergence of unreasonable demands for unity within the majority, and the identification of some members of the majority as disloyal minority-sympathizers or even traitors.

3. As shown in many cases, ethnic hegemony is a basic source of instability both internally and internationally. Although it is impossible to predict precisely what might happen in a particular situation, on the whole the result of promoting ethnic hegemony is likely to be destabilizing. The contradiction between the proclaimed commitment to democracy and the loyalty to the aims of a hegemonic state invites instability. Thus, for example, long-term hegemony is likely to lead to separatism (e.g., the case of Francoist Spain, Chechnya and other parts of the old Russian and Soviet empires, Former Yugoslavia, Sri Lanka, Cyprus, and numerous other cases). Separatist movements of all types are obviously greatly destabilizing (Spencer 1998). They are inevitable consequences of hegemonic rule.

What Taras and Ganguly (1998, 2006) call "ethno-secessionist movements" are often reactions to overly aggressive hegemonic policies that radicalize their victims (more often than not, permanently).

4. Aggressive hegemonic behavior often results in massive bloodshed, as has been documented extensively by several scholars (Gurr 1993, 2000). The link between hegemony and violence is rather direct although not inevitable. It is possible, as Lustick's control model suggests, that a subordinate group will accept its fate and offer minimal resistance to ethnic domination (1979). Contemporary politics suggest that this is a rare response. When a subordinate group resists domination, the hegemonic group might take a strong, violent action against it, particularly if it views its position as weakening in the long run. The cases of East Pakistan, Nigeria, Rwanda, the Former Yugoslavia, and many others have resulted in the killing of large numbers of people identified by members of the hegemonic group as enemies of "their" state.

More specifically, hegemonic states and the dominant majorities that they claim to represent often adopt policies designed to homogenize their political systems and even their societies. Homogenizing a polity could possibly be achieved by politically marginalizing the minority or totally dominating it, a result that could (although is unlikely to) be achieved peacefully or without large-scale bloodshed. Homogenizing a society requires the physical removal of the minorities, and it could easily result in large-scale violence. Therefore, in many situations genocide or ethnocide is organically linked to hegemony. Genocidal operations have been carried out by hegemonic states such as Iraq, Rwanda, Serbia, Nigeria, Pakistan, Burundi, and Burma. Genocide is, of course, the most severe policy that a hegemonic polity might carry out against those considered its ethnic enemies. Less severe policies include expulsion of the types seen in Bosnia, Kosovo, Israel, and Czechoslovakia.

A third consequence of hegemonic policy is forced assimilation, discussed by many scholars (Taras and Ganguly 2006, 14; McGarry and O'Leary 1993, 16–22). This is a situation in which minority members are forced to give up "elements of their cultural, linguistic, religious, and/or national identity" (Schneckener and Wolff 2004, 21) and become, in effect, members of the hegemonic nation. In some situations hegemony does not lead to forced assimilation because neither of the groups involved in a conflict believe it can be done or is even interested in doing it (e.g., Arabs in Israel). There are, nevertheless, many situations in which assimilation has been attempted: the Hungarians tried to Magyarize the Slovaks prior to World War I, the Italians under Mussolini tried to Italianize the Germans of South Tyrol (1922–39), the Turks refused to recognize the existence of a Kurdish nation (thus assuming assimilation), the Bulgarians tried to assimilate the Turks in the 1970s and 1980s, Francoist Spain attempted to turn Catalans into Spaniards between 1939–75, and so forth.

Nonhegemonic polities may often engage in "civic integration" (McGarry and O'Leary 1993, 17) or "inter-ethnic integration" (Horowitz 1985, 587), trying to create civic, national, or patriotic identity among their diverse groups. These projects, often typical to immigrant societies such as Australia or the United States, are based on the principles of equal citizenship for all individuals, tolerance toward all groups, and no coercive assimilation, although there is the presumption that the language and culture of the majority, or that of the founding people, is to be prominent in society as a whole. Such civic integration, although often not as neutral as it is claimed to be, is quite different from coercive assimilation within hegemonic states where there are already distinct groups with a formed identity of their own.

Different "methodologies" of hegemonism are, of course, not mutually exclusive. Some hegemonic polities have used them simultaneously. Harsh policies of population transfer (i.e., expulsion), let alone genocidal practices, are often unavailable to hegemonic elites. In such situations these elites may be forced to choose, by necessity, softer techniques to maintain or enhance their hegemony.

In general, hegemonic policy is based on a Hobbesian, realist perspective on human relations, including intergroup relations. It is the belief that the stronger group in a sociopolitical situation must rule the weaker group and that the relationship between them is inevitably conflictual. This realist, conflictual position has been challenged over the last few decades by a more liberal position, reflected in consociationalism, federalism of all types, cantonal and autonomal schemes, and so forth. These alternatives to hegemonic control are based on the assumption that stability and justice cannot be achieved unless the power of the socially dominant group is curtailed by the state. Liberal democracy, with its emphasis on individual rights, is based on the very same assumption: it establishes political equality among individuals despite the recognition that socioeconomically there is no equality.

In the final analysis, both hegemonic and inclusive solutions to intergroup relations in deeply divided societies are based on the way in which people construct their reality, not by the way reality is. Constitutional designs are merely reflections of that constructed reality. If people of different nationalities and ethnicities can imagine equality and view it as a necessary element of their political life, then they might be open to inclusive solutions. They resort to hegemonic solutions if they cannot imagine such possibilities.

Many of the cases presented in this volume (particularly in Chapters 4 and 5), cases of both gradual and fundamental transformation, suggest that hegemonic political systems are capable of adopting creative, enlightened, and constitutionally imaginative solutions to internal ethnic conflict. In all such cases – successes in the face of long-term and bitter conflict – close cooperation between the state, leading elements within the ethnic majority, and moderate elements within the minority were necessary conditions for progress toward better interethnic relations. Political compromise is never easy, particularly not in a democracy, however, a commitment to peaceful resolution of ethnic conflict and political ingenuity could bring about considerable improvement in a conflictual environment.

On the whole, the gradual approach to political change seems to be more promising than the radical or megaconstitutional approach. Yet relations between ethnic or national groups living in the same political space could easily deteriorate to a level in which only radical solutions are available. In those situations, political engineering – the redesigning of the political order – is at a premium.

References

Abu-Laban, Yasmeen and Daiva Stasiulis. 1992. "Ethnic Pluralism under Siege: Popular and Partisan Opposition to Multiculturalism," *Canadian Public Policy* 18(4), 365–86.

Acton, Lord Emerich Ed. 1907. "Nationality," in J. N. Figgis and R. V. Laurence, eds., *The History of Freedom and Other Essays* (London: Macmillan and Co. Limited).

Ahern, Bertie. 2003. "In Search of Peace: The Fate and Legacy of the Good Friday Agreement," *Harvard International Review* (Winter), 26–31.

Aklaev, Airat R. 1999. *Democratization and Ethnic Peace: Patterns of Ethnopolitical Crisis Management in Post-Soviet Settings* (Aldershot, UK: Ashgate).

Almond, Gabriel. 1956. "Comparative Political Systems," *Journal of Politics* 18, 391–409.

Anderson, Benedict. 1983. *Imagined Communities: Reflections on the Origins and the Spread of Nationalism* (London: Verso).

Arel, Dominique, 2001. "Political Stability in Multinational Democracies: Comparing Language Dynamics in Brussels, Montreal and Barcelona," in Alain-G. Gagnon and James Tully, eds., *Multinational Democracies* (Cambridge and New York: Cambridge University Press), 65–89.

Argun, Betigul Ercan. 1999. "Universal Citizenship Rights and Turkey's Kurdish Question," *Journal of Muslim Minority Affairs* 19(1), 85–104.

Aronoff, Myron. 1989. *Israeli Visions and Divisions: Cultural Change and Political Conflict* (New Brunswick, NJ: Transaction Press).

Aronoff, Myron and Pierre Atlas, 1998. "The Peace Process and Competing Challenges to the Dominant Zionist Discourse," in Ilan Peleg, ed., *The Middle East Peace Process: Interdisciplinary Perspectives* (Albany: State University of New York Press), 41–60.

Azaryahu, Maoz. 1995. *State Cults: Independence Celebrations and the Fallen, 1948–1956* (Sde Boker: Ben-Gurian University of the Negev Press) (Hebrew).

Bahcheli, Tozun. 2000. "Searching for a Cyprus Settlement," *Journal of Federalism*, 30(1–2), 203–16.

Baker, Judith, ed. 1994. *Group Rights* (Toronto: University of Toronto Press).

Baker, Pauline H. 1996. "Conflict Resolution Versus Democratic Governance: Divergent Paths to Peace?" in Chester A. Crocker and Fen Osler Hampson, with Pamela Aall, eds., *Managing Global Chaos* (Washington, DC: UPIS Press), 563–71.

Barber, Benjamin. 1985. "How Swiss Is Rousseau?" *Political Theory* 13, 475–95.

Barry, Brian. 1975. "Review Article: Political Accommodation and Consociational Democracy," *British Journal of Political Science* 5 (October), 477–505.

———. 2001. *Culture and Equality: An Egalitarian Critique of Multiculturalism* (Cambridge, MA: Harvard University Press).

Barzilai, Gad and Ilan Peleg. 1994. "Israel and Future Borders: Assessment of a Dynamic Process," *Journal of Peace Research* 31(1), 49–63.

Barziali, Gad, Efraim Yuchtman-Yaar, and Zeev Segal. 1996. *The High Court of Justice in View of Israeli Society* (Tel Aviv: Tel Aviv University Press) (Hebrew).

Basta, Lidja R. and Thomas Fleiner, eds. 1996. *Federalism and Multiethnic States: The Case of Switzerland* (Fribourgs Switzerland: Institut du federalisme).

Beaufays, Jean. 1995. "Observations on Switzerland: A Model for Belgium," in Brown-John, C. Lloyd, ed., *Federal-Type Solutions and European Integration* (Lanham, NY and London: University Press of America).

Bennum, Mervyn and Marilyn D. Newitt. 1995. *Negotiating Justice: A New Constitution for South Africa* (Exeter, UK: University of Exeter Press).

Ben-Porat, Guy. 2006. Global Liberalism, Local Popularism: Peace and Conflict in Israel/Palestine and Northern Ireland (Syracuse, NY: Syracuse University Press).

Benvenisti, Meron. 2000. *Sacred Landscape: The Buried History of the Holy Land since 1948* (Berkeley: University of California Press).

Berg, Eiki. 2002. "Local Resistance, National Identity and Global Swings in Post-Soviet Estonia," *Europe-Asia Studies* 54(1), 109–22.

Bew, Paul. 2003. "Paisleyism Cannot Be Appeased: The DUP Has Nothing to Offer to a Much Needed Culture of Tolerance," *Guardian*, December 4.

Bissoondath, Neil. 1994. *Selling Illusions: The Cult of Multiculturalism in Canada* (Toronto: Penguin).

Black, Max, ed. 1962. *The Importance of Language* (Englewood Cliffs, NJ: Prentice-Hall).

Blum, Andrew. 2001. "Recognition as Protection/Recognition as Threat: Understanding the Link between Minority Rights and Ethnic Hostility," *Nationalism and Ethnic Politics* 7(2) (Summer), 95–124.

Bocock, Robert. 1986. *Hegemony* (Chichester [West Sussex]: E. Horwood; New York: Tavistock Publications).

Bogdanor, Vernon. 1999a. "Devolution: Decentralization or Disintegration?" *The Political Quarterly*, 185–94.

———. 1999b. "The British-Irish Council and Devolution," *Government and Opposition* 34(3) (Summer), 287–98.

———. 2001. *Devolution in the United Kingdom* (Oxford: Oxford University Press).

Bohn, David Earle. 1980. "Consociational Democracy and the Case of Switzerland," *The Journal of Politics* 42 (1) (February), 165–79.

Bollen, Kenneth and Juan Diez Medrano. 1998. "Who Are the Spaniards? Nationalism and Identification in Spain," *Social Forces* 77(2) (December), 587–622.

Bonime-Blanc, Andrea. 1987. *Spain's Transition to Democracy: The Politics of Constitution Making* (Boulder, CO: Westview Press).

Bradbury, Jonathan and James Mitchell. 2001. "Devolution: New Politics for Old?" *Parliamentary Affairs* 54, 257–75.

———. 2002. "Devolution and Territorial Politics: Stability, Uncertainty and Crisis," *Parliamentary Affairs* 55, 299–316.

Brass, Paul, ed. 1985. *Ethnic Groups and the State* (London: Croom Helm).

———. 1999. *The Politics of India since Independence* (Cambridge and New York: Cambridge University Press).

Breton, Raymond. 1984. "The Production and Allocation of Symbolic Resources: An Analysis of the Linguistic and Ethnocultural Fields in Canada," *Canadian Review of Sociology and Anthropology* 21, 123–40.

———. 1986. "Multiculturalism and Canadian Nation-Building," in Alan Cairns and Cynthia Williams, eds., *The Politics of Gender, Ethnicity and Language in Canada* (Toronto: University of Toronto Press), 27–66.

———. 1992. *Why Meech Failed* (Toronto: C. H. Howe Institute).

Brooks, Stephen. 1993. *Social Policy in Canada* (Toronto: McClleland and Stewart).

———. 1996. *Canadian Democracy* (Toronto: Oxford University Press).

Brubaker, Rogers. 1996. *Nationalism Reframed: Nationhood and the National Question in the New Europe* (New York: Cambridge University Press).

———. 2004. "In the Name of the Nation: Reflections on Nationalism and Patriotism," *Citizenship Studies* 8(2) (June), 115–27.

Burg, Steven L. 1996. *War or Peace? Nationalism, Democracy and American Foreign Policy in Post-Communist Europe* (New York: New York University Press).

Burgess, Michael, 2001. "Competing-National Visions: Canada-Quebec Relations in a Comparative Perspective," in Alain-G. Gagnon and James Tully, eds., *Multinational Democracies* (Cambridge and New York: Cambridge University Press), 279–99.

Butora, Martin and Zora Butorova. 1993. "Slovakia: The Identity Challenges of the Newly Born State," *Social Research* 60(4) (Winter), 705–36.

———. 1999. "Slovakia's Democratic Awakening," *Journal of Democracy* 10(1) (January), 80–95.

Byman, Daniel and Stephen Van Evera. 1998. "Why They Fight: Hypotheses on the Causes of Contemporary Deadly Conflict," *Security Studies* 7(3) (Spring), 1–50.

Camilleri, Joseph and Richard Falk. 1992. *The End of Sovereignty? The Politics of a Shrinking and Fragmented World* (Aldershot UK: Edward Elgar).

Cannon, Gordon E. 1982. "Consociationalism vs. Control: Canada as a Case Study," *Western Political Quarterly* 35(1) (March), 50–64.

Carr, Raymond, ed. 2000. *Spain: A History* (Oxford: Oxford University Press).

Carrillo, Ernesto. 1997. "Local Government and Strategies for Decentralization in the 'State of the Autonomies,'" *Publius* 27(4) (Fall), 39–63.

Cash, John D. 1998. "The Dilemmas of Political Transformation in Northern Ireland," *Pacifica Review* 10(3), 227–34.

Cederman, Lars-Erik. 1997. *Emergent Actors in World Politics: How States and Nations Develop and Dissolve* (Princeton: Princeton University Press).

Central Intelligence Agency, World Factbook, http://www.cia.gov/cia/publications/factbook/.

Chadda, Maya, 2004. "Between Consociationalism and Control: Sri Lanka," in Ulrich Schneckener and Stefan Wolff, eds., *Managing and Settling Ethnic Conflicts* (New York: Palgrave), 94–114.

Christopher, A. J. 1995. "Post-Apartheid South Africa and the Nation-State," in Anthony Lemon, ed., *The Geography of Change in South Africa* (Chichester, UK: Wiley), 3–18.

Clarance, William. 2002. "Conflict and Community in Sri Lanka," *History Today* 52(7) (July), 41–7.

Coakley, John. 1992. "The Resolution of Ethnic Conflict: Toward a Typology," *International Political Science Review* 13(4), 343–58.

———. ed. 1993. *The Territorial Management of Ethnic Conflict* (London: Cass).

———. 1994. "Approaches to the Resolution of Ethnic Conflict: The Strategy of Non-territorial Autonomy," *International Political Science Review* 15(3), 217–314.

Coates, Crispin. 1998. "Spanish Regionalism and the Future of the European Union," *Parliamentary Affairs* 51(2) (April), 259–71.

Cobban, Alfred. 1969. *The Nation State and National Self-Determination*, rev. ed. (London: Fontana).

Cohen, Asher and Bernard Susser. 1996. "From Accommodation to Decision: Transformation of Israel's Religio-Political Life," *Journal of Church and State* 38(4), 817–39.

Colomer, Josep M. 1991. "Transitions by Agreement: Modeling the Spanish Way," *American Political Science Review* 85(4) (December), 1283–1302.

———. 1995. *Game Theory and the Transition to Democracy: The Spanish Model* (London: Edward Elgar).

———. 1998. "The Spanish 'State of Autonomies': Non-Institutional Federalism," *West European Politics* 21(4) (October) 40–52. Published also in Paul Heywood, ed., *Politics and Policy in Democratic Spain: No Longer Different?* (London: Frank Cass), 40–52.

Commission on Security and Cooperation in Europe. 1994. *Human Rights and Democratization in the Czech Republic* (September), 1–32.

Connolly, William E. 1991. *Identity/Difference, Democratic-Negotiations of Political Paradox* (Ithaca, NY: Cornell University Press).

Cornell, Svante E. 2001. "The Kurdish Question in Turkish Politics," *Orbis* 45(1) (Winter), 31–46.

Craig, Gerald M. 1963. *Lord Durham's Report* (Toronto: McClleland and Stewart).

Crawford, Neta and Audie Klotz, eds. 1999. *How Sanctions Work: Lessons from South Africa* (London: St. Martin's Press).

Crick, Bernard, ed. 1991. *National Identities: The Constitution of the United Kingdom* (Oxford: Blackwell).

Cullen, Kevin. 2005. "The Love of the Irish," *Boston Globe*, July 10.

Dahl, Robert, 1971. *Polyarchy, Participation and Observation* (New Haven, CT: Yale University Press).

———. 1989. *Democracy and Its Critics* (New Haven, CT: Yale University Press).

Datta, Rekha. 1999. "Hindu Nationalism or Pragmatic Party Politics? A Study of India's Hindu Party," *International Journal of Politics Culture and Society* 12(4), 573–87.

De Villiers, Bertus. 1994. "Forward" in Bertus de Villiers, ed., *Evaluating Federal Systems* (Netherlands: Martinus Nijhoff Publishers).

DeVotta, Neil. 2005. "From Ethnic Outbidding to Ethnic Conflict: The Institutional Bases for Sri Lanka's Separatist War," *Nations and Nationalism* 11(1), 141–59.

Diamond, Larry and Marc F. Plattner, eds. 1999. *Democratization in Africa* (Baltimore: Johns Hopkins University Press).

Diamond, Larry, Juan Linz, and Seymour Martin Lipset. 1990. *Politics in Developing Countries: Comparing Experiences with Democracy* (Boulder, CO: Lynne Riener Publishers).

Don-Yehiya, Eliezer. 1999. *Religion and Political Accommodation in Israel* (Jerusalem: The Floersheimer Institute for Policy Studies).

Douglas, Neville. 1998. "The Politics of Accommodation, Social Change and Conflict Resolution in Northern Ireland," *Political Geography* 17(2) (February), 209–29.

Dowty, Alan. 1999. "Is Israel Democratic? Substance and Semantics in the 'Ethnic Democracy' Debate," *Israel Studies* 4 (Fall), 1–15.

———. 2000. *The Jewish State: A Century Later* (Berkeley: University of California Press).

Draper, Theodore. 1993. "The End of Czechoslovakia," *New York Review of Books*, January 23.

Dreidger, Leo. 1996. *Multi-Ethnic Canada* (Toronto: Oxford University Press).

Duchacek, Ivo. 1973. *Power Maps: Comparative Politics of Constitutions* (Santa Barbara, CA: ABC Clio).

———. 1987. *Comparative Federalism: The Territorial Dimension of Politics* (Lanham, MD: University Press of America; Philadelphia: Center for the Study of Federalism).

Duchacek, Ivo, Daniel Latouche, and Garth Stevenson, eds. 1988. *Perforated Sovereignties and International Relations: Trans-Sovereign Contacts in Subnational Governments* (Westport, CT: Greenwood Press).

Dumont, Paul. 1984. "The Origins of Kemalist Ideology," in Jacob M. Landau, ed., *Ataturk and the Modernization of Turkey* (Boulder, CO: Westview Press), 25–44.

du Toit, B. M. 1991. "The Far Right in Current South African Politics," *Journal of Modern African Studies* 29(4), 627–67.

Ehrlich, Thomas. 1974. *Cyprus 1958–1967: International Crises and the Rule of Law* (New York and London: Oxford University Press).

Ergil, Dogu. 2000a. "Identity Crises and Political Instability in Turkey," *Journal of International Affairs* 54(1) (Fall), 43–62.

———. 2000b. "The Kurdish Question in Turkey," *Journal of Democracy* 11(3) (July), 122–35.

Erk, Jan. 2003. "Swiss Federalism and Congruence," *Nationalism and Ethnic Politics* 9 (2), 50–74.

Evans, Peter, Dietrich Rueschmeyer, and Theda Skocpol. 1985. *Bringing the State Back In* (Cambridge and New York: Cambridge University Press).

Fisher, Ronald J. 2001. "Cyprus: The Failure of Mediation and the Escalation of an Identity-Based Conflict to an Adversarial Impasse," *Journal of Peace Research* 38(3), 307–26.

Fleiner, Thomas. 2002. "Recent Developments in Swiss Federalism," *Publius* 32(2) (Spring), 97–123.

Flynn, M. K. 2001. "Constructed Identities in Iberia," *Ethnic and Racial Studies* 24(5) (September), 703–18.

Fossas, Enric. 2001. "National Plurality and Equality," in Raquejo Ferran, ed., *Democracy and National Pluralism* (New York: Routledge), 64–83.

Franchi, V. and T. M. Swart. 2003. "From Apartheid to Affirmative Action: The Use of 'Racial' Markers in Past, Present and Future Articulations of Identity among South African Students," *International Journal of Intercultural Relations* 27(2) (March), 209–37.

Freedom House, Annual Survey of Political Rights and Civil Liberties.

Freitag, Markus and Adrian Vatter. 2004. "Political Institutions and the Wealth of Regions: Swiss Cantons in Comparative Perspective," *European Urban and Regional Studies* 11 (October), 291–301.

Friedman, Steven. 2004. "South Africa: Building Democracy after Apartheid," in E. Gyimah-Boadi, ed., *Democratic Reform in Africa: The Quality of Progress* (Boulder, CO: Lynne Riener Publishers), 235–62.

Friel, Brian. 1981. *Translations (a play)* (London and Boston: Faber and Faber).

Fukuyama, Francis. 1992. *The End of History and the Last Man* (New York: Free Press; Toronto: Maxwell Macmillan Canada; New York: Maxwell Macmillan International).

Gagnon, Alain-G. 2001. "The Moral Foundation of Asymmetrical Federalism: A Normative Exploration of the Case of Quebec and Canada," in Alain-G. Gagnon and James Tully, *Multinational Democracies* (Cambridge and New York: Cambridge University Press), 319–37.

Gagnon, Alain-G. and James Tully, eds. 2001. *Multinational Democracies* (Cambridge and New York: Cambridge University Press).

Gallagher, Tom. 1992. "Autonomy in Spain: Lessons for Britain?" in Bernard Crick, ed., *National Identities: The Constitution of the United Kingdom* (Oxford: Blackwell), 119–33.

Gallie, W. B., 1962. "Essentially Contested Concepts," in Max Black, ed., *The Importance of Language* (Englewood Cliffs, NJ: Prentice-Hall), 121–46.

Ganguly, Rajat. 2004. "Sri Lanka's Ethnic Conflict: At a Crossroads between Peace and War," *Third World Quarterly* 25(5), 903–18.

Gann, L. H. and Peter Duignan, 1981. *Why South Africa Will Survive?* (London: Croom Helm).

———. 1991. *Hope for South Africa?* (Stanford, CA: Hoover Institution Press).

Gellner, Ernest. 1983. *Nations and Nationalism* (Oxford: Blackwell).

———. 1997. *Nationalism* (New York: New York University Press).

Gentile, Emilio. 2006. *Politics as Religion* (Princeton: Princeton University Press).

Ghai, Jash, ed. 2000. *Autonomy and Ethnicity: Negotiating Competing Claims in Multiethnic States* (Cambridge and New York: Cambridge University Press).

Ghanim, Asad. 2001. The Palestinian-Arab Minority in Israel, 1948–2000: A Political Study (Albany: State University of New York Press).

Giddens, Anthony. 2000. *The Third Way and its Critics* (Cambridge: Polity Press).

Giliomee, Hermann. 1995. "Democratization in South Africa," *Political Science Quarterly* 110(1) (Spring), 83–105.

———. 2003. *The Afrikaners: Biography of a People* (Charlottesville: University of Virginia Press; Cape Town: Tafelberg Publishers).

Giliomee, Hermann and Jannie Gagiano, eds. 1990. *The Elusive Search for Peace: South Africa, Israel and Northern Ireland* (Cape Town: Oxford University Press).

Giliomee, Hermann and Lawrence Schlemmer. 1989. *From Apartheid to Nation-Building: Contemporary South African Debates* (Cape Town: Oxford University Press).

Gloppen, Siri. 1997. *South Africa: The Battle over the Constitution* (Aldershot, UK and Brookfield, VT: Ashgate/Dartmouth).

Goldberg, David Theo. 2002. *The Racial State* (Oxford: Blackwell Publishers).

Gramsci, Antonio. 1971. *Selections from the Prison Notebooks* (New York: International Publishers).

Greenfeld, Leah. 1992. *Nationalism: Five Roads to Modernity* (Cambridge, MA: Harvard University Press).

Greenway, H. D. S. 2001. "Hindu Nationalism Clouds the Face of India," *World Policy Journal* 18(1) (Spring), 89–105.

Greenwood, Davyd. 1985. "Castilians, Basques and Andalusians: An Historical Comparison of Nationalism," in Paul Brass, ed., *Ethnic Groups and the State* (London: Croom Helm), 202–27.

Guelke, Adrian. 1992. "Ethnic Rights and Majority Rule: The Case of South Africa," *International Political Science Review* 13(4), 415–32.

———. 1996. "The Impact of the End of the Cold War on the South African Transition," *Journal of Contemporary African Studies* 14(1) (January), 87–100.

———. 1999. *South Africa in Transition: The Misunderstood Miracle* (London and New York: T. B. Tauris).

———. 2004. "The Politics of Imitation: The Role of Comparison in Peace Processes," in Adrian Guelke, ed., *Democracy and Ethnic Conflict: Advancing Peace in Deeply Divided Societies* (Houndmills, Basingstoke, Hampshire and New York: Palgrave Macmillan), 168–83.

———. 2005. *Rethinking the Rise and Fall of Apartheid* (Houndmills, Basingstoke, Hampshire and New York: Palgrave Macmillan).

Gunter, Michael M. 1997. *The Kurds and the Future of Turkey* (New York: St. Martin's Press).

Gurr, Ted Robert. 1993. *Minorities at Risk: A Global View of Ethnopolitical Conflict* (Washington, DC: USIP Press).

———. 2000. *People versus States: Minorities at Risk in the New Century* (Washington, DC: USIP Press).

Gwyn, Richard. 1995. *Nationalism without Walls: The Unbearable Lightness of Being Canadian* (Toronto: McClleland and Stewart).

Habermas, Jurgen. 1998. *The Inclusion of the Other* (Cambridge, MA: MIT Press).

Hadar, Leon T. 1999. "Israel in the Post-Zionist Age: Being Normal and Loving It," *World Policy Journal* 16(1) (Spring), 76–86.

Harding, Jeremy. 2004. "What to Wear to School," *London Review of Books* 26(4) (February 19).

Harel-Shalev, Ayelet. 2006. "The Status of Minority Languages in Deeply Divided Societies: Urdu in India and Arabic in Israel – A Comparative Perspective," *Israel Studies Forum* 21(2), 28–57.

Hauss, Charles. 2001. *International Conflict Resolution* (London and New York: Continuum).

Hayden, Robert. 1992. "Constitutional Nationalism in the Formerly Yugoslav Republics," *Slavic Review* 51(4) (Winter), 654–73.

Hazareesingh, Sudhir, ed. 2002. *The Jacobin Legacy in Modern France: Essays in Honor of Vincent Wright* (Oxford and New York: Oxford University Press).

Hazell, R. 2000. "Regional Government in England: Three Policies in Search of a Strategy," in S. Chen and T. Wright, eds., *The English Question* (London: Fabian Society).

Hazony, Yoram. 2000. *The Jewish State* (New York: Basic Books).

Henrard, Kristin. 2003. "Post-Apartheid South Africa: Transformation and Reconciliation," *World Affairs* 166(1) (Summer), 37–55.

Hertzberg, Arthur. 1997. *The Zionist Idea: A Historical Analysis and Reader* (Philadelphia: Jewish Publication Society).

Herzl, Theodor. 1988 (orig. pub. 1896). *The Jewish State* (New York: Dover Publication).

Hilde, Sigurd. 1999. "Slovak Nationalism and the Break-up of Czechoslovakia," *Europe-Asia Studies* 51(4) (June), 647–66.

Hintjens, Helen M. 1999. "Explaining the 1994 Genocide in Rwanda," *The Journal of Modern African Studies* 37(2), 241–86.

Hitchens, Christopher. 1989. *Hostage to History: Cyprus from the Ottomans to Kissinger*, 2nd ed. (New York: The Noonday Press).

Hobsbawm, Eric. 1990. *Nations and Nationalism since 1780* (Cambridge and New York: Cambridge University Press).

Hooghe, Liesbet. 1993. "Belgium: From Regionalism to Federalism," in John Coakley, ed., *The Territorial Management of Ethnic Conflict* (London: Cass, 44–68).

Hoole, H. R. R. 1998. "The Tamil Secessionist Movement in Sri Lanka (Ceylon): A Case of Secession by Default?" in Metta Spencer, ed., *Separatism: Democracy and Disintegration* (Lanham, MD: Rowman and Littlefield Publishers, Inc.), ch. 11, 253–79.

Horowitz, Donald L. 1985. *Ethnic Groups in Conflict* (Berkeley: University of California Press).

_____. 1991a. *A Democratic South Africa?: Constitutional Engineering in a Divided Society* (Cape Town: Oxford University Press).

_____. 1991b. "Making Moderation Pay," in Joseph Montville, ed., *Conflict and Peacemaking in Multiethnic Societies* (Lexington, MA: Lexington Books).

Huntington, Samuel. 1991. *The Third Wave: Democratization in the Late Twentieth Century* (Norman: University of Oklahoma Press).

_____. 1993. "The Clash of Civilizations," *Foreign Affairs* 72(3) (Summer), 22–49.

_____. 1996. "Democracy for the Long Haul," *Journal of Democracy* 7(2) (April), 3–13.

_____. 2002. *Who Are We? The Challenges to America's National Identity* (Cambridge: Cambridge University Press).

Icduygu, Ahmet, David Romano, and Ibrahim Sirkeci. 1999. "The Ethnic Question in an Environment of Insecurity: The Kurds of Turkey," *Ethnic and Racial Studies* 22(6) (November), 991–1010.

Inglehart, Ronald. 1990. *Culture Shift in Advanced Industrial Society* (Princeton: Princeton University Press).

Isaac, Kalpana. 1996. "Sri Lanka's Ethnic Divide," *Current History* 95(600) (April), 177–81.

Jenkins, John R. G. 1986. *Jura Separatism in Switzerland* (Oxford: Clarendon Press).

Jenkins, Simon. 2003. "The Good Friday Agreement is Brain-Dead," *Times* (London), October 22.

Jiryis, Sabri. 1969. *The Arabs of Israel* (Beirut: Institute for Palestine Studies).

Johns, Michael. 2002. "Assessing Risk Assessment: A Baltic Test," *Nationalism and Ethnic Politics* 18(1) (Spring), 105–28.

Joseph, Joseph S. 1999. *Cyprus: Ethnic Conflict and International Politics* (New York: St. Martin's Press).

Juergensmeyer, Mark. 1993. *The New Cold War? Religious Nationalism Confronts the Secular State* (Berkeley: University of California Press).

Kaplan, Robert D. 1994. "The Coming Anarchy," *Atlantic Monthly* 273(2) (February), 44–76.

_____. 2000. *The Coming Anarchy: Shattering the Dreams of the Post Cold War* (New York: Random House).

Karmis, Dimitrios and Alain-G. Gagnon. 2001. "Federalism, Federation and Collective Identities in Canada and Belgium: Different Routes, Similar Fragmentation," in Alain-G. Gagnan and James Tully, eds., *Multinational Democracies* (Cambridge and New York: Cambridge University Press).

Kaufmann, Eric P., ed. 2004. *Rethinking Ethnicity: Majority Groups and Dominant Minorities* (London and New York: Routledge).

Kearney, H. 1991. "Four Nations or One?" in Bernard Crick, ed., *National Identities: The Constitution of the United Kingdom* (Oxford: Blackwell).

Kearney, R. N. 1985. "Ethnic Conflict and The Tamil Separatist Movement in Sri Lanka," *Asian Survey* 25(9), 898–917.

Keating, Michael. 2001a. "So Many Nations, So Few States: Territory and Nationalism in the Global Order" in Alain-G. Gagnon and James Tully, eds., *Multinational Democracies* (Cambridge and New York: Cambridge University Press), 39–64.

———. 2001b. *Nations against the State: The New Politics of Nationalism in Quebec, Catalonia and Scotland* (Houndmills, Basingstoke, Hampshire and New York: Palgrave Macmillan).

Keating, Michael and John McGarry. 2001a. "Introduction" in Michael Keating and John McGarry, eds., *Minority Nationalism and Changing International Order* (Oxford: Oxford University Press), 1–15.

———, eds. 2001b. *Minority Nationalism and Changing International Order* (Oxford: Oxford University Press).

Kedar, Alexander. 2000. "A First Step in a Difficult and Sensitive Road: Preliminary Observations on Qaadan vs. Katzir," *Israeli Studies Bulletin* 16(1) (Fall), 3–11.

Keyman, E. Fuat. 1995. "On the Relation between Global Modernity and Nationalism: The Crisis of Hegemony and the Rise of (Islamic) Identity in Turkey," *New Perspective in Turkey* 13 (Fall), 93–120.

Killian, Caitlin. 2003. "The Other Side of the Veil: North African Women in France Respond to the Headscarf Affair," *Gender and Society* 17(4), 567–90.

Kimmerling, Baruch. 1983. *Zionism and Territory* (Berkeley: Institute of International Studies, University of California).

Kinzer, Stephen. 2006. "Kurds in Turkey: The Big Change," *The New York Review of Books* 53(1) (January 12), 34–6.

Kirch, Aksel, Marika Kirch, and Tarmo Tuisk. 1993. "Russians in the Baltic States: To Be or Not to Be?" *Journal of Baltic Studies* 24(2), 173–88.

Kirisci, Kemal and Gareth M. Winrow. 1997. *The Kurdish Question and Turkey: An Example of Trans-State Ethnic Conflict* (London: Frank Cass).

Kivisto, Peter. 2002. *Multiculturalism in a Global Society* (Oxford and Malden, MA: Blackwell Publishing).

Klotz, Audie. 1995. *Norms in International Relations: The Struggle against Apartheid* (Ithaca, NY: Cornell University Press).

Kohn, Hans. 1944. *The Idea of Nationalism: A Study in its Origins and Background* (New York: Macmillan).

———. 1956. *Nationalism and Liberty: The Swiss Example* (London: Allen and Union Ltd.).

Kopanic, Michael J. 1999. "A Brief Historical Background of Hungarians in Slovakia," *Central Europe Review* 1(2) (July).

Kopecky, Petr. 2000. "From 'Velvet Revolution' to 'Velvet Split': Consociational Institutions and the Disintegration of Czechoslovakia," in Michael Kraus and Allison Stanger, eds., *Irreconcilable Differences? Explaining Czechoslovakia's Dissolution* (Lanham, MD: Rowman and Littlefield Publishers), 69–86.

Kotze, H. J. 1996. "The New Parliament: Transforming the Westminster Heritage" in M. Faure and J. E. Lane, eds., *South Africa: Designing New Political Institutions* (London: Sage).

———. 1998. "South Africa: From Apartheid to Democracy," in M. Dogan and J. Higley, eds., *Elites, Crises, and the Origins of Regimes* (Lanham, MD: Rowman and Littlefield Publishers), 213–36.

_____. 2000. "The State and Social Change in South Africa," *International Social Science Journal* 52 (March), 79–94.

Kraus, Michael and Allison Stanger, eds. 2000. *Irreconcilable Differences? Explaining Czechoslovakia's Dissolution* (Lanham, MD: Rowman and Littlefield Publishers).

Kretzmer, David. 1990. *The Legal Status of the Arabs in Israel* (Boulder, CO: Westview).

Kristeva, Julia. 1991. *Strangers to Ourselves* (New York: Columbia University Press).

Kymlicka, Will. 1995. *Multicultural Citizenship: A Liberal Theory of Minority Rights* (Oxford: Clarendon Press).

_____. 1998. *Finding Our Way: Rethinking Ethnocultural Relations in Canada* (Oxford: Oxford University Press).

_____. 2002. "The Impact of Group Rights on Fear and Trust: A Response to Offe," *Hagar* 3(1), 19–36.

Kyriakides, Stanley K. 1968. *Cyprus: Constitutionalism and Crisis Government* (Philadelphia: University of Pennsylvania Press).

Laczko, Leslie S. 1994. "Canada's Pluralism in Comparative Perspective," *Ethnic and Racial Studies* 17(1) (January), 20–41.

Lahav, Pnina. 1997. *Judgment in Jerusalem: Chief Justice Simon Agranat and the Zionist Century* (Berkeley: University of California Press).

Laitin, David D. 1986. *Hegemony and Culture: Politics and Religious Change among the Yoruba* (Chicago: University of Chicago Press).

Lancaster, Thomas D. 1997. "Nationalism, Regionalism, and State Institutions: An Assessment of Opinions in Spain," *Publius* 27(4) (Fall), 115–33.

Lapidoth, Ruth. 1996. *Autonomy: Flexible Solutions to Ethnic Conflicts* (Washington, DC: USIP Press).

Laponce, Jean. 1987. *Languages and Their Territories* (Toronto: University of Toronto Press).

Leff, Carol Skalnik. 1988. *National Conflict in Czechoslovakia: The Making and Remaking of a State* (Princeton: Princeton University Press).

_____. 1995. "Czech and Slovak Nationalism in the Twentieth Century," in Peter F. Sugar, ed., *Eastern European Nationalism in the Twentieth Century* (Washington, DC: American University Press), 103–62.

_____. 2000. "Inevitability, Probability, Possibility: The Legacies of the Czech-Slovak Relationship, 1918–1989, and the Disintegration of the State," in Michael Kraus and Allison Stanger, eds., *Irreconcilable Differences? Explaining Czechoslovakia's Dissolution* (Lanham, MD: Rowman and Littlefield Publishers), 29–48.

Lenaerts, Koen. 1996. "Constitutionalism and the Many Faces of Federalism," *American Journal of Comparative Law* 38, 205–63.

Lester, Alan. 1998. *From Colonization to Democracy: The New Historical Geography of South Africa* (London and New York: I. B. Tauris).

Lieven, Dominic and John McGarry. 1993. "Ethnic Conflict in the Soviet Union and Its Successor States," in John McGarry and Brendon O'Leary, eds., *The Politics of Ethnic Conflict Regulation* (London and New York: Routledge), 62–83.

Lijphart, Arend. 1968. *The Politics of Accommodation: Pluralism and Democracy in the Netherlands* (Berkeley: University of California Press).

_____. 1977. *Democracy in Plural Societies: A Comparative Exploration* (New Haven, CT: Yale University Press).

_____. 1980. "Federal, Confederal, and Consociational Options for the South African Plural Society," in Robert I. Rotberg and John Barratt, eds., *Conflict and Compromise in South Africa* (Cape Town: David Philip), 51–75.

———. 1984. *Democracies: Patterns of Majoritarian and Consensus Government in Twenty-one Countries* (New Haven, CT: Yale University Press).

———. 1996. "The Puzzle of Indian Democracy: A Consociational Interpretation," *American Political Science Review* 90(2) (June), 258–68.

———. 1997. *Democracy in Plural Societies: A Comparative Exploration* (New Haven, CT: Yale University Press).

Linder, Wolf. 1994. *Swiss Democracy: Possible Solutions to Conflict in Multicultural Societies* (New York: St. Martin's Press).

Linz, Juan. 1985. "De la crisis del Estado unitario el Estado de las Autonomias," in Fernando Fernandez Rodrigue, ed., *La Espana de las Autonomias* (Madrid: Instituto de Estudios se Administracion Local), 527–672.

Linz, Juan, and Alfred Stepan, 1996a. *Problems of Democratic Transition and Consolidation* (Baltimore: Johns Hopkins University Press).

———. 1996b. "Toward Consolidated Democracies," *Journal of Democracy* 7(2) (April), 14–33.

Lustick, Ian. 1979. "Stability in Deeply Divided Societies: Consocialionalism vs. Control," *World Politics* 31(3), 325–44.

———. 1980a. "The Quiescent Palestinians: The System of Control over Arabs in Israel," in K. Nakhleh and E. Zureik, eds., *The Sociology of the Palestinians* (New York: St. Martin's Press) 64–83.

———. 1980b. *Arabs in the Jewish State: Israel's Control of a National Minority* (Austin: University of Texas Press).

———. 1993. *Unsettled States, Disputed Lands: Britain and Ireland, France and Algeria, Israel and the West Bank-Gaza* (Ithaca, NY: Cornell University Press).

Mackey, Eva. 1999. *The House of Difference: Cultural Politics and National Identity in Canada* (London and New York: Routledge).

Malova, Darina. 1994. "The Relationships between Political Parties and Civil Society in Postcommunist Czech-Slovakia," in Sona Szomolanyi and Grigorji Meseznikov, eds., *The Slovak Path of Transition – to Democracy?* (Bratislava, Slovakia: Slovak Political Science Association), 111–58.

———. 2001. "Slovakia: From the Ambiguous Constitution to the Dominance of Informal Rules," in Jan Zielonka, ed., *Democratic Consolidation in Eastern Europe, Volume I: Institutional Engineering* (Oxford: Oxford University Press), 346–77.

Maphai, Vincent T. 1999. "The New South Africa: A Season for Power-Sharing," in Larry Diamond and Marc F. Plattner, eds., *Democratization in Africa* (Baltimore: Johns Hopkins University Press), 94–108.

Martiniello, Marco, ed. 1998. *Multicultural Policies and the State: A Comparison of Two European Societies*, European Research Centre on Migration and Ethnic Relations (Utrecht: Utrecht University Press).

McAllister, Laura. 2000. "The New Politics in Wales: Rhetoric or Reality?" *Parliamentary Affairs* 53(3) (July), 591–604.

McGarry, John. 2002. "'Democracy' in Northern Ireland: Experiments in Self-Rule from the Protestant Ascendancy to the Good Friday Agreement," *Nations and Nationalism* 8(4), 451–74.

McGarry, John and Brendan O'Leary, eds. 1993. *The Politics of Ethnic Conflict Regulation* (London and New York: Routledge).

———. 2004a. "Stabilizing Northern Ireland Agreement," *Political Quarterly* 75(3), 213–25.

_____. 2004b. *The Northern Ireland Conflict: Consociational Engagements* (Oxford: Oxford University Press).

McKittrick, David. 2003. "Northern Ireland Elections: Careful Planning behind Changes to Political Landscape," *Independent* (London), November 29.

McRae, Kenneth, ed. 1974. *Consociational Democracy: Political Democracy in Segmented Societies* (Toronto: McClleland and Stewart).

McRoberts, Kenneth. 1988. *Quebec: Social Change and Political Crisis* (Toronto: McClleland and Stewart).

_____. 1997. *Misconceiving Canada: The Struggle for National Unity* (Toronto: Oxford University Press).

Mearsheimer, John. 1990. "Back to the Future," *International Security* 15(1) (Summer), 5–56.

Medding, Peter. 1990. *The Founding of Israeli Democracy, 1949–1967* (Oxford and New York: Oxford University Press).

Melman, Yossi. 2002. "Killing Moslems, Burn Mosques, Dream of a Hindu State," *Ha'aretz*, July 14 (Hebrew).

Memmi, Albert. 1967. *The Colonizer and the Colonized* (Boston: Beacon).

Migdal, Joel. 1988. *Strong Societies and Weak States: State-Society Relations and State Capabilities in the Third World* (Princeton: Princeton University Press).

_____. 2001. *Through the Lens of Israel: Explorations in State and Society* (Albany: State University of New York Press).

Milgram, Stanley. 1974. *Obedience to Authority* (New York: Harper and Row).

Mill, John Stuart. 1958 (orig. pub. 1861). *Considerations of Representative Government* (New York: New York Liberal Arts Press).

Miller, David. 1995. *On Nationality* (Oxford: Clarendon Press).

Misra, Amatendu. 1999. "Politics of the Hindu Right: Emergence and Growth of the Bharatiya Janata Party," *Politics, Administration and Change* 32, (July–December), 36–55.

Mitchell, James. 2000. "New Parliament, New Politics in Scotland," *Parliamentary Affairs* 53(3) (July), 605–21.

Mitchell, Timothy. 1991. "The Limits of the State," *American Political Science Review* 85(1), 77–96.

Montville, Joseph, ed. 1991. *Conflict and Peacemaking in Multiethnic Societies* (Lanham, MD: Lexington Books).

Moodie, T. Dunbar. 1975. *The Rise of Afrikanerdom* (Berkeley, University of California Press).

Moodley, Kogila. 1983. "Canadian Multiculturalism as Ideology," *Ethnic and Racial Studies* 6(3), 320–31.

Moreno, Luis. 1997. "Federalization and Ethnoterritorial Governance in Spain," *Publius* 27(4), 65–84.

_____. 2001a. "Ethnoterritorial Concurrence in Multinational Societies: The Spanish Comunidades Autonomas," in Alain-G. Gagnon and James Tully, eds., *Multinational Democracies* (Cambridge and New York: Cambridge University Press), 201–22.

_____. 2001b. *The Federalization of Spain* (London: Frank Cass).

Moreno, Luis and Carlos Trilles. 2005. "Decentralization and Welfare Reform in Andalusia," *Regional and Federal Studies*, 15(4), 519–35.

Morris-Hale, Walter, 1996. *Conflict and Harmony in Multi-ethnic Societies: An International Perspective* (New York: Peter Lang).

Mouffe, Chantal. 2002. "Which Public Sphere for a Democratic Society?" *Theoria* 99, (June), 55–65.

Murphy, A. B. 1989. "Territorial Politics in Multiethnic States," *Geographical Review* 79), 410–21.

Murray, Martin J. 1994. *A Revolution Deferred: The Painful Birth of Post-Apartheid South Africa* (New York and London: Verso).

Mutlu, Servet. 1995. "Population of Turkey by Ethnic Groups and Provinces," *New Perspectives on Turkey* 12, (Spring), 33–60.

———. 1996. "Ethnic Kurds in Turkey: A Demographic Study," *International Journal of Middle East Studies* 28), 517–41.

Nairn, Tom. 2001. "Farewell Britannia," *New Left Review* 7, 55–74.

Nakhleh, Khalil, and Elia Zureik, eds. 1980. *The Sociology of the Palestinians* (New York: St. Martin's Press).

Necatigil, Zaim M. 1998. *The Cyprus Question and the Turkish Position in International Law*, 2nd ed. (New York: Oxford University Press).

Newbury, Catherine. 1988. *The Cohesion of Oppression: Clientship and Ethnicity in Rwanda, 1860–1960* (New York: Columbia University Press).

———. 1995. "Background to Genocide: Rwanda," *Issue: A Journal of Opinion* 23(2), 12–17.

Noel, S. J. R. 1971a. "Political Parties and Elite Accommodation: Interpretations of Canadian Federalism," in J. Peter Meekison, ed., *Canadian Federalism: Myth or Reality*, 2nd ed. (Toronto: Metheum).

———. 1971b. "The Prime Minister's Role in Consociational Democracy," in Thomas A. Hoskin, ed., *Apex of Power: The Prime Minister and Political Leadership in Canada* (Scarborough, Ontario: Prentice-Hall Canada).

Nordlinger, Eric A. 1972. *Conflict Regulation and Divided Societies* (Cambridge, MA: Harvard University Press).

O'Connor, Kevin. 2003. *The History of the Baltic States* (Westport, CT: Greenwood Press).

O'Donell, Guilermo and Philippe Schmitter. 1986. *Transition from Authoritarian Rule: Tentative Conclusions about Uncertain Democracies* (Baltimore: Johns Hopkins University Press).

O'Leary, Brendan. 1999. "The Nature of the British-Irish Agreement," *New Left Review* 233), 66–96.

———. 2001a. "An Iron Law of Nationalism and Federation? A (neo Diceyian) Theory of the Necessity of a Federal Staatvolk and the Consociational Rescue," *Nations and Nationalism* 7(3), 273–96.

———. 2001b. "The Protection of Human Rights under the Belfast Agreement," *Political Quarterly* 72(3) (July–September), 353–65.

Offe, Claus. 1998. "Homogeneity and Constitutional Democracy: Coping with Identity Conflicts through Group Rights," *Journal of Political Philosophy* 6(2), 113–41.

———. 2002. "Political Liberalism and Group Rights and the Politics of Fear and Trust," *Hagar* 3(1), 5–17.

Ohmae, Kenichi. 1995. *The End of the Nation State: The Rise of Regional Economies* (New York: Free Press).

Ortiz, Carmen. 1999. "The Use of Folklore by the Franco Regime," *The Journal of American Folklore* 112(446), 479–96.

Ott, F. et al. 1996. "Ethnic Anxiety: A Case Study of Resident Aliens in Estonia (1990–1992)," *Journal of Baltic Studies* 27(1), 21–46.

Page, Don. 2000. "The Canadian Experience with Multiculturalism: Is It Relevant Elsewhere?" in Robert B. Tapp, ed., *Multiculturalism: Humanist Perspectives* (Amherst, NY: Prometheus Books), 35–50.

Paltiel, Khayyam Zev. 1987. "Group Rights in Canadian Constitution and Aboriginal Claims to Self-Determination," in Robert J. Jackson, Doreen Jackson, and Nicolas Baster Moore, ed., *Contemporary Canadian Politics* (Scarborough, Ontario: Prentice Hall Canada).

Patten, Alan. 2001. "Liberal Citizenship in Multiethnic Societies," in Alain-G. Gagnon and James Tully, *Multinational Democracies* (Cambridge and New York: Cambridge University Press), 279–98.

Peled, Yoav. 1992. "Ethnic Democracy and Legal Construction of Citizenship: Arab Citizens of the Jewish State," *American Political Science Review* 86(2), 432–43.

Peled, Yoav and Doron Navot. 2005. "Ethnic Democracy Revisited: On the State of Democracy in the Jewish State," *Israel Studies Forum* 20(1) (Summer), 3–27.

Peleg, Ilan. 1994. "Otherness and Israel's Arab Dilemma," in Laurence J. Silberstein and Robert L. Cohn, eds., *The Other in Jewish Thought and History: Construction of Jewish Culture and Identity* (New York: New York University Press), 258–80.

_____. 1995. *Human Rights in the West Bank and Gaza* (Syracuse: Syracuse University Press).

_____. 1998a. "Israel's Constitutional Order and Kulturkampf: The Role of Ben Gurion," *Israel Studies* 3(1), 230–50.

_____, ed. 1998b. *The Middle East Peace Process: Interdisciplinary Perspectives* (Albany: State University of New York Press).

_____. 1998c. "The Peace Process and Israel's Political Kulturkampf," in Ilan Peleg, ed., *The Middle East Peace Process: Interdisciplinary Perspectives* (Albany: State University of New York Press), 237–63.

_____. 2000. "Israel as a Liberal Democracy: Civil Rights in the Jewish State," in Laurie Eisenberg and Neil Caplan, eds., *Review Essays in Israel Studies: Books on Israel, Vol. 5* (Albany: State University of New York Press), 63–80.

_____. 2001. "Culture, Ethnicity and Human Rights in Contemporary Biethnic Democracies: The Case of Israel and Other Cases," in Lynda Bell, Andrew Nathan, and Ilan Peleg, eds., *Negotiating Culture and Human Rights* (New York: Columbia University Press), 303–33.

_____. 2002-3. "Israel between Democratic Universalism and Particularist Judaism: Challenging a Sacred Formula," *Report to the Oxford Centre for Hebrew and Jewish Studies*, 5–20.

_____. 2003a. "Ethnic Constitutional Orders and Human Rights: Historical, Comparative Analysis," in David Forsythe and Patrice McMahon, eds., *International Human Rights and Diversity* (Lincoln: University of Nebraska Press), 279–96.

_____. 2003b. "The Middle East: Israel," in Edward. A. Kolodziej and Marvin Weinbaum, eds., *A Force Frofonde: The Power, Politics, and Promise of Human Rights* (Philadelphia: University of Pennsylvania Press), 113–27.

_____. 2004a. "Transforming Hegemonic Ethnic Orders to Pluralist Regimes in Ethnically Divided Societies," in Adrian Guelke, ed., *Democracy and Ethnic Conflict: Advancing Peace in Deeply Divided Societies* (New York: Palgrave Macmillan), 7–25.

_____. 2004b. "Jewish-Palestinian Relations in Israel: From Hegemony to Equality?" *International Journal of Politics, Culture and Society* 17(3) (Spring), 415–37.

Peleg, Ilan and Dov Waxman. 2006. "Achieving Liberal-Multiculturalism in Deeply Divided Societies: A Comparison of the Challenges for Palestinians in Israel and Kurds in Turkey." Paper presented at the twenty-second annual meeting of the Association for Israel Studies, Banff, Canada, May 28.

Pettai, V. and K. Hallik. 2002. "Understanding Processes of Ethnic Control: Segmentation, Cooptation and Dependency in Post-Soviet Estonia," *Nations and Nationalism* 8(4), 505–29.

Physicians for Human Rights. 1994. *Rwanda 1994: A Report of the Genocide* (London: Physicians for Human Rights).

Pilkington, Colin. 2002. *Devolution in Britain Today* (Manchester, UK: Manchester University Press).

Piper, L. 2002. "Nationalism without a Nation: The Rise and Fall of Zulu Nationalism in South Africa's Transition to Democracy, 1975–1999," *Nations and Nationalism* 8(1) (January), 73–95.

Pithart, Petr and Metta Spencer. 1998. "The Partition of Czechoslovakia," in Matta Spencer, ed., *Separatism: Democracy and Disintegration* (Lanham, MD: Rowman and Littlefield Publishers), 185–204.

Presthus, Robert. 1973. *Elite Accommodation in Canadian Politics* (Cambridge: Cambridge University Press).

Prunier, G. 1995. *The Rwanda Crisis 1959–1994: History of a Genocide* (London: Hurst).

Rabinowitz, Dan, Asad Ghanem, and Oren Yiftacel, eds. 2000. *After the Rift: New Directions for Government Policy Toward the Arab Population in Israel*, November.

Rabushka, Alvin and K. A. Shepsle. 1972. *Politics in Plural Societies: A Theory of Democratic Instability* (Columbus, OH: Charles A. Merrill Publishing Company).

Radu, Michael. 2001. "The Land of Many Crossroads: The Rise and Fall of the PKK," *Orbis* 45(1) (Winter), 47–63.

Rajashekara, H. M. 1997. "The Nature of Indian Federalism: A Critique," *Asian Survey* 37(3) (March), 245–53.

Rawls, John. 1971. *A Theory of Justice* (Cambridge, MA: Belknap Press of Harvard University Press).

Renan, Ernest. 1996. "What Is a Nation?" in Geoff Eley and Ronald Grigor Suny, eds., *Becoming National: A Reader* (New York and Oxford: Oxford University Press), 41–55.

Requejo, Ferran, ed. 2001a. *Democracy and National Pluralism* (New York: Routledge).

————. 2001b. "Political Liberalism in Multinational States: The Legitimacy of Plural and Asymmetrical Federalism," in Alain-G. Gagnon and James Tully, eds., *Multinational Democracies* (Cambridge: Cambridge University Press), 110–32.

Resnick, P. 1999. "Toward a Multinational Federalism: Asymmetrical and Confederal Alternatives," in F. Leslie Seidle, ed., *Seeking a New Canadian Partnership: Asymmetrical and Confederal Options* (Montreal: Institute for Research and Public Policy), 71–89.

Rex, John. 1998. "Multiculturalism and Political Integration in Europe," in Marco Martiniello, ed., *Multicultural Policies and the State: A Comparison of Two European Societies*, European Research Centre on Migration and Ethnic Relations (Utrecht: Utrecht University Press), 11–24.

Reynolds, Andrew. 1999–2000. "A Constitutional Pied Piper: The Northern Irish Good Friday Agreement," *Political Science Quarterly* 114 (Winter), 613–37.

Rhodes, Matthews. 1995. "National Identity and Minority Rights in the Constitutions of the Czech Republic and Slovakia," *East European Quarterly* 29(3) (September), 347–69.

Rotberg, Robert I. 2002. *Ending Autocracy, Enabling Democracy* (Cambridge, MA: World Peace Foundation; Washington, DC: Brookings Institution Press).

Rothchild, Donald and Victor Olurunsola, eds. 1986. *State vs. Ethnic Claims: African Policy Dilemmas* (Boulder, CO: Westview Press).

Rothchild, Joseph. 1974. *East Central Europe between the Two World Wars* (Seattle: University of Washington Press).

Rothman, Jay. 1997. *Resolving Identity-Based Conflict in Nations, Organizations and Communities* (San Francisco: Jossey-Bass Publishers).

Rouhana, Nadim. 1997. *Palestinian Citizens in an Ethnic Jewish State: Identities in Conflict* (New Haven, CT: Yale University Press).

Rudolph, Joseph R. and Robert J. Thompson. 1985. "Ethnoterritorial Movements and the Policy Process: Accommodating Demands in the Developed World," *Comparative Politics* 17(3) (April), 291–311.

Russell, Peter H. 1994. "The Politics of Mega-constitutional Change: Lessons for Canada," in Bertus de Villiers, ed., *Evaluating Federal Systems* (The Netherlands: Martinus Nijhoff), 30–40.

Russett, Bruce. 1993. *Grasping the Democratic Peace: Principles for a Post-Cold War World* (Princeton: Princeton University Press).

Rutland, Peter. 1993–1994. "Thatcherism, Czech-style: Transition to Capitalism in the Czech Republic," *Telos* 93 (Winter), 103–24.

Rychlik, Jan. 2000. "The Possibilities for Czech-Slovak Compromise, 1989–1992," in Michael Kraus and Allison Stanger, eds., *Irreconcilable Differences? Explaining Czechoslovakia's Dissolution* (Lanham, MD: Rowman and Littlefield Publishers), 49–66.

Saatci, Mustafa. 2002. "Nation-states and Ethnic Boundaries: Modern Turkish Identity and Turkish-Kurdish Conflict," *Nations and Nationalism* 8(4) (October), 549–64.

Safran, William. 1991. "Ethnicity and Pluralism: Comparative and Theoretical Perspectives," *Canadian Review of Studies in Nationalism* 18 (1–2), 1–12.

_____. 1994. "Non-separatist Policies Regarding Ethnic Minorities: Positive Approaches and Ambiguous Consequences," *International Political Science Review* 15(1), 61–80.

Safran, William and Ramon Maiz, eds. 2000. *Identity and Territorial Autonomy in Plural Society* (London: Frank Cass).

Salomone, S. D. "The Dialectics of Turkish National Identity: Ethnic Boundary Maintenance and State Ideology," pt. II, *East European Quarterly* 23(2) (June 1989), 225–48.

Samson, Ivo. 1989. "Slovakia: Misreading the Western Message," in Jan Zielonka and Alex Pravda, eds., *Democratic Consolidation in Eastern Europe, Volume II: International and Transnational Factors* (Oxford: Oxford University Press), 363–82.

Sandel, Michael. 1982. *Liberalism and the Limits of Justice* (Cambridge and New York: Cambridge University Press).

Sartori, Giovanni. 1968. "Political Development and Political Engineering," *Public Policy* 17, 261–98.

_____. 1997. "Understanding Pluralism," *Journal of Democracy* 8(4), 58–69.

Schlesinger, Arthur. 1992. *The Disuniting of America* (New York: W. W. Norton).

Schmid, Carol L. 1981. *Conflict and Consensus in Switzerland* (Berkeley: University of California Press).

_____. 2001. *The Politics of Language: Conflict, Identity, and Cultural Pluralism in Comparative Perspective* (Oxford: Oxford University Press).

Schnapper, Dominique. 2004. "The Concept of 'Dominant Ethnicity' in the Case of France," in Eric P. Kaufmann, eds. *Rethinking Ethnicity: Majority Groups and Dominant Minorities* (London and New York: Routledge), 102–15.

Schneckener, Ulrich and Stefan Wolff, eds. 2004. *Managing and Settling Ethnic Conflicts* (London: Hurst).

Seidle, F. Leslie, ed. 1999. *Seeking a New Canadian Partnership: Asymmetrical and Confederal Options* (Montreal: Institute for Research and Public Policy).

Senn, Alfred Erich and Graham Smith, eds. 1996. *The Nationalities Question in the Post-Soviet States* (London: Longman).

Shafir, Gershon and Yoav Peled. 1998. "Citizenship and Participation in an Ethnic Democracy," *Ethnic and Racial Studies* 21(3) (May), 408–27.

———. 2002. *Being Israeli: The Dynamics of Multiple Citizenship* (Cambridge and New York: Cambridge University Press).

Shamir, Michal and John L. Sullivan. 1983. "The Political Context of Tolerance: The United States and Israel," *American Political Science Review* 77(4) (December), 911–28.

———. 1985. "Jews and Arabs in Israel: Everybody Hates Somebody, Sometimes," *Journal of Conflict Resolution* 22(2) (June), 288–305.

Shapiro, Yonathan. 1996a. *Politicians as a Hegemonic Class: The Case of Israel* (Tel-Aviv: Sifriat Poalim) (Hebrew).

———. 1996b. "Where Has Liberalism Disappeared in Israel?" *Zmanim* (Winter), 92–101 (Hebrew).

Share, Donald. 1986. *The Making of Spanish Democracy* (New York: Praeger).

Sheridan, William. 1987. "Canadian Multiculturalism: Issues and Trends" (Ottawa: Library of Parliament).

Shirlow, Peter. 2001. "Devolution in Northern Ireland/Ulster/the North/Six Counties: Delete as Appropriate," *Regional Studies* 35(8) (November), 743–52.

Simeon, Richard and Daniel-Patrick Conway. 2001. "Federalism and the Management of Conflict in Multinational Societies," in Alain-G. Gagnon and James Tully, *Multinational Democracies* (Cambridge and New York: Cambridge University Press), 338–65.

Singer, Marshall R. 1992. "Sri Lanka's Tamil-Sinhalese Ethnic Conflict: Alternative Solutions," *Asian Review* 32(8) (August), 712–22.

Sisk, Timothy. 1995. *Democratization in South Africa: The Elusive Social Contact* (Princeton: Princeton University Press).

———. 1996. *Powersharing and International Mediation in Ethnic Conflicts* (Washington, DC: USIP Press).

Skocpol, Theda. 1985. "Bringing the State Back In: Strategies of Analysis in Current Research," in Peter B. Evans, Dietrich Rueschemeyer, and Theda Skocpol, eds., *Bringing the State Back In* (Cambridge and New York: Cambridge University Press), 3–37.

Smiley, Donald. 1979. "French-English Relations in Canada and Consociational Democracy," in Milton J. Esman, ed., *Ethnic Conflict in the Western World* (Ithaca, NY: Cornell University Press).

Smith, Anthony. 1971. *Theories of Nationalism* (Malden, MA: Blackwell).

———. 1986. *The Ethnic Origins of Nations* (Malden, MA: Blackwell).

———. 1991. *National Identity* (London: Penguin).

———. 2004. "Ethnic Cores and Dominant Ethnies," in Eric P. Kaufmann, ed., *Rethinking Ethnicity: Majority Groups and Dominant Minorities* (London and New York: Routledge), 17–30.

Smith, David J. 2003. "Minority Rights, Multiculturalism and EU Enlargement: The Case of Estonia," *Journal of Ethnopolitics and Minority Issues in Europe*, 1, 1–38.

Smith, Rogers M. 1988. "The 'American Creed' and the American Identity: The Limits of Liberal Citizenship in the United States," *Western Political Quarterly* 41(2) (June), 225–51.

Smooha, Sammy. 1990. "Minority Status in an Ethnic Democracy: The Status of the Arab Minority in Israel," *Ethnic and Racial Studies* 13(3) (July), 389–413.

———. 1997. "Ethnic Democracy: Israel as an Archetype," *Israel Studies* 2(2) (Fall), 198–241.

———. 2002. "Types of Democracy and Modes of Conflict Management in Ethnically Divided Societies," *Nations and Nationalism* 8(4), 423–31.

Smooha, Sammy and Theodor Hanf. 1992. "The Diverse Mode of Conflict-regulation in Deeply Divided Societies," *International Journal of Comparative Sociology* 33(1–2), 26–47.

Snyder, Jack. 2000. *From Voting to Violence: Democratization and Nationalist Conflict* (New York: W. W. Norton).

Somer, Murat. 2004. "Turkey's Kurdish Conflict: Changing Context, and Domestic and Regional Implications," *Middle East Journal* 58(2) (Spring), 235–53.

Sparks, Allister. 1990. *The Mind of South Africa: The Story of the Rise and Fall of Apartheid* (London: Heinemann).

———. 1994. *Tomorrow is Another Country: The Inside Story of South Africa's Negotiated Revolution* (Sandton, South Africa: Struik Book Distribution).

Spencer, Metta, ed. 1998. *Separatism: Democracy and Disintegration* (Lanham, MD: Rowman and Littlefield Publishers).

Spencer, Philip and Howard Wollman. 2002. *Nationalism: A Critical Introduction* (London: Sage).

Spinner, Jeff. 1994. *The Boundaries of Citizenship: Race, Ethnicity and Nationality in the Liberal State* (Baltimore: Johns Hopkins University Press).

Spinner-Halev, Jeff. 2002. "Unoriginal Sin: Zionism and Democratic Exclusion in Comparative Perspective," *Israel Studies Forum* 18(1) (Fall), 26–56.

Steinberg, Gerald. 2000. "The Poor in Your Own City Shall Have Precedence: A Critique of the Katzir-Qaadan Case and Opinion," *Israel Studies Bulletin* 16(1) (Fall), 12–22.

Steinberg, Jonathan. 1996. *Why Switzerland?* 2nd ed. (Cambridge: Cambridge University Press).

Sternhell, Zeev. 1995. *Nation-Building or Model Society: Nationalism and Socialism in the Israeli Labor Movement, 1904–1940* (Tel-Aviv: Am Oved) (Hebrew).

Stewart, P. and Peter Shirlow. 1999. "Northern Ireland between Peace and War?" *Capital and Class* 69), 6–16.

Stuligross, David. 1999. "India's Vision and the BJP," *Current History* 98(632) (December), 422–32.

Suleiman, Michael W. 1967. *Political Parties in Lebanon: The Challenge of Fragmented Political Culture* (Ithaca, NY: Cornell University Press).

Tamir, Yael. 1993. *Liberal Nationalism* (Princeton: Princeton University Press).

Taras, Raymond C. and Rajat Ganguly. 1998. *Understanding Ethnic Conflict: The International Dimension* (New York: Longman).

———. 2006. *Understanding Ethnic Conflict: The International Dimension*, 3rd ed. (New York: Longman).

Tarlton, Charles D. 1965. "Symmetry and Asymmetry as Elements of Federalism: A Theoretical Speculation," *Journal of Politics* 27(4), 861–74.

Tatar, Peter. 1994. "The Circumstances of the Preparation and Acceptance of the Slovak Constitution," in Irena Grudzinska Gross, ed., *Constitutionalism and Politics* (Bratislava, Slovakia: Slovak Committee of the European Cultural Foundation), 318–20.

Taylor, Charles. 1965. "Symmetry and Asymmetry as Elements of Federalism: A New Theoretical Speculation," *Journal of Politics* 27(4), 861–74.

———. 1992. "The Politics of Recognition," in Amy Gutmann, ed., *Multiculturalism and the Politics of Recognition* (Princeton: Princeton University Press), 25–74.

———. 2001. "Forward" in Alain-G. Gagnon and James Tully, eds., *Multinational Democracies* (Cambridge and New York: Cambridge University Press).

Taylor, Peter. 1994. "The State as a Container," *Progress in Human Geography* 18(2), 151–62.

Taylor, Rupert. 1990. "South Africa: Consociation or Democracy?" *Telos* 85, 17–32.

———. 1991. "The Myth of Ethnic Division: Township Conflict on the Reef," *Race and Class* 33 (October–December), 1–14.

Tetley, William. 1982. "Language and Education Rights in Quebec and Canada," *Law and Contemporary Problems* 45, 177–217.

Theophanous, Andreas. 2000. "Cyprus, the European Union and the Search for a New Constitution," *Journal of Southern Europe and the Balkans* 2(2), 213–33.

Uvin, Peter. 1997. "Prejudice, Crisis and Genocide in Rwanda," *African Studies Review* 40(2) (September), 91–115.

Van Bruinessen, Martin. 1996. "Kurds, Turks and the Alevi Revival in Turkey," *Middle East Report* (200) (July–September), 7–10.

Van Creveld, Martin. 1999. *The Rise and the Decline of the State* (Cambridge and New York: Cambridge University Press).

Van de Meeren, R. 1996. "Three Decades in Exile: Rwandan Refugees 1960–90," *Journal of Refugee Studies* 9(3), 252–67.

Van der Berghe, A. C. 1981a. "Protection of Ethnic Minorities: A Critical Appraisal," in R. G. Wirsirg, ed., *Protection of Ethnic Minorities: Comparative Analysis* (Oxford: Pergamon Press), 343–55.

———. 1981b. *Ethnic Phenomenon* (New York: Elsevier).

Van der Berghe, Pierre. 2002. "Multicultural Democracy: Can It Work?" *Nations and Nationalism* 8(4), 433–49.

Van Zyl Slabbert, Frederik. 1983. "Sham Reform and Conflict Resolution in a Divided Society," *Journal of African and Asian Societies* 18 (1–2), 34–48.

Van Zyl Slabbert, Frederik and David Welch. 1979. *South Africa's Options: Strategies for Sharing Power* (Cape Town: David Philip).

Vincent, Andrew. 2002. *Nationalism and Particularity* (Cambridge: Cambridge University Press).

Voutat, Bernard. 1992. "Interpreting National Conflict in Switzerland: The Jura Question," in John Coakley, ed., *The Social Origins of Nationalist Movements: The Contemporary West European Experience* (London and Newbury Park, CA: SAGE Publications).

———. 1996. "Objectivation sociale et motivations politiques: La question nationale dans la Jura Suisse," *Reveu Francaise de Science Politique* 46(1), 30–51.

———. 2000. "Territorial Identity in Europe: The Political Process of the Construction of Identities in Corsica, the Basque Country, Italy, Macedonia and the Swiss Jura," *Contemporary European History* 9(2), 285–94.

Walker, Lee and Paul C. Stern, eds. 1993. *Balancing and Sharing Power in Multiethnic Societies: Summary of a Workshop* (Washington, DC: National Academy Press).

Waxman, Dov. 2000. "Islam and Turkish National Identity: A Reappraisal," *Turkish Yearbook of International Relations* (30), 1–22.

———. 2004. "Hegemony Lost: The Crisis of National Identity in Israel and Turkey." Paper presented at the annual meeting of the International Studies Association, Jerusalem, March 18.

Weber, Eugene. 1976. *Peasants into Frenchmen: The Modernization of Rural France, 1870–1914* (Stanford: Stanford University Press).

Weiss, Linda. 1998. *The Myth of the Powerless State* (Ithaca, NY: Cornell University Press).

Welsh, David. 1993. "Domestic Politics and Ethnic Conflict" in Michael Brown, ed., *Ethnic Conflict and International Security* (Princeton: Princeton University Press), 43–60.

Wilford, Rick. 2000. "Designing the Northern Ireland Assembly," *Parliamentary Affairs* 53), 577–90.

Williams, Cynthia. 1986. "The Changing Nature of Citizen Rights," in Alan Cairns and Cynthia Williams, eds., *Constitutionalism, Citizenship and Society in Canada* (Toronto: University of Toronto Press).

Wolchik, Sharon L. 1991. *Czechoslovakia in Transition: Politics, Economics and Society* (London and New York: Pinter).

———. 1993. "The Politics of Ethnicity in Post-Communist Czechoslovakia," *East European Politics and Societies* 8(1) (December), 153–88.

———. 2000. "The Impact of Institutional Factors on the Breakup of the Czechoslovak Federation," in Michael Kraus and Allison Stanger, eds., *Irreconcilable Differences? Explaining Czechoslovakia's Dissolution* (Lanham, MD: Rowman and Littlefield Publishers), 87–106.

Xydis, Stephen G. 1973. *Cyprus: The Reluctant Republic* (The Hague: Mouton).

Yadgar, Y. 2002. "From the Particularistic to the Universalistic: National Narratives in Israel's Mainstream Press, 1967–1997," *Nation and Nationalism* 8(1) (January), 55–72.

Yanai, Natan. 1989. "Ben-Gurion's Concept of Mamlachtiut and the Forming Reality of The State of Israel," *Jewish Political Studies Review* 1 (1–2), 151–78.

Yegen, Mesut. 1996. "The Turkish State Discourse and the Exclusion of Kurdish Identity," *Middle Eastern Studies* 32(2) (April), 216–29.

———. 1999. "The Kurdish Question in Turkish State Discourse," *Journal of Contemporary History* 34(4) (October), 555–68.

Yiftachel, Oren. 1992a. "The Concept of Ethnic Democracy and its Applicability to the Case of Israel," *Ethnic and Racial Studies* 15(1) (January), 125–37.

———. 1992b. "The State, Ethnic Relations and Democratic Stability: Lebanon, Cyprus and Israel," *GeoJournal* 28 (November), 319–22.

———. 1998. "Democracy or Ethnocracy? Territory and Settler Politics in Israel/Palestine," *Middle East Report* 207 (Summer), 8–13.

———. 2000a. "Ethnocracy, Geography and Democracy: Comments on the Politics of the Judaization of Israel," *Alpaiim* 19, 78–105 (Hebrew).

———. 2000b. "Ethnocracy and Its Discontents: Minorities, Protests, and the Israeli Polity," *Critical Inquiry* 26(4) (Summer), 725–56.

———. 2001. "Centralized Power and Divided Space: 'Fractured Regions' in the Israeli 'Ethnocracy,'" *GeoJournal* 53, 283–93.

———. 2006. *Ethnocracy: Land and Identity Politics in Israel/Palestine* (Philadelphia: University of Pennsylvania Press).

Yiftachel, Oren and Asad Ghanem. 2004a. "Understanding 'Ethnocratic' Regimes: The Politics of Seizing Contested Territories," *Political Geography* 23(6) (August), 647–76.

———. 2004b. "Toward a Theory of Ethnocratic Regimes: Learning from the Judaization of Israel/Palestine," in Eric P. Kaufmann, ed., *Rethinking Ethnicity: Majority Groups and Dominant Minorities* (London and New York: Routledge), 179–97.

Yiftachel, Oren and Alexandre Kedar. 2000. "Landed Power: The Making of the Israeli Land Regime," *Teoria U'Vikoret* 16, 67–100.

Young, Iris Marion. 1990. *Justice and the Politics of Difference* (Princeton: Princeton University Press).

———. 2000. *Inclusion and Democracy*. (Oxford Political Theory). (Oxford: Oxford University Press).

Young. Robert A. 1994. *The Breakup of Czechoslovakia* (Kingston, Ontario: Queens University Institute of Inter-Governmental Relations).

Zajac, Petr. 2000. "Czechoslovakia after 1989: The Reason for the Division," in Michael Kraus and Allison Stanger, eds., *Irreconcilable Differences? Explaining Czechoslovakia's Dissolution* (Lanham, MD: Rowman and Littlefield Publishers), 259–68.

Zakaria, Fareed. 1997. "The Rise of Illiberal Democracy," *Foreign Affairs* 76(6), 22–43.

———. 2003. *The Future of Freedom: Illiberal Democracy at Home and Abroad* (New York: W. W. Norton).

Zerubavel, Yael. 1995. *Recovered Roots: Collective Memory and the Making of Israeli National Tradition* (Chicago: University of Chicago Press).

Zvidrin, Peteris. 1992. "Changes in the Ethnic Composition of Latvia," *Journal of Baltic Studies* 23(4), 359–68.

Index